Vietnam and the Transformation of American Life

Problems in American History

Series editor: Jack P. Greene

Each volume focuses on a central theme in American history and provides greater analytical depth and historiographic coverage than standard textbook discussions normally allow. The intent of the series is to present in highly interpretive texts the unresolved questions of American history that are central to current debates and concerns. The texts will be concise enough to be supplemented with primary readings or core textbooks and are intended to provide brief syntheses to large subjects.

Forthcoming titles in this series:

Vietnam and the Transformation of American Life

Robert Buzzanco

University of Houston

First published 1999

Reprinted (twice)1999

Blackwell Publishers Inc
350 Main Street
Malden, Massachusetts 02148, USA

Blackwell Publishers Ltd
108 Cowley Road
Oxford OX4 1JF, UK

Library of Congress Cataloging in Publication Data
Buzzanco, Robert.
    Vietnam and the transformation of American life/Robert Buzzanco.
      p. cm.—(Problems in American history)
    Includes bibliographical references (p.) and index.
    ISBN 1-57718-093-3 (alk. paper).— ISBN 1-57718-094-1 (pbk. : alk. paper)
    1. Vietnamese Conflict, 1961-1975—United States. 2. Vietnamese Conflict, 1961-1975—Influence. 3. United States—Civilization—1970- . I. Title. II. Series.
DS558.B92   1999
959.704'3373—dc21   98-45677
                                          CIP

British Library Cataloguing in Publication Data
A CIP catalogue record for this book is available from the British Library

Typeset in 11 on 13pt Sabon
by Ace Filmsetting Ltd, Frome, Somerset
Printed and bound in Great Britain
by T. J. International Limited, Padstow, Cornwall

This book is printed on acid-free paper

Contents

Acknowledgments

I would like to extend my deepest appreciation to those colleagues and friends who helped me in the process of preparing this book. Among those who read various chapters – at least those whom my increasingly frazzled mind can still remember – are Maggie Jaffe, Leigh Fought, Austin Allen, Dwight Watson, Bill Walker, Richard Blackett, and Landon Storrs. Steve Mintz and Ken Lipartito deserve special merit for reading the entire manuscript; and Amy Elizabeth Blackwell was a great critic and editor, and joined the Kelso/Buzzanco home as sister and aunt and best friend as well. At Blackwell, I was blessed to have an expert and patient editor in Susan Rabinowitz. I hope she forgives me for my poor sense of time.

Finally, I would like to thank my wife, Jane Kelso, for her support and patience, and dedicate this book to my son, Kelsey Sandino Buzzanco. While I was working on this project he became interested in the 1960s, mostly from watching old repeats of *The Wonder Years* on cable TV. He was at first disdainful of me: "Dad, it's the 1990s now, get out of the sixties." Eventually, however, he began to ask questions about the era and gave me a chance to tell him that it was a serious time, full of attempts to create a more just and democratic society. May he and his young comrades in the twenty-first century try to do the same!

Bob Buzzanco
Houston, Texas
12 June 1998

To Kelsey and His Generation

Be Realistic, Demand the Impossible!

The War Comes Home. LBJ slumps over in anguish as he listens to son-in-law Marine Captain Chuck Robb's taped account of the war in Vietnam.

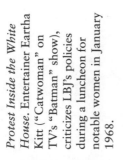

Protest Inside the White House. Entertainer Eartha Kitt ("Catwoman" on TV's "Batman" show), criticizes LBJ's policies during a luncheon for notable women in January 1968.

New Administration, Same Old Problems. LBJ speaks with his eventual successor, Richard Nixon, in the summer of 1968. Despite Nixon's promise to end the war quickly, he did not have any greater success than Johnson in extricating the United States from Vietnam.

Overcoming Personal Animosities. LBJ and Bobby Kennedy campaign together in 1964. Four years later Kennedy, a critic of Johnson's war policies, would run for president and help force LBJ to withdraw from the campaign.

Introduction: Intersection – The Vietnam War and the Social and Political Movements of the 1960s

Martin Luther King, Jr possessed greater moral authority than any other American in the 1960s. He had stood up to police dogs and fire hoses; mobilized millions – black and white, northern and southern – to agitate for civil rights; managed boycotts and marches; successfully lobbied for civil rights laws; stirred untold numbers worldwide with his passionate oratory; and won the 1964 Nobel Peace Prize. Yet one of the more dramatic and historically significant episodes of his life has not become a central element of King's public legacy, as have Birmingham, Selma, the March on Washington, and other events we celebrate in our history books and, in the United States, in the media during the second week of January.

Speaking at the Riverside Baptist Church in New York City on 4 April 1967 – by eerie coincidence exactly a year before he was slain in Memphis – Martin Luther King publicly broke ranks with the policies of President Lyndon B. Johnson and the white establishment as he condemned American involvement in the Vietnam War – Johnson's war, the liberals' war. The war in Vietnam had already and would continue to intersect with the compelling social and political movements of that era, but King's sermon in New York perhaps more clearly and strikingly developed the ways in which the issues of Vietnam, civil rights, race and class at home, and the promise and shortcomings of liberalism were interconnected than other episodes in the 1960s.

To King, there was a "very obvious and almost facile

connection" between the US war in Vietnam and the struggle for civil rights and against poverty at home. Just as the Civil and Voting Rights Acts of 1964–5 and Lyndon B. Johnson's "Great Society" had begun to confront the crises of race and class at home, the United States began pouring soldiers and resources into Southeast Asia. With that military buildup, King watched the commitment to domestic justice and equality "broken and eviscerated as if it were some idle political plaything of a society gone mad on war." At the same time, Vietnam was showcasing the government's hypocrisy on racial matters, as African-Americans and other minorities were dying in extraordinarily high proportions in the early years of the war even though they accounted for a small percentage of the population. "We were taking the black young men who had been crippled by our society," King charged, "and sending them eight thousand miles away to guarantee liberties in Southeast Asia which they had not found in southwest Georgia and East Harlem."

As a result, Americans faced the "cruel irony" of watching black and white American boys kill and die together in the service of a country "that has been unable to seat them together in the same schools." Because of these circumstances, King, who had developed a strong relationship with the Johnson White House and the liberal establishment, had to speak out; he "could not be silent in the face of such cruel manipulation of the poor." At home, as the Reverend saw it, racial division had become increasingly contentious, with urban uprisings in the north becoming as common as anti-black violence in the south had been earlier in the decade. Abroad, especially in Vietnam, US actions were marked by mayhem and destruction as well, as American soldiers, weapons, and airplanes inflicted massive levels of damage on the residents of a small agrarian society. The United States, King thus concluded, was "the greatest purveyor of violence in the world today."

Not four years earlier King dreamed of an America in which "little black boys and black girls will be able to join hands with little white boys and white girls and walk together as brothers and sisters." Violence in Vietnam, however, had brought them together, and Americans watched those black and white boys "in brutal solidarity burning down the huts of a poor village" though "they would never live together on the same block in Detroit." As King saw it, the commitment to racial reconciliation and social improvement was dying on the battlefields of Vietnam, causing a rupture in the social fabric unlike any in the twentieth century. He thus called on all Americans to confront the impact of the war. "These are the times for real choices and not false ones," he lectured. "We are at the moment when our lives must be placed on the line if our nation is to survive its own folly. Every man of humane convictions must decide on the protest that best suits his convictions, *but we must all protest.*"[1]

King's words are an appropriate starting point for this work because they so powerfully describe the impact of the Vietnam War on other aspects of American society in the 1960s. There is, to be sure, already a significant body of literature on this period. Scholars, public officials, and the popular media have lectured on and analyzed the major events of the period – Vietnam, civil rights, political upheaval, cultural conflict, Women's Liberation, student unrest, and others – to no end, but at times in isolation from each other. The war in Indochina and the domestic crises of that generation indeed were integral and cohesive parts of the same process. Though many of the principal political and cultural movements of that decade preceded America's large-scale commitment to Vietnam, the war ultimately shaped them in new ways, variously radicalizing, co-opting, or shattering them.

Vietnam and the domestic crises of the 1960s must be understood as unique yet connected consequences of the economic and cultural environment produced in the aftermath of World War II. After 1945, the United States had unrivaled power, but had assumed leadership of a troubled world. The forces of *nationalism* – usually described as Communist by American leaders – were disrupting the US vision of a new world order, especially in the Third World and particularly in Vietnam. Closer to home, blacks, women, workers, students, and others would eventually mobilize to seek greater democracy, often in the streets of major American cities. To face both challenges, foreign and domestic, America's leaders pursued a strategy of *containment*, preventing the political left and forces of nationalism abroad from spreading, while also containing movements for participatory democracy at home. In both cases, the United States tried to limit movements that were based upon the idea that individual citizens – be they Vietnamese peasants, poor African-Americans, or middle-class college students – should have a decisive voice in choosing the nature of their society.

That effort to contain nationalism and democracy in turn motivated many of those whom American leaders opposed – Communists and Vietnamese patriots led by Ho Chi Minh, student protestors on American campuses, African-American activists, champions of women's liberation – to more forcefully, and at times violently, press their agendas. Such tension was already evident by the later 1950s as the United States began to assume greater control over the civil war in Vietnam, while also trying to direct protests over civil rights at home along more manageable and less threatening paths. Those movements for popular democracy nonetheless achieved success or expanded in the early 1960s. The Civil Rights Act of 1964 outlawed discrimination in public accommodations; the Voting Rights Act a year later extended suffrage to millions of black southerners; the Free Speech Movement (FSM) motivated huge numbers of college students to rethink the role of the university; the Student Nonviolent Coordinating Committee (SNCC) and Students for a Democratic Society (SDS) became the most influential organizations of student activists in the 1960s; and music, film, and literature began to explore new, often previously taboo, areas.

While such movements existed in their own right, ultimately all were transformed by the growing commitment in Vietnam, which by the mid-1960s had become a major war and, ultimately, the nation's primary concern, if not obsession. Because of Vietnam, as Martin Luther King charged, other issues were downplayed, ignored, or dismissed. The growing expense of the war meant that less funding was available to address the "War on Poverty" at home. The US attempt to crush Vietnamese nationalism caused millions of Americans – many, but by no means all, young – to question the morality, if not legitimacy, of the government's behavior, and they often took to the streets to express their opinions. Perhaps most importantly, Vietnam exposed the inconsistency in the world-view of the liberal establishment: it was not possible – as Athens had discovered over two millennia earlier – to have a full-fledged democracy at home while extending one's empire abroad. The dreams of a great society indeed were dying on the battlefields of Vietnam. Likewise, the anger and energy of young students, blacks, women, and others was being fueled by the war. In all instances, Vietnam was a transformative event. Just as World Wars I and II fundamentally altered the nature of American society in the 1920s and 1940s, the war in Vietnam would do likewise in the 1960s.

Prior to the American military commitment to Vietnam and the domestic upheavals of the 1960s, the United States had enjoyed over a decade of economic growth and apparent stability. Despite war in Korea, occasional recession, and growing dissent from southern blacks, most Americans seemed content. Workers were relatively well paid; the GI Bill was allowing more young men than ever to attend college; women were supposed to be relieved from housework by technological innovation; suburban tract housing was readily available; and Americans had access to more consumer goods, services, and entertainment than even thought possible just a generation earlier. The country liked President "Ike" Eisenhower, and Beaver Cleaver, and Lucille Ball; the kids loved that new "rock and roll" music; and, aside from the threats posed by the Soviet Union and "Red" China, all seemed right with the world.

Below this exaggerated litany of harmony and conformity, however, lay forces that would rock the next generation. Though poverty and racial, gender, and ethnic discrimination were mostly rendered invisible by the media and popular culture, democratic movements were bubbling up in a number of places. In Montgomery, Alabama, King, a young minister, achieved national recognition by successfully desegregating the public bus lines through the tactics of boycott. In Greenwich Village, "Beat" poets and folk singers were challenging the conformity of postwar American life. The seeds of the women's movements of the 1960s were beginning to sprout, as women, often through labor and civil rights activism, asserted their own political agenda, while on a more personal level began to challenge sexual double standards, especially when liberated by the development of the birth control pill. At the same time, American youth, especially on college campuses, were starting to question or rebel against the university establishment and then society at large. By the early years of the 1960s, these forces would coalesce into various politico-cultural movements of decided significance and, against the overwhelming backdrop of the Vietnam War, fundamentally alter American life.

The purpose of this book, then, is to examine the Vietnam War and the political and social movements of the 1960s. Though it is in part a narrative of the major developments of that decade, it is more so an interpretive work with a common thread running through it – the nature of US involvement in Vietnam and the significance of the war for the various movements at home. The major theme is fairly straightforward: *Vietnam was a transformative event, with the war and opposition to it reshaping American life.* Vietnam generated the largest mass protest movement in US history; it exposed the limits of liberal reform; the war forestalled anti-poverty and civil rights progress and radicalized movements associated with those issues; helped bring other movements into existence, like Women's Liberation or the Counterculture; and provoked a backlash that continues to influence American politics and society to this day.

Although the major point of this work is that Vietnam and the movements at home were interrelated, I have organized the book into two parts – Vietnam and the Movements of the 1960s – to make it easier to use. In the courses I have taught, in which I cover this material, I have found that the subject matter flows best when demarcated this way rather than lumping everything together in a chronological narrative of the decade. Part I will thus cover the Vietnam War. We will examine the major issues regarding the war: political and social conditions in Vietnam; the reasons for American involvement; the development of US policy; criticism of the war, both internally, as from the military, and externally, as from the Peace Movement; the experience of soldiers; and the legacy of America's quarter-century of war in Indochina. The war, we shall see, was a product of America's mission to assume world leadership after World War II, was flawed badly from the outset, and was never likely to succeed. It was, most Americans believed, not only a mistake but morally wrong.

In Part II, we will look into some of the principal domestic issues of the 1960s, and show how they affected each other and, importantly, were connected with the war in Vietnam. First, we will consider the impact of the war, namely on the emergence of the New Left and the shattering of the postwar liberal consensus; next, we will investigate the ways in which Vietnam helped alter, hurt, or create dominant social movements such as Civil Rights and Women's Liberation; and finally, we will look at the cultural impact of the Vietnam generation. Not only did the war and social movements affect America politically, but they also changed the ways Americans created or enjoyed films, music, sports, and other cultural forms. These movements generally shared a commitment to democracy and social justice – though their own behavior could at times become extreme – and a belief that the American people – old and young, female and male, black and white, poor as well as wealthy – should have a voice in determining their lives. They often rejected traditional politics or the established culture and tried to create new organizations, institutions, and cultural relationships. Sometimes, the movements succeeded: southern racial segregation was abolished, students gained a measure of independence and autonomy within the university, a new and alternative culture took root. In the end, however, the state and other authority figures contained these movements or they were internally divided and their ultimate goals were not achieved. In any event, America was a much different place by the end of the 1960s than it had been at the outset of that decade.

Although our discussion of them is separated into two parts, it should remain clear that the war and the social movements were part of the same, interrelated historical process. Vietnam, civil rights, politics, and culture all played off each other and helped shape, and were shaped by, each other. They are separated here mainly to make it less complex to try to learn about them. Though Vietnam and the movements of the 1960s may be represented by different sections in this book, they are unquestionably linked historically and are part of the same process that transformed American life.

This study is important then not only as a means to provide a history of an important era but to draw a bridge to the present as well. Vietnam and the 1960s are still with us, visibly, today. To George Bush, victory in the Persian Gulf in 1991 signified the end of the "Vietnam syndrome." Whenever the United States has contemplated military involvement abroad, the media and politicians make constant reference to Vietnam. Likewise, the political movements of the 1960s still provide crucial points of reference. The right-wing tide of the 1980s and 1990s – demonstrated by the Reagan, Bush, and Clinton presidencies – represents in no small way a backlash against the 1960s. Politicians today in both major parties rail against the Great Society and the liberalism of a previous generation as harshly as critics did during that decade. Culturally too, the 1960s live on, whether in movies like *The Big Chill, Rambo,* or *Forrest Gump* or in the social protest music of Billy Bragg, Public Enemy, Tracy Chapman, and others, or in the anti-1960s political views of conservative media celebrity Rush Limbaugh, right-wing judge Robert Bork, and Republican Speaker of the House of Representatives Newt Gingrich.

As we enter a new century, our future is shaped by our past. America's role in the world today, its social system, racial antagonisms, gender relations, and culture can be traced back to an earlier generation when the United States tried to contain a war of national liberation in Vietnam and various democratic movements at home. The triumphs and shortcomings of that era fundamentally transformed the United States and made it what it is today.

Part I

The Vietnam War

I

Containment, Liberalism, and Vietnam: Background to the American War

On the third night of Tet, the Vietnamese lunar new year, in 1788, the Emperor Quang Trung, leader of the Tay Son movement, drove on Hanoi with his elephant brigade. The Tay Son, mostly a peasant group, aimed to conquer the Chinese forces of Sun Shiyi which had invaded and occupied northern Vietnam just weeks earlier. Quang Trung's army shocked and routed the Chinese troops, who panicked as they fled across the Red River, causing a pontoon bridge to break and large numbers of Sun's soldiers to drown. Shortly thereafter, the Qing dynasty recognized Quang Trung's state and withdrew from Vietnam. The Tay Son had ousted the Chinese and gained national independence.

Precisely 180 years later, in 1968, another force of Vietnamese nationalists, inspired by Ho Chi Minh and others, many of them peasants like the Tay Son, staged a similar uprising at the beginning of Tet. Despite suffering significant losses, the Vietnamese troops – the Viet Cong (VC) in the south and the People's Army of Vietnam (PAVN) in the north – faced another great power, the United States, and ultimately sent a clear message to the American public and its political and military leaders: the war in Vietnam would not be won! Though the fighting continued until 1975 when the southern capital of Saigon either fell or was liberated, depending on one's perspective, by the early months of 1968 the United States was facing up to the failure of its efforts to preserve an anti-Communist government in the southern half of Vietnam.

Peasant nationalists living in an underdeveloped Asian nation, led by a frail, goateed old man who wore simple clothes and sandals, had stood up to and overcome the greatest power in the world. The spirit of Quang Trung lived on in Ho Chi Minh, and the Americans suffered the same fate as the Qing.

Vietnam: Nationalism, Communism, and Resistance

The paths to 1968 and 1975 were long in the making. The ideals and ideologies that drove the Vietnamese independence movement – anti-colonialism, national liberation, Communism – had been developing well before the Americans came to Vietnam. Indeed, the successful war against the United States grew out of political seeds planted well over a century earlier. Not long after French colonizers arrived in the 1860s with gunboats and troops to take over the area collectively known as Indochina – including Tonkin, Annam, and Cochinchina in Vietnam, as well as Cambodia and Laos – natives in the region began to protest and resist the brutal French rule, especially in Vietnam. By the turn of the twentieth century, Vietnamese poets and revolutionaries, often one and the same, were agitating for dignity and national sovereignty. After World War I, when the underdeveloped world was simply not included in President Woodrow Wilson's call for an end to colonialism, the Vietnamese independence movement grew and became increasingly radical under the leadership of Ho and others. During World War II, those nationalists, collectively referred to as the Viet Minh, resisted Japanese occupation, often with the support of the United States. Japan's defeat in that war, it seemed, meant that Vietnam would finally regain its independence, and in September 1945, Ho even proclaimed the establishment of the Democratic Republic of Vietnam (DRVN) with its capital in the north at Hanoi. International politics, however, intervened and the French moved back into Indochina and resumed control, as oppressively as ever. Thus began what we now call the "First Indochina War."

From 1945 to 1954, the Viet Minh, with huge popular backing from most levels of Vietnamese society, fought the French and finally defeated them in 1954, after the decisive battle of Dien Bien Phu. Again, however, an outside power, this time the United States, snatched victory from Ho and the Viet Minh. Rather than recognize the DRVN, the United States and other nations – both American-allied and Communist – divided Vietnam along its seventeenth parallel. In the northern half, Ho would govern the DRVN; below the seventeenth parallel, the United States essentially invented the Republic of Vietnam (RVN), and for the next two decades would pour billions of dollars, millions of tons of equipment, and hundreds of thousands of soldiers into Vietnam to try to preserve it. In 1945, Vietnam had been little more than an afterthought for US policymakers. It eventually became the centerpiece in the Cold War, the site of America's longest, most difficult, and most divisive war. Why Vietnam?

The "Burdens" of Power

World War II created a new global order. Before 1940, Britain, France, and Germany all claimed power to rival the United States, as well as extensive formal empires; the United States was mired in economic depression and was limiting its international political commitments; while the Bolshevik regime was still solidifying internal power in the Soviet Union and hoping to avoid wider European conflict. Faced with the rise of the Nazis in the 1930s, the British and French appeased Adolf Hitler, the Soviet Union agreed to a non-aggression treaty, and the United States basically sat on its hands. Hitler's attacks against Poland, France, Britain, and the Soviet Union, however, finally dragged the major powers into world war (with a huge assist from the Japanese strike at Pearl Harbor, of course) and shattered the existing world order. After World War II, the United States and Soviet Union would emerge as the dominant powers, respectively leading the forces of Capitalism and Communism. Britain and France were facing the losses of their colonies. Germany had to rebuild and de-Nazify its bombed-out country. In Asia, the corrupt and ineffective Chinese government of Jiang Jieshi was trying to fend off the onslaught of the Chinese Communist Party (CCP), led by Mao Zedong, while the Japanese, with American direction and aid, were being transformed into the foundation for Capitalist expansion and anti-Communism in Asia.

The United States had interests in all those areas. In Europe, Americans hoped to rebuild Britain, Germany, France, Italy, and other countries along Capitalist lines to provide resources and markets while also using those areas to prevent the Soviet Union from spreading Communism beyond Eastern Europe. In Asia, the Roosevelt and Truman administrations strongly supported Jiang Jieshi against the CCP, though it was clear to American diplomatic and military officials that Mao's victory was likely, if not inevitable. In Japan, American dollars aimed to rebuild that country along free market lines as well, again both to provide opportunities for American businesses and to stop the Left.

In both Europe and Asia, the United States pursued an overall strategy of containment, preventing Communism from spreading beyond its already established borders. In Europe, American economic aid, through programs like the Marshall Plan, and military support, best demonstrated by the creation of the North Atlantic Treaty Organization (NATO), helped maintain a heavily armed truce throughout the Cold War. In Asia, however, the Cold War became hot as the United States sought to first contain and then roll back Communism, first in Korea and more particularly in Vietnam. To American policymakers, Third World nationalism – in India, Guatemala, the Congo, Iran, Vietnam, and scores of other places – was not distinguishable from Communism; nationalist movements trying to eliminate outside control were viewed as probable enemies. American leaders took a clearly defined and often simplistic "Us versus Them" approach to the Cold War. As a result, the United States violently tried to contain the Vietnamese Revolution even though Ho had hoped to develop strong ties with America, had never been particularly close to Stalin, and though supported by Mao, held a traditional Vietnamese distrust of China. Containment, except in rare instances such as Yugoslavia, did not allow for nuance, and so the United States went to war to contain, then roll back, the Vietnamese national liberation forces. A generation later, the United States left Indochina in defeat.

The Liberals' War?

America's containment strategy flowed naturally out of the world liberal system it had established. The term "liberal" today means something much different than it did in the immediate post-World War II period, and that shift in definition was in large measure caused by the Vietnam War. Today, liberals are derided as advocates of big government who want to take away the hard-earned money of working people and redistribute it to the poor and minorities. Culturally, a liberal is often perceived as permissive and lacking traditional values. Liberals, in Richard Nixon's famous phrase from the 1972 campaign, favored "amnesty, acid, and abortion." While the truth of such stereotypes can be questioned, the effectiveness of the post-Vietnam attack on liberalism is quite clear. The war shattered the liberal consensus in the later 1960s and ushered in new world and domestic orders. Since that time, American politicians and pundits such as Nixon, Ronald Reagan, George Will, Rush Limbaugh, Bill Clinton, and countless others have gained power and fame by criticizing the liberalism of an earlier generation.

But liberalism was not always the caricature that Newt Gingrich and others have made it out to be. In the World War II era, liberalism was the organizing principle for the United States to establish hegemony over the globe and unparalleled economic progress and social reform at home. In that period, liberalism was equated with Capitalist expansion, free markets, increases in production at home, good wages, and domestic reform to stabilize the American economic and social systems. Liberals had conducted World War II; established a global economy after the war based on free trade, private investment, and transnational corporations; tried to transport American culture abroad ("Coca-colonization" as critics dubbed it); fostered economic growth at home through a Keynesian system of military spending; and pursued civil rights for African-Americans to end the shame of the southern apartheid system and expand the domestic market as well.

Liberalism, however, also brought with it aggression on a global scale. In their efforts to remake the world along liberal, Capitalist lines after World War II, American leaders such as Secretaries of State Dean Acheson and John Foster Dulles and President John F. Kennedy, among others, essentially held that the United States had the privilege of intervening in the affairs of nations that were not following the US model or were acting too independently. Thus, when nationalist or Leftist governments like those of Jawaharlal Nehru in India, Mohammed Mossadegh in Iran, Jacobo Arbenz in Guatemala, Sukarno in Indonesia, Fidel Castro in Cuba, Patrice Lumumba in the Congo, and many others were perceived as challenging America's economic or strategic interests – oil in Iran, fruit in Guatemala, investments in Cuba, anti-Communist security in South Asia – the United States was compelled to act. Accordingly, the United States facilitated the overthrows of Arbenz, Mossadegh, and Sukarno, boycotted Castro, or tilted toward Pakistan. But nowhere did the United States try as hard or for as long to get its way as in Vietnam.[1]

Given the liberal world-view, the effort to make a new world guided by Capitalism, free markets, private investment, and political pluralism may have made conflicts such as Vietnam inevitable anyway, especially given the growth of Nationalist-Socialist-Communist movements in the aftermath of World War II. Vietnam, perhaps, had the bad fortune to become the test case for global liberalism. Even if one does not accept the concept of historical inevitability, it does seem clear that the American war in Vietnam was produced by forces that preceded the 1950s and had significance for all points on the globe, not just Indochina.

On to Vietnam

"Most of the men I commanded were like Rambo," Captain J. B. Wilcox explained in an interview with Mark Slackmeyer in the comic strip *Doonesbury*; "they wanted to win. But I had my orders: 'Don't win. We're not here to win. Take it easy on the enemy.' "[2] Garry Trudeau's satire of the *Rambo* movies of the 1980s still draws laughs, but also offers a realistic depiction of a popular view about Vietnam. Many supporters of the war – politicians, military officials, media representatives – have an explanation for the US defeat there: Americans actually won the war on the battlefield but were sold out at home. The United States, many of them argued, lost because weak politicians did not authorize American forces to take the measures necessary to win, anti-war protestors undermined the war effort, and the media was too critical. Had the Americans invaded North Vietnam, dropped more bombs, or activated the Reserves, the war might well have been won.[3] Indeed, as he began the Gulf War, George Bush told a national television audience that "our troops . . . will not be asked to fight with one hand tied behind their back."[4]

Such views, while attractive to large numbers of Americans, do not make good history. In fact, the United States, in its efforts to contain nationalism and Communism in Vietnam, employed a full array of the military assets at its disposal. From the 1960s – when John F. Kennedy began to send in military personnel and helicopters, and approve the use of napalm and chemicals against the enemy, to the American withdrawal in January 1973, following the so-called Christmas Bombings just weeks earlier – the United States inflicted massive damage against Vietnam, both north and south of the seventeenth parallel. Indeed, American forces destroyed the land of their ally, the RVN in the south, as much as that of their foe, the DRVN in the north. Using its vastly superior technology, the American military pulled few punches in Indochina. In the decade prior to the end of the war, the United States dropped 4.6 million tons of bombs on Vietnam and another 2 million tons on Cambodia and Laos. American forces sprayed over 11 million gallons of Agent Orange, an herbicide containing dioxin, a cancer-causing agent, and dropped over 400,000 tons of napalm. The impact of such warfare was immense: over 9,000, or about 60 percent, of southern hamlets were destroyed, as were 25 million acres of farmland and 12 million acres of forest. American bombs created about 25 million craters, many still containing active ordnance today. Most tragically, the Vietnamese suffered about 2 million deaths in the war, the Cambodians and Laotians had about 300,000 killed, and a greater number was wounded. And by 1975, there were 15 million refugees in Indochina and nearby countries. All in a nation roughly the size of New Mexico.[5]

Ironically, many of the men who were responsible for that warfare, senior military officers, had hoped to avoid such destruction. Vietnam was very much a civilian's war. Liberals in the John F. Kennedy and Lyndon B. Johnson administrations made the crucial decisions to fight there and to constantly escalate the conflict. But from the 1950s on, a significant number of ranking military leaders had argued against war in Vietnam. They believed that it was not an area of vital importance to US security, that the enemy had the capability to fight a long-term guerrilla war on its own terrain, that the allied government and military of the RVN was corrupt and weak, and that America's heavy firepower would be ineffective or counterproductive. At the same time, huge numbers of American soldiers – in Vietnam and on bases in the United States, Europe, and elsewhere – were suffering from low morale, discipline problems, drug abuse, racial conflict, or were actively involved in the anti-war movement.

The United States, then, dropped more bombs on Vietnam than were used by all countries in World War II *combined*. At the peak of the war, it had over 500,000 soldiers in the country and overall spent perhaps $200–300 billion to wage war there. America's military leaders were divided and often pessimistic about their chances for victory, while maybe a majority of soldiers were stoned, angry at their officers or each other, or opposed to the war. To somehow conclude from these conditions that the United States "won" all the battles, or was not allowed to "win" by politicians and protestors at home, or fought with hands tied behind their backs, is a convenient and often popular alibi. An examination of America's motives, its role, and its actions in Vietnam indicates otherwise.

2

Why (Not) Vietnam? The Vietnamese, the French, and the Americans to 1960

The area that today encompasses Indochina emerged as a coherent community in the first millennium BC, and its people have spent the better part of the next twenty-five centuries fighting off foreign invaders. According to their creation myth, the Vietnamese descended from dragons and fairies, and the traits embodied by these characters – the fierceness of the dragon and the serendipity of fairies – would serve them time and again throughout their history. At various times, the Chinese, French, Japanese, and Americans would try to take over Vietnam; all ultimately met harsh resistance and failure.

In the second century BC, the Chinese conquered Vietnam and, until the decline of the Tang dynasty in the tenth century AD, held control there, although patriots such as the Trung Sisters (*c.* AD 40) or Lady Trieu (*c.* AD 245), and others, led uprisings against the Chinese in this period. In 939, the Vietnamese gained their independence and then lived under the Ly and Tran dynasties, both with capitals at Hanoi in northern Vietnam, for the next four centuries. In the late 1200s, Mongol armies from China invaded Vietnam, only to be defeated by the forces of Tran Hung Dao, perhaps the first in a long line of nationalist heroes whose strategic brilliance would be used to repel foreign invasions. Tran inspired the Vietnamese to fight the Mongols, whose "ambassadors stroll about in our streets with conceit, using their owls' and crows' tongues to abuse our court, flexing their goats' and dogs' bodies to threaten our ministers . . . They

have extracted silver and gold from our limited treasures."
The Chinese, however, again invaded Vietnam at the beginning of the fifteenth century and held control until repelled
by the armies of Le Loi, who established the Le dynasty in
1428. Le Loi too expressed strong nationalist sentiments,
boasting that "we have our own mountains and rivers, our
own customs and traditions." Centuries later, Ho Chi Minh
would convey thoughts similar to those of Tran Hung Dao
and Le Loi and, like them, he would use his "virile, martial
patriotism" to oust the invaders.[1]

The French Connection

Foreign adventurers and imperialists, however, would continue to challenge Vietnamese autonomy. In the sixteenth century, Portuguese traders arrived in Vietnam to develop silk
and spice markets and established a settlement along the coast
of central Vietnam at Da Nang. The Portuguese left after a
century, their fantasies of riches from Vietnam unfulfilled.
Other Europeans, particularly French Jesuits, remained interested, however, and by the mid-1800s posed a great challenge
to Vietnamese independence. In the early nineteenth century
the northern and southern provinces had been unified under
the Nguyen dynasty, centered at Hué, a bit northwest of Da
Nang. The Nguyen, however, administered Vietnam errati-
cally, could not maintain harmony between the north and
south, and had to contend with tax protests, smallpox, lo-
custs, and constant breaks in the Red River dike system. In
1858, a French fleet with three thousand troops arrived in Da
Nang and began to attack the Nguyen and, within a decade,
had established control over Vietnam. In 1862, a collaborator in the Vietnamese court ceded the southern third of Vietnam, Cochinchina, to the French, and it became a French
colony with its capital at Saigon. A year later, hoping to create a trade route along the Mekong River all the way into
China, the French established a protectorate in Cambodia,
which lay immediately west of Cochinchina. But the Mekong

was not navigable to China's borders, so the French turned their attention northward, and by the 1880s they held protectorates in the central (Annam) and northern (Tonkin) regions of Vietnam, and in Laos, north of Cambodia and west of Vietnam, as well. For the next seven decades, this area would be known as French Indochina.

Like the forces of Tran Hung Dao or the Tay Son, Vietnamese nationalists in the 1880s and thereafter began to rebel against the brutal conditions created by an outside power. The French established rubber plantations and coal mines with Vietnamese workers virtually enslaved, and the colonial administration used corvée labor – forcing peasants to work on public projects like roads or bridges in place of paying taxes – to build up the infrastructure. In a short story by the Vietnamese writer Ngo Tat To, he illustrates the burdens of life under the French and their Vietnamese lackeys. A woman, Mrs Dau, travels to the home of Representative Que, a collaborator with the French, to negotiate the release of her husband from prison, where he had been sent for not being able to pay his "body tax." In exchange for Mr Dau's freedom, his wife is forced to trade four valuable puppies, and, tragically, her daughter Ty. Adding insult to injury, before gaining her husband's release, she also has to pay a body tax for her brother-in-law, even though he had died months earlier. On her way out, Mrs Dau's fine is increased because she had paid in coin, not paper currency, and there was a "transfer fee" as well.[2]

Ngo Tat To's story not only reveals the colonial administration established by the French, but also the role of the Vietnamese upper classes who worked with the Europeans to exploit their own people. To the Vietnamese, those countrymen, usually large landholders and converts to Catholicism, were a threat to national sovereignty. Nationalists might refer to a collaborator as a "God-cursed traitor who acted like a worm in one's bones," while Court officials were "cowards excessively anxious to save their lives." Confronted by such Francophiles, nationalists pledged to fight – often in verse:

We possess our life, but we must know how to give it up
Shall we remain silent and thereby earn the reputation of cowards?
As long as there exist people on this earth, we shall exist
As long as there is water, we must bail it out
We must read the Proclamation on the victory over the Wu
We shall follow the example of those who exterminated the Mongols[3]

In fact, the greatest patriot of this generation was a poet, Phan Boi Chau, a founder of the "Association for the Modernization of Vietnam" in 1904. To Phan, the Vietnamese Mandarin class as well as the French had refused to listen to the people, who, for their part, did not assert themselves strongly enough. As a result, Phan saw a land "splashed with blood. The whole country has a tragic hue." Phan and other nationalists believed that Japan, where the monarch and the people allegedly respected each other, could serve as a model for the too-often greedy and selfish Vietnamese, and many of them began a "Travel East" movement to encourage young nationalists to train and raise funds in China and Japan. These poets–freedom fighters, however, also saw great hope in the future. To Phan, almost all Vietnamese had reason to forcefully oppose French rule. As he explained:

> Ten thousand Vietnamese can at least kill one hundred Frenchmen,
> One thousand Vietnamese can kill ten Frenchmen,
> One hundred Vietnamese can kill one Frenchman.
> In this way four to five hundred thousand Vietnamese can wipe out four to five thousand Frenchmen!
> Those grey-eyed, heavily-bearded people cannot live if Vietnam is to live![4]

Phan's words describing the extent of Vietnam's will to resist would be prophetic in the coming decades as his ideological descendants would come to the fore.

The New Left

The generation of Vietnamese nationalists that came of age in the aftermath of World War I would carry on the tradition of Tran Hung Dao, Quang Trung, Phan Boi Chau, and others and ultimately gain national independence and make a revolution. By the 1920s, younger, more militant patriots, inspired by the likes of Lenin, the Russian revolutionary Bakunin, and the Chinese revolutionary politician Sun Yatsen, and imbued with the growing spirit of anti-colonialism, were moving to the forefront of the resistance, led by a young Annamite born in 1890 who was variously called Nguyen Sinh Cung, Nguyen Tat Thanh, and Nguyen Ai Quoc, but who would become known to the world as Ho Chi Minh. As a young boy, so the legend goes, he sat at the feet of Phan Boi Chau and listened to his nationalist poetry; he heard his father, a civil servant, attack the French administration and refuse to learn its language, thereby getting fired from his job, although the French made up charges of drunkenness and embezzlement to justify the dismissal; and he saw his neighbors in Nghe An, in Annam, forced to do corvée labor.

Ho quite obviously was raised on resistance. Phan Boi Chau even tried to persuade Ho's father to send the young man to Japan or China to be educated, but instead he enrolled his son in the program of French studies at Hué. There he saw imperial troops violently suppress a tax rebellion and his father lose his job, so Ho dropped out and became a merchant seaman. After two years at sea, he spent the early war years in London, then moved on to Paris in late 1917. In France, he fit in with a large group of East Asian expatriates, radicals, and Socialists and began to develop the political ideology and strategy that would take him through the next half century. In Paris, Ho allegedly worked as a pastry chef by day – until, the joke goes, he was fired for refusing to bake Napoleons – and helped draw up a program for Vietnamese liberation with his leftist compatriots by night.

At this time, adopting the name Nguyen Ai Quoc ("Nguyen the Patriot"), he apparently rented a tuxedo and tried to arrange a visit with Woodrow Wilson to discuss his plans for Vietnam while the American president was attending the postwar peace conference at Versailles. Wilson, despite his anti-imperialist rhetoric, had little interest in the non-white colonies, so Ho turned even further to the left, befriending Chinese Communists like Zhou Enlai and Liu Shaoqi, joining the

Parti Communiste Français and the Comintern (Communist International), and making his first trip to the Soviet Union, where he wrote articles using the name Nguyen O Phap, or "Nguyen the anti-French." In Moscow, the Comintern appointed Ho to organize the "League of East Asian Oppressed Peoples" in Guangdong, China, the site of Phan Boi Chau's exile and the center of the Vietnamese resistance in Asia. While there, Ho, now known as "Wong," and other Vietnamese radicals at the Whampoa Military Academy, which had been established by Sun Yatsen, were trained by both Jiang Jieshi and Zhou, who would become blood rivals in the Chinese Civil War. As Ho's major biographer, Jean Lacouture, explains, while in China Ho "began a practical course in political philosophy and behaved in general in the manner of a secular saint, chopping wood, stopping the barber from beating his wife . . . and feeding the little boy; he played a role that was part Buddha and part Lenin-in-Finland."[5]

Reds

As a consequence of his time in Guangdong, Ho's nationalism merged more strongly than ever with his study of Communism, and he also began developing contacts with many other Vietnamese Leftists who would help him make the Revolution, including Ho Tung Mau, Le Hong Phong, Le Hong Son, and, especially, Pham Van Dong, Truong Chinh, and, later, Vo Nguyen Giap. In February 1930, many of them formally established the Indochinese Communist Party (ICP, or the "Dang Cong San Dong Duon."). With an appeal to both "the oppressed colonies and the exploited working class," the ICP offered a ten-point program that stressed nationalist objectives such as ousting the French and establishing Vietnamese independence, along with Communist goals such as land redistribution, while also promising civil rights, public education, and equality between men and women.[6] The establishment of the ICP, however, was marked by a strategic dispute between Nguyen Ai Quoc and many of his comrades. Quoc

(Ho) had announced that the Vietnamese resistance should be peasant-led but also should seek the active support of middle-class landlords, based on their common hatred of the French. But in October 1930, under pressure from the Comintern and the far left of the ICP, the Party deleted references to such alliances from its program and stated that it would be "the party of the working class." At that point, "there was no longer any doubt that the movement led by Ho Chi Minh was dedicated to social revolution" as well as national liberation.[7]

While the ICP debated the relative places of nationalism and class struggle, the Vietnamese and the French took to the streets. From the 1930s forward, Ho and the Party would often have to respond to pressures for action from below, and that was the case in 1930 and 1931. Ho was in Hong Kong (where he was now known as "Tong Van So") in the early months of 1930, as workers, protesting the dire impact of the world depression on their wages and prices, spontaneously staged strikes at a Haiphong cement works, a Saigon rubber plantation, and a Nam Dinh textile mill, while also organizing work stoppages and demonstrations at various sites in Tonkin and Annam on 1 May, International Labor Day. The most serious actions took place in Ho's home region of Nghe Tinh, in northern Annam. Peasants and workers there had established "soviets" to guide the protests and, in some cases, had unseated the local administration, reduced rents, and redistributed land, all without any centralized control from the ICP. Ironically, Ho and the French authorities both were displeased with these rebellions. The Nghe Tinh uprising lacked effective organization, so Ho feared that the French would crush it and seriously damage the entire movement. He was right. The French did respond fiercely. In September 1930, their airplanes bombed thousands of peasants as they marched in protest. Local police arrested over 1,000 Vietnamese suspected of being Communists or taking part in the rebellions, executed over 80 protestors, and handed long prison sentences to over 400 others. The ICP estimated that, nationwide, over 2,000 militants were killed and over 50,000 arrested, including Pham Van Dong, Truong Chinh, and Vo

Nguyen Giap in Vietnam, and Ho in Hong Kong. Bad planning and a lack of weapons, along with the French repression, caused the ICP severe damage; Ho's efforts to build up an organized and disciplined movement would have to begin from scratch.

Although in disarray in the aftermath of the Nghe Tinh affair, the Party would emerge from the French attacks stronger than before. Exile groups in China and Thailand would oversee protest activities, and in Vietnam remnants of the ICP met underground and published a newspaper while peasant strikes and demonstrations occurred in 1932–3 despite the French crackdown. More importantly, world politics, as they would repeatedly, created conditions that Ho and his allies would exploit to Vietnamese advantage. The 1933 rise of Adolf Hitler and the Nazis alarmed Europeans, especially the Left. As a result, many nations, including France, moved into their "Popular Front" phase, establishing governments that included all anti-Fascist elements, including Socialists and Communists. The French government thus took a less harsh view of the Vietnamese resistance, offering amnesty to thousands of political prisoners, allowing the ICP to exist on a "semi-legal" basis if it renounced violence, and even accepting the election of two Communists to the Saigon city council. This Vietnamese "glasnost" also enabled Pham Van Dong, Truong Ching, Le Duan, and Vo Nguyen Giap to openly organize and rise to leadership in the ICP.

Despite the political opening in Vietnam, Ho remained abroad after his release from Hong Kong prison. In Moscow, Stalin was suspicious of Ho's versions of nationalism and peasant Communism. The Soviet leader expected Popular Fronts to be under the authority of local Communists, but Ho insisted that the ICP *not* demand leadership of the movement in Vietnam but instead "show itself to be its most loyal, active and sincere member." Many ICP members, however, challenged Ho on this point as well. In an article in the *Communist Review* Vietnamese party leaders criticized Ho's "opportunist theories" about working with non-Communist groups and attacked him for his "erroneous and collaborationist tactics" of accepting rich peasants and bourgeoisie into the anti-French campaign.[8]

Ho accordingly spent the 1930s organizing from outside Vietnam, principally in China. Although criticized for his attempts to work with "class enemies," he understood and emphasized as an overall organizing principle the one issue certain to appeal to all layers of Vietnamese society – *land*. Indeed, the Vietnamese struggle in the 1930s, and thereafter, revolved around the central issue of land ownership. French landholders and Vietnamese collaborators held vast tracts of the countryside. In Cochinchina, for instance, just 6,200 landlords owned over half the rice acreage, while another 60,000 owned about 40 percent. The remaining 4.5 million Vietnamese held little land or were tenants, with 60 percent of the rural population (approximately 2.7 million) altogether landless. In Tonkin, 2 percent of the landholders controlled nearly half of the rice lands, and tenants on those plantations had to pay their landlords between 40 and 60 percent of their crops as rent. Worse, these percentages were fixed amounts based on a "normal" year's yield. If flood, drought, or other such problems occurred, rents could reach 80 percent or higher in real terms.

And the War Came

Wars fundamentally transform social conditions, and just as the Vietnam War would change America in the 1960s, World War II was a major turning point in the Vietnamese struggle for national liberation and social revolution. While Popular Front politics and land issues undoubtedly helped the ICP and nationalist movement, the world war brought great difficulty to Vietnam but also created the conditions for future struggle and, in the long run, success. The path from the outset of World War II to the war against the Americans, however, involved more twists and turns than is easily imagined, with shifts in alliances and enemies, changes in strategies, and apparent and real victories, with frequent setbacks, constant along the way. Indeed, the American phase of Vietnam's wars can be directly linked to the events of 1939–45. Though the United States had little knowledge of or interest in Vietnam during the war, American leaders would make it a central battleground in their efforts to remake the world after World War II.

As war broke out in Europe in the fall of 1939, the situation in Vietnam for the resistance was, as always, precarious, and quite confusing as well. In Asia, the Japanese were trying to establish what they called the Greater East Asian Co-Prosperity Sphere, an alliance of Asian states under Japan's control. Already brutally occupying China and Korea, Japan could be expected to expand throughout the continent. Thus Ho Chi Minh, along with Pham Van Dong and Vo Nguyen Giap, operating out of southern China, trained Jiang Jieshi's troops in guerrilla warfare to use against the Japanese. Simultaneously, the French began another crackdown in Vietnam. Because the Soviet Union had signed a non-aggression treaty with Hitler in August 1939, Communists everywhere were held in greater suspicion, and the French declared the ICP to be illegal and arrested over 2,000 activists, mostly from urban areas. Eventually, however, the French repression forced the nationalists to shift their focus to the countryside, thus building the foundation for later struggle, and once more demonstrating the Vietnamese capacity to take advantage of apparent setbacks. Though under attack at home by France and threatened externally by the Japanese, Ho and his comrades working out of China were able to revitalize and expand the resistance.

In November 1939, meeting at Gia Dinh Province near Saigon, the ICP broadened its appeal beyond those attracted to Vietnamese Communism and established the "Anti-imperialist National United Front" with national liberation, not class struggle, as its number one goal. The conflict with the French, however, took a new turn in 1940, and events in both Europe and Asia would again change the direction of Vietnamese efforts. In Europe, German armies swept through France in just weeks, causing the government to fall and be replaced by a Nazi puppet state with its capital at Vichy. At the same time, Japan was unable to force China to surrender and so set its sights on Indochina, demanding that the French close railway traffic from Hanoi to southern China because shipments of war-related items into the Kunming area were being used against Japanese troops. The French gave in on that point and in August gave the Japanese military facilities and transit rights through Indochina, and allowed them to station troops in Tonkin. In September 1940, Japanese troops thus landed at Haiphong, along the northern coast; another outside power was entering Vietnam.

Immediately, Japan's forces began to attack French troops at outposts along the Chinese border, aided by the Vietnamese troops of Prince Cuong De, a nationalist who naively believed Japan's promise to grant his country independence. After brief skirmishing in Bac Son, the Japanese withdrew and the French crushed Cuong De's troops. Amid the various conflicts, however, the Vietnamese Communists were able to move into the vacuum and establish control, again without any central orders from ICP leadership. Once more, as in Nghe Tinh in 1930–1, the Vietnamese rebels, disorganized and outgunned, had to retreat, but spontaneous uprisings soon took place in western Cochinchina (November 1940) and Nghe An (January 1941). These rebellions too were premature and ineffective, but forced the leadership of the resistance in the ICP to hold a general conference to discuss the future of their movement. Thus in May 1941, it met in Pac Bo, along the Chinese border. For the first time in thirty years, the man now calling himself Ho Chi Minh ("He Who Enlightens") entered into his homeland. In Pac Bo, Ho lived in a cave he named "Karl Marx" with a stream next to it that he called "Lenin," and he secretly wrote and distributed a newsletter titled *Viet Lap*, or "Independent Vietnam."

The Pac Bo meeting was a crucial step in the liberation struggle, for there Ho and the ICP established the *Viet Nam Doc Lap Dong Minh*, "The League for Vietnamese Independence," better known as the *Viet Minh*. Ho and the Viet Minh stressed nationalist sentiments, emphasizing Vietnamese history and culture. They called on all "rich people, soldiers, workers, peasants, intellectuals, employees, traders, youth, and women who warmly love your country" to join the cause. "National liberation is the most important problem," he insisted. "We shall overthrow the Japanese and French and their jackals in order to save people from the situation between boiling water and boiling heat."[9] Ho and his chief military officer, Vo Nguyen Giap, an expert in Maoist guerrilla warfare, also decided on the military strategy to be used against the occupying forces. The Japanese, with an eye on the oil fields of the Dutch East Indies (Indonesia), had entered Indochina in force in the summer of 1941, ousted French officials, and set up a brutal administration of their own which, between 1941 and 1945, created conditions of famine and dire poverty that would kill between one and two million Vietnamese. Some ICP hardliners were urging prompt military action against the Japanese, but Ho and Giap cautioned that the Viet Minh was not yet prepared for battle, and instead they advocated patience and building up an armed movement until Japan was weakened and on the verge of defeat by the Americans and others.

Before taking on the Japanese, however, Ho would again have to contend with his old friends and enemies – and they were often one and the same – in China. In 1942, he traveled to China again, but this time was arrested by authorities of the same army he had just trained. Jiang Jieshi feared Ho's independent, nationalist streak and wanted to establish a puppet Vietnamese party of his own. While serving his fifteen-month sentence under terrible conditions in Chinese prison, Ho continued to work for liberation, often defiantly challenging his captors in verse:

> Being chained is a luxury to compete for.
> The chained have somewhere to sleep, the unchained haven't . . .
> The State treats me to its rice,
> I lodge in its palaces,
> Its guards take turns escorting me.
> Really, the honor is too great . . .

Ho's saga then took another twist upon his release, as the Chinese began *paying* him, perhaps as much as $100,000 per month, to fight against the Japanese and for Vietnamese independence.[10]

Inside Vietnam, however, Vo Nguyen Giap had different plans from Ho. In July 1944, at Giap's urging, the Revolutionary Committee of Cao Ban Region voted to begin armed struggle against the Japanese in the northern provinces. While Ho agreed that "the phase of peaceful revolution is behind us," he also warned Giap that "the time for general insurrection has not yet come." Instead, Ho wanted to establish a "brigade of liberation" with political, not military, aims. Toward that end, in December 1944 he established the "Propaganda Unit for National Liberation," which "shows by its name that greater importance should be attached to the political side than the military side." At the same time, Ho sought "national resistance by the whole people," who would be mobilized and armed for a long, guerrilla struggle. Again he stressed patience. Although "we may not have strength on our side," he saw "no reason for simply letting ourselves be crushed." Finally, as he said goodbye to Giap, he reminded him, "Stealth, continual stealth. Never attack except by surprise. Retire before the enemy has a chance to strike back." It was advice Giap would never forget, and Ho's general ideas from the summer of 1944 would serve the Vietnamese cause well time and again in the coming years.[11]

To the August Revolution

In some ways, late 1944 marks the beginning of the armed struggle, as Ho envisioned the Propaganda Unit as the "embryo" of a Vietnamese Liberation Army. Accordingly, Viet Minh guerrillas, at times fighting with French troops, began engaging the Japanese in Thai Nguyen Province, northeast of Hanoi not far from the Chinese border, and even successfully convinced several French garrisons to desert. Viet–French cooperation was not typical, however. Anticipating that the allied powers would defeat a badly weakened Japan in 1945, the French planned to regain full control over Indochina after the war. A year prior, Ho had offered economic concessions and issued moderate demands – political autonomy with full independence delayed for ten years – but the French would not consider negotiations on those, or any, terms. Worse, the French were preparing for a concentrated assault on the Viet Minh in March 1945, and Giap's forces, outnumbered and outgunned, might have been crushed. Again, though, "the gods were on Ho's side" as the Japanese, on 9 March 1945 (just three days before the planned French attack), arrested and jailed every French official with even the slightest authority. The Japanese then returned Emperor Bao Dai to the throne and nullified the 1884 treaty that had established French control over Indochina. Any thoughts of Vietnamese independence, however, were short-lived as the Japanese maintained their authority and placed their own Vietnamese puppets in power.

Although the events of March 1945 seemed to be another setback to the movement, they worked to Viet Minh advantage ultimately. By attacking the French, Japan prevented them from destroying Viet Minh bases and capturing its leaders. And the Japanese army, now in charge, was not as experienced or efficient in dealing with the resistance. The Japanese had come as conquerors but ironically "acted as a catalyst, leading to a fundamental transformation of Vietnamese political configurations," as Huynh Kim Khanh, an authority on Vietnamese affairs in this period, put it. "By bending the French will, setting limits to their political monopoly, and finally destroying their power," he explained, "the Japanese exposed . . . the myth of the white man's invincibility and . . . the bankruptcy of the concept of the 'white man's burden.'"[12] As a result, Ho again had a window of opportunity. With the French out of the way, the Viet Minh declared the Japanese the new number one enemy, and Giap began moving units southward for armed struggle. Ho's strategic concepts of the "favorable moment" and concentrating against "the main adversary" had fortuitously converged. Though still warning against "overadventurousness," Ho nonetheless saw the movement entering a new phase, and in June 1945 he established a "free zone" of Viet Minh areas and united the various military units into an "Army of Liberation." Throughout

Vietnam, the conditions seemed ripe for revolution. Labor unrest was rising, Communist propaganda units were successfully recruiting, peasants – angry and hungry due to famine – were joining the cause, and Viet Minh fighters were even seizing government granaries to feed the people. By mid-1945, all northern provinces had active Viet Minh organizations, while over 100,000 peasants in the central region had enlisted in the resistance as well.

In the summer of 1945, the Viet Minh and other nationalists were prepared for power and liberation. The years of exile, repression, famine, and struggle seemed to be leading inexorably to the recreation of an independent Vietnam. Western leaders had been critical of colonialism during World War II; the French had been ousted by Japan; and the atomic bombings of Hiroshima and Nagasaki in August 1945 had ended the Japanese hope of establishing an Asian empire. In Vietnam, Ho called for a "national insurrection" at the ICP's Ninth Plenum, and the Party's Secretary General, Truong Chinh, took direction of the uprising. On 16 August, Ho addressed the National Liberation Committee, introduced the movement's new flag – a gold star on a red background – and emotionally called for a countrywide rebellion and described the Front for national independence: "At present, the Japanese army is crushed. The National Salvation Movement has spread to the whole country. The . . . Viet Minh has millions of members from all social strata: intellectuals, peasants, workers, businessmen, soldiers, and from all nationalities . . . In the Front our compatriots march side by side without discrimination to age, sex, religion, or fortune."[13]

Inspired by Ho's appeal and energized by Japan's defeat, Viet Minh forces conducted mass rallies and seized control in various villages and towns in the northern and central regions in mid-August. In Hanoi, ICP cadre and local militia units overthrew Japanese authorities in a bloodless coup, and in late August Viet Minh representatives traveled to the Imperial Capital at Hué to demand Bao Dai's abdication. Facing the prospects of losing his throne or his life, he formally resigned on 25 August, and four days later invested Ho with the Confucian Mandate of Heaven and handed over to him the imperial sword and seal. As the French scholar Philippe Devillers observed, "ten days after the Japanese capitulation, the Vietminh controlled the entire territory of Vietnam. With disconcerting ease, through the combined effects of negotiation, infiltration, propaganda, and – above all – Japanese 'neutrality,' it had gained power."[14] After a lifetime of struggle, Ho and his fellow nationalist-Communists had achieved independence and gained power – it seemed. Thus on 2 September 1945, Ho faced a half million of his fellow Vietnamese in Ba Dinh Square in Hanoi and proclaimed the independent Democratic Republic of Viet-Nam [DRVN], with himself as president and minister of foreign affairs. Ho's words that day were quite remarkable, and ironic: "All men are created equal," he began; "they are endowed by their Creator with certain unalienable rights; among these are Life, Liberty, and the pursuit of Happiness." He deliberately chose words from the United States Declaration of Independence to connect the Vietnamese Revolution with other such historical movements, to announce to the world the democratic nature of the DRVN, and to try to convince America of his good intentions. After a long condemnation of the French and Japanese, Ho concluded that "Vietnam has the right to be a free and independent country – and in fact is so already," and he was "now convinced that the Allied Nations [then organizing the United Nations] . . . will not refuse to acknowledge the independence of Viet-Nam."[15] Ho, this time, was wrong. His country was still occupied, with British, Chinese, and French military forces deployed in Vietnam and all preferring that a regime other than his be in charge.

Independence Denied

Ho assumed control of a "nation" that had received no international recognition and was structurally damaged by the years of occupation and the recent famine. The Vietnamese lacked technology and capital and had suffered at least one million deaths from the famine of 1944–5, with another million likely to die by the end of the year. In some areas, bodies were just piled up along the roadside. The new government, then, had to deal with fundamental problems like hunger and poverty simply to stem the disaster. Accordingly, Ho took a moderate approach in his domestic policies and foreign affairs, trying to respond to the crisis at home but not frighten off foreign observers. He abolished the head tax and removed restrictions on the transport of rice from the southern to the northern regions. Ho also announced an austerity program, encouraging an already hungry people to fast, but also intensifying cultivation and banning the distillation of liquor to save grains for food. To somewhat ameliorate those hardships, the DRVN also began a land reform program in which it seized property from French and Japanese holders and their collaborators for redistribution. To gather public support and assure other nations, the government accepted the concept of private property and did not proclaim the establishment of a Communist society. In fact, the DRVN, as Ho envisioned it, should be a broad alliance of all patriotic groups, including progressive bourgeoisie and large landowners. Toward that end, the ICP formally dissolved itself on 11 November. Though Communism would remain a vital force in Vietnamese life, the DRVN would have a Vietnamese, not Communist, government.

None of these measures seemed to matter to the French, who quickly moved to restore control in Indochina. At war's end, Jiang Jieshi's Chinese troops were occupying northern Vietnam, while British troops were stationed in the south. The British, however, delayed in disarming the Japanese and, using French prisoners of war and their own Indian troops, overthrew the Viet Minh committee in charge of Saigon. In the north, France announced that its forces would replace the Chinese, who were only too happy to leave Vietnam and get back to China to confront Mao's CCP in their own civil war. Britain too would quit Vietnam, ceding its responsibility to the French. France, despite its collapse in 1940 and collaboration with the Nazis in World War II, would be back in control of Vietnam. For Ho, it was a nightmarish scenario. World War II, the years of resistance, famine, struggle, and ultimate success notwithstanding, the Vietnamese liberation movement found itself in much the same situation it had been a decade earlier.

Indeed, the French were determined to turn back the clock. Their commander, General Jean Leclerc, publicly promised that they would retain control over Indochina, by force of arms if necessary. Thus Ho, lacking international support and trying to rebuild at home, had to negotiate with his former colonial masters. The French, however, were not of one mind on Vietnam. Jean Sainteny, the French representative to the talks with Ho, did not believe his country could afford to commit soldiers and resources to Vietnam, and he was impressed to some degree by the revolution there, a view shared by some of the younger French officers. But older colonial administrators still viewed the Viet Minh as a rebel band, not terribly popular and unlikely to hold onto power. Sainteny, for his part, was thus predisposed to deal with Ho, a position Leclerc came to share as well. In fact, Leclerc, in early 1946, cabled Paris that it was urgent to settle the Vietnam situation and suggested it be prepared to discuss "independence" to conclude an agreement. Ho was flexible as well, stating his willingness to negotiate membership in the French Union as a precondition to later autonomy.

Ho, Sainteny, and Leclerc all sought accommodation, and so reached an agreement in March 1946. In the pact, France agreed to "recognize the Republic of Viet Nam as a free state having its own government, its own parliament and its own finances, and forming part of the Indochinese Federation and the French Union." In return, Ho accepted France's continued economic and cultural influence in the north and the deployment of 15,000 of its troops there. Hated as the French were, Ho figured that it was better to have them in Vietnam rather than the traditional Chinese enemy. As he reminded his critics in Hanoi, "Don't you remember your history? The last time the Chinese came, they stayed a thousand years. The French are foreigners. They are weak. Colonialism is dying.

The white man is finished in Asia. But if the Chinese stay now, they will never go. As for me, I prefer to sniff French shit for five years than eat Chinese shit for the rest of my life."[16]

Though Ho had hedged his bets by advising Viet Minh units to conduct guerrilla operations in the south while he negotiated, many of his associates berated him as a traitor, a puppet of the French, and a sellout. In an open letter, many Viet Minh followers lamented, "little did we suspect that we should have to renounce all hope after [the March pact]. You have signed an agreement to accept self-government, not independence! The strength of our faith in you in the days when your name stood for the great revolutionary idea is equaled today by the rage in our hearts – we are ashamed that we should have chosen the wrong elder . . . But the Vietnamese people never lose hope for long . . . They will continue along the path which you have been unable to follow to the end."[17]

Such criticism seemed more valid than ever in mid-1946. On 1 June, the High Commissioner in southern Vietnam, Admiral Thierry d'Argenlieu, declared that Cochinchina was "a free state having its own government, its own parliament, its own army and its own finances, forming part of the Indochinese Federation and the French Union." D'Argenlieu's proclamation came just as Ho was en route to a conference with the French at Fontainebleau Palace, outside of Paris. Immediately, the Vietnamese delegation walked out in protest and the talks were suspended, but Ho stayed behind to try to cobble together some type of deal. While at Fontainebleau, he and Sainteny developed a strong working relationship, with the French representative calling Ho a "person of the highest caliber" whose "intelligence, vast culture, unbelievable energy, and total unselfishness had earned him unparalleled prestige and popularity in the eyes of his people."[18] Ho had similar feelings about Sainteny and so both sought ways to avoid war throughout the summer of 1946. In September, after more compromises by Ho, the parties signed the Fontainebleau Agreement, which reaffirmed the March pact, gave France new economic concessions in the north in exchange for "democratic rights" in Cochinchina, and established a cease-fire in the southern half of the country beginning on 30 October. The agreement did not mention independence or even discuss the relationship between Vietnam and the French Union. Again, the Vietnamese would have to wait for national liberation and autonomy.

From Haiphong to Dien Bien Phu

Despite Ho's efforts to reconcile with the French and pacify Viet Minh hardliners, skirmishing between the two sides continued into the fall. Then, in November, the French began to provoke the Vietnamese, first by trying to seize control of Haiphong harbor in order to keep Chinese weapons from entering Vietnam. Days later, after the Viet Minh fired on a French ship in the harbor at Haiphong, the French, violating Fontainebleau, ordered all Vietnamese troops removed from the area. General Jean Valluy, the French commander in Vietnam, instructed the officer in charge at Haiphong, Colonel Dèbes, "to give a harsh lesson" to the Viet Minh. "By every means at your disposal you must take control of Haiphong and bring the government and the Vietnamese army to repentance."[19] On 23 November, Dèbes did just that, ordering a full evacuation of Haiphong. Three hours later, with the Viet Minh still in positions there, Dèbes opened fire and called in naval artillery support. By the end of the day, over 6,000 Vietnamese had died, another 25,000 were wounded, and Haiphong had fallen to the French. The DRVN then declared the agreements with the French null and void and, on 19 December, General Giap called for armed resistance. The next day Ho appealed to the entire population to rise against the French: "Men and women, old and young, regardless of creeds, political parties, or nationalities, all the Vietnamese must stand up to fight the French colonialists to save the Fatherland. Those who have rifles will use their rifles; those who have swords will use their swords; those who have no swords will use spades, hoes, or sticks. Everyone must endeavor to oppose the colonialists and save his country . . . The hour for national salvation has struck! We must sacrifice even our last drop of blood to safeguard our country."[20] The First Indochina War was about to begin.

Barely a year after gloriously proclaiming Vietnamese independence with Thomas Jefferson's words, Ho Chi Minh faced war against a European power while being accused of "rightist deviationism" and "bourgeois opportunism" by many of his own followers. But again, through unrivaled strategic skills, and at times what appeared to be magic, Ho rallied his people and emerged victorious. In 1954, the Viet Minh defeated the French and appeared to have won national independence. As in 1945–6, however, things were not as they appeared to be.

As the war began, French forces held huge advantages over the Vietnamese in terms of manpower, weapons, transport, and military organization. Native forces, however, were fighting in their own country for their own liberation and livelihood. In warfare, Napoleon estimated, morale was overwhelmingly – 90 percent he believed – the most important factor, far more crucial than material, and the Vietnamese proved that repeatedly, though they were fierce fighters as well. The French Union Forces (FUF) – comprising French and Vietnamese troops – grew from 70,000 men in the early 1940s to over 500,000 by 1954; the French Expeditionary Corps (FEC), the occupying army, increased from 70,000 troops at the outset of World War II to 115,000 in 1947, and 180,000 by the 1950s; the Vietnamese National Army (VNA), created by the French and consisting of Vietnamese soldiers, had about 375,000 troops in it by 1954. General Giap, meanwhile, had about 300,000 Viet Minh and militia fighters under his charge, with only a third equipped with small arms initially, and no naval or air forces. Even as they acquired military supplies from China during the war, Ho and Giap would always be outgunned by the French and their western supporters.

But in the end technological power would not be decisive. The Viet Minh controlled the loyalty of the population and Vietnamese morale remained high. To his people, Ho was a daily living symbol of resistance and freedom, and he was one of them. As one of his assistants, Hoang Quoc Viet, described it, he "used to live among the peasants, wear brown cotton clothes like theirs, and live by the same restrictions as everybody else." This was the "Uncle Ho" persona that the world would come to know in the following decades. In addition to this "common touch," Ho could be a hardheaded military strategist, telling a French official that "you would kill ten of my men for every one I killed of yours. But even at that rate you would be unable to hold out, and victory would go to me."[21] The French Minister of War did not really disagree with Ho's assessments. "It is evident that the greater part of the country remains in the hands of the Viet Minh," he recognized. "I do not think that we should undertake the conquest of French Indochina. It would necessitate an expeditionary corps of at least 500,000 men." And General Leclerc questioned the possibility of military success altogether, conceding that "the capital problem is now political. It is a question of coming to terms with an awakening xenophobic nationalism."[22]

French military superiority, all sides recognized, would not be the key factor in the war. Like the American rebels in their war for independence against the British in the 1770s and 1780s, the Viet Minh was more dedicated to its cause, willing to sacrifice, familiar with its own land, politically popular, and maintained discipline and morale. And that would make all the difference. The Vietnamese were fighting a "people's war." All segments of their society – including women, children, and the aged – contributed to the resistance; indeed, one of the more crucial support groups was that of "combat mothers," older women who adopted soldiers into their own families. Militarily, people's war, derived from Maoist doctrine in the Chinese Civil War, emphasized constant movement and flexibility. As Truong Chinh explained, "if the enemy attacks us from above, we will attack him from below. If he attacks us in the North, we will respond in Central or South Vietnam, or in Cambodia and Laos. If the enemy penetrates one of our territorial bases, we will immediately strike hard at his belly and back . . . cut off his legs, destroy his roads."

Such tactics would anger and frustrate the French, with one of their officers complaining "if only the Vietnamese would face us in a set battle, how we would crush them!"[23] Ho and Giap realized that too, and would spend the next generation eluding French, and American, forces.

Ultimate victory, however, would not come without great difficulty and cost to the Viet Minh. Beginning around 1950, Giap, contrary to people's war doctrine, began large-scale engagements with the French. In October the Viet Minh attacked enemy forts along the Chinese border, with the French losing 6,000 troops and large numbers of mortars, trucks, machine guns, and rifles. Hoping to build on that success, Giap, in January 1951, began a general offensive, hoping for a Tet victory. About 15,000 Viet Minh who had been hiding in the mountains outside the Red River delta launched a "human wave" attack on French garrisons at Vinh Yen, near Hanoi. But the French reacted forcefully, rushing in reserves and dropping American-made napalm bombs on Giap's men. One Viet Minh, Ngo Van Chieu, described the French bombardment: "Another plane approaches and spews more fire. The bomb falls behind us and I feel its fiery breath which passes over my entire body. Men flee, and I can no longer restrain them. There is no way to live under that torrent of fire which runs and burns all in its route."[24] The French thus repulsed the assault on Vinh Yen with 6,000 Viet Minh killed. Giap did not retreat, though, striking French positions along the delta. In bitter fighting, the French held. The Viet Minh suffered more heavy losses and had little reason to celebrate Tet. In the spring, the situation worsened when Giap tried to cut off the French by sea by occupying Haiphong. The battle, "Operation Hoang Hoa Tham II," ended in another defeat. Just two months later, in the battle of "Ha Nam Ninh," French aircraft and armor blunted Giap's charges. By mid-June, the Viet Minh was backtracking and bloodied.

After the early 1951 setbacks, many of Giap's comrades criticized him harshly for being unduly aggressive and impatient, and even called for his removal. Ho intervened on behalf of his commander, but he and Giap also shifted to a strategy of *protracted war* – from then on, the Viet Minh would try to spread out French forces in defensive positions throughout the country so that they could be attacked in smaller engagements and, in time, French morale would collapse. When the time and conditions were right, Giap could then conduct big-unit engagements to gain decisive victories. Beginning in mid-1951, the Viet Minh, working with local tribes, successfully struck at many French district capitals in the mountains of the northwest, and did the same in league with Communit Pathet Lao guerrillas in Laos. Also at this time Chinese Communist forces, flush off their 1949 victory in their civil war, sent larger quantities of arms, equipment, and supplies to Ho – thousands of tons monthly by the end of the war – while a quarter million Chinese troops along the border served as a warning to the French and others against expanded warfare.

The French were thus concerned about the Viet Minh's growing capabilities, so General Jean de Lattre de Tassigny, their commander, directed his troops to seize the town of Hoa Binh, at the southern edge of the Red River delta, to disrupt Giap's communications network and reduce the movement of supplies and troops. The Viet Minh took huge losses – over 50 percent of its 40,000 troops were killed or wounded – but managed to blunt the offensive, infiltrate the entire delta area, and move freely in and out of liberated zones. Finally, frustrated and weary from chasing Viet Minh troops, the French withdrew from Hoa Binh in February 1952. French morale began to slip, as their enemy infiltrated or bypassed supposedly secure points along the "de Lattre Line." Indeed, French soldiers had so much difficulty clearing Viet Minh from the major north–south route, Highway 1, that they began to bitterly refer to it as "*la rue sans joi,*" the street without joy.

By 1953, French prospects were fading. Their new commander, General Henri Navarre, proposed a major expansion of the Vietnamese National Army, reinforcing French forces in Indochina and attacking Viet Minh positions in the delta. The United States backed the "Navarre Concept" with $400 million in aid. Navarre, however, blundered terribly. To secure access to the delta and cut enemy supply routes into Laos,

Navarre established a base at an isolated mountain valley near the Laotian border in northwest Vietnam. It was Dien Bien Phu, and it was destined to become one of the more memorable battle scenes of the twentieth century.

Navarre committed 12 battalions (about 15,000 soldiers), ten tanks, and six aircraft to Dien Bien Phu. In the surrounding hills the local commander, Colonel Christian de Castries, had further protected the main base by establishing strongpoints in the surrounding hills and, with typical élan, had named them after his mistresses: Beatrice, Gabrielle, Dominique, Elaine, and Claudine. The French, it seemed, were confident and daring the Viet Minh to attack. Giap took his time, though. The area near Dien Bien Phu seemed impassable, but thousands of Vietnamese peasants cut trails by hand, laid roads, and moved supplies as much as 500 miles to the front by bicycle and on foot. As four divisions of combat troops (about 50,000 men) moved on the base, they were daily bombed and napalmed by the French Air Force, but the advance continued. At times dragging heavy artillery by rope for fifty miles, the Viet Minh's dedication and willingness to sacrifice was decisive. At one point, a veteran of the Dien Bien Phu campaign related, a rope being used to pull a heavy artillery piece broke and a Vietnamese soldier dove in front of it to prevent it from rolling downhill, dying in the process. Meanwhile, de Castries, legend has it, was bringing in local prostitutes for his troops. The Viet Minh, to be sure, was emotionally and physically prepared for battle and was positioned to attack in the early months of 1954. When they reached Dien Bien Phu, Giap's men and material disappeared into caves they had dug into the hillsides, and they encroached on the French via the hundreds of miles of tunnels and trenches they had dug clandestinely.

For the French, the waiting was the hardest part, with Navarre even dropping leaflets on the Vietnamese daring them to fight. Giap moved according to his own pace, however, and finally struck on 13 March 1954. Initially Giap advanced his units en masse to try to overrun French positions on the perimeter, but such tactics cost him dearly, with about 2,000

Viet Minh lost in the first few days of battle alone. At that point, the commander became patient, digging and operating out of trenches while raining artillery on the French in the valley below. In time, French forces began to take heavy casualties, and the airfield at Dien Bien Phu became inoperable. By April, the Viet Minh were successfully assaulting fire bases along the perimeter as Giap's strategy of "steady attack and steady advance" was paying off. The commander pressed the attack throughout April and the French, taking heavy losses and short on supplies, were in dire straits. On 6 May, Dien Bien Phu fell. Ho Chi Minh, it once more seemed, was primed to become president of an independent Vietnam.

Vietnam, America, and the Cold War

The Viet Minh defeat of the French, it appeared, had cleared the way for Ho, as in 1945, to proclaim independence and assume the presidency of Vietnam. That would not happen. Just as the French had returned to Indochina to prevent the establishment of the DRVN after World War II, the United States would thwart Vietnamese autonomy after Dien Bien Phu, and in the process set off the Second Indochina War – one that would continue until 1975. Indeed, the Vietnamese Revolution, throughout the 1940s and early 1950s, was closely linked to various international developments. While the United States had little knowledge of or interest in Vietnam at the end of World War II, it quickly became an important national interest due to factors that lay far beyond Indochina, including the Cold War, European politics, and western economic expansion.

Ho had sought American support throughout his struggle against the French. In 1943, he initiated contacts with US intelligence agents in southern China, and the Viet Minh, it was reported, helped rescue American pilots downed behind Japanese lines, and may have even received light armaments from the Office of Strategic Services (OSS). Just as he had approached Woodrow Wilson at Versailles, Ho wrote letters to

President Harry S. Truman in 1945 seeking friendship and
assistance, but Washington, DC never even acknowledged his
overtures. In 1945 and 1946, various American military officials had close contact with the Viet Minh and came away
impressed. One OSS agent called Ho "an awfully sweet guy."
Other American operatives in Hanoi had helped him write
and translate his declaration of independence speech in September 1945. Major Allison Thomas, head of an intelligence
mission to Indochina, wrote quite positive reports about the
Viet Minh to his superiors. And General Philip Gallagher, a
US adviser in northern Vietnam, called Ho "an old Bolshevik," but nonetheless hoped that the Vietnamese "could be
given their independence." Even General George Marshall,
who served as both Secretary of State and of Defense, understood early on that the French "have no prospect" of victory
in Vietnam, and he warned that their war against the Viet
Minh "will remain a grievously costly enterprise, weakening
France economically and all the West generally in its relations
with Oriental peoples." And the Joint Chiefs of Staff (JCS)
recognized in 1949 that it was the "widening political consciousness and the rise of militant nationalism" among the
Vietnamese that was motivating the war against France; any
attempt to stop the Viet Minh would thus be "an anti-histori-
cal act likely in the long run to create more problems than it
solves and cause more damage than benefit."[25]

Despite these prophetic military warnings regarding the
danger of intervention in Vietnam, the United States became
progressively more involved there. Although US military officials saw Ho's popularity, the rise of nationalism, and French
weakness as huge barriers to success, American civilian officials took an opposite view. To them, it was crucial to support
France and stop Asian Communism. Over the military's objections, then, the United States began to send hundreds of
millions of dollars to French Indochina, even though Air Force
Chief of Staff Hoyt Vandenberg compared it to "pouring
money down a rathole."[26] To American officials in the White
House and Department of State, such policy was necessary
for three interrelated reasons: to maintain French support in

the European Cold War, to contain Communism in Asia, and to encourage economic development. Whereas military officers looked at conditions *inside* Vietnam and saw great risks, civilian officials had a *global* outlook and they saw Vietnam as part of a much larger contest – the Cold War.

Supporting France

During World War II, President Franklin Delano Roosevelt spoke often of the need to end European colonialism in Asia and Africa. While Roosevelt's rhetoric encouraged nationalist groups in the Third World, many were suspicious of western motives. Even Ho, though he wrote to Truman for support, nonetheless complained that the Americans were "only interested in replacing the French . . . They want to reorganize our country and control it. They are capitalists to the core."[27] US behavior bore him out. Although not thrilled with the French re-entry into Vietnam, the United States believed that events in Europe were much more important than those in Indochina and did not want to alienate its allies in Paris. After 1945, the United States was pursuing containment, and to do this cooperation from the western Europeans – the British, Germans in the western zones, and of course the French – was essential. Complicating matters, French President Charles De Gaulle was trying to re-establish his country's prestige and influence after the débâcle of Vichy, while the political Left – the Communist and Socialist Parties and the trade unions – was quite popular and netting impressive numbers of votes in free elections. If the United States tried to push France out of Vietnam, American officials feared, it might endanger De Gaulle politically and encourage the Left, which in turn could lead to the loss of a valuable ally in the fight against Euro-Communism.

Asian Communism

Although containment, as envisioned by its intellectual father, the American diplomat George Frost Kennan, was to be applied politically in Europe, the focus of the Cold War shifted eastward and led to hot wars in Asia. At the end of World War II, the United States had two principal economic-strategic objectives in Asia: to rebuild Japan along western, capitalist lines and to maintain the pro-American government of Jiang Jieshi in China. While America met its goals in Japan, China appeared to be a disaster. When, in 1949, Mao won the Civil War and established a Communist government in the world's most populated country (about a half billion), American leaders found it imperative to halt any other such advances in Asia. As a result, the United States intervened in the Korean War in 1950 to prevent victory by the nationalist-Communist forces of Kim Il Sung. In Vietnam, the spectre of Mao loomed just as large. Despite US military recognition of Ho's nationalist credentials, American civilian officials saw him simply as a Communist, a puppet of Mao and Stalin. From 1949 on, then, US policy toward Vietnam would be determined according to the greater need to keep the People's Republic of China (PRC) isolated and to make sure that unfriendly governments did not emerge in proximity to Japan. "The East is Red," Chinese Communists boasted, but "the West is Ready," Americans responded.

Economic Development

The escalating Cold War and the extension of containment had a powerful economic component, which was a fundamental and vital factor in the US intervention into Vietnam. In 1945, at war's end, the United States hoped to construct a "new world order" based on free trade and global investment. The major barrier to that, however, was a shortage of American dollars in Europe. Because of this "dollar gap," other nations, especially the British and French, could not buy American goods, thus hurting both the European and US economies and hampering Japanese reconstruction in Asia, which depended in large measure on trade with Southeast Asia, including Indochina. To address those problems, American leaders believed that it was necessary to purchase goods from Europe's colonies in Southeast Asia, and thus put dollars into their hands that would in turn be used to buy products made in the United States. But in the two most important areas – British Malaya and French Indochina – Communist insurgencies were already strong and growing. Thus, to help the domestic economy and rebuild their allies, American officials had to support the British and French wars against the Malayan Communists and the Viet Minh. As Andrew Rotter, who has given the most attention to this subject, explains, "if British economic recovery required British control of Malaya, so it must be. If the security of Malaya demanded support for the French-sponsored, anti-Communist government in Vietnam, the United States would offer its support."[28]

Civilian Hawks and Military Doves

The combination of these factors – maintaining French support in the Cold War, containing Asian Communism, expanding markets – created a new sense of urgency with regard to Vietnam. Thus in 1950 the United States supported the return of the deposed Emperor Bao Dai from the brothels and casinos of the Riviera to the Vietnamese throne. Bao Dai did not have a deep interest in governance and would rather be playing baccarat or escorting beautiful blondes, but his presence gave the appearance of legitimacy. So the United States recognized his government and sent $25 million, mostly in military aid, to Indochina in the spring, and another $130 million later that year. Giap saw the American support as a watershed: "The aggressive war waged by the French colonialists," he pointed out, "gradually became a war carried out with 'US dollars' and 'French blood.' It was really a 'dirty war.'"[29] Despite that support, American military officials remained staunchly opposed to US involvement in Vietnam. "France will be driven out of Indochina," the Army's Chief of Staff J. Lawton Collins predicted, and was "wasting time and equipment trying to remain there." If the French requested air or naval support, the JCS insisted, "they will have to be told point blank that none will be committed."

Indeed, military officials – despite the intensity of the Cold War – continued to recognize that the Viet Minh's appeal was widespread. Ho enjoyed the support of 80 percent of the population, Army planners reported, yet 80 percent of his followers were *not* Communists.[30]

The Truman and Eisenhower administrations, however, essentially disregarded military warnings regarding Vietnam. While armed forces officers might have recognized the political and military peril of war against the Viet Minh, civilian officials had more global concerns. Vietnam was thus a pawn in a geopolitical Cold War game. Though not strategically or even economically critical in its own right, Vietnam became the centerpiece in the effort to contain Communism when viewed within the context of French needs, Chinese Communism, and economic development. So Charles Cabell, an Air Force General and JCS official, might conclude that "terrain difficulties and the guerrilla nature of Vietminh operations" would make it impossible to dislodge the enemy, but President Eisenhower and Secretary of State John Foster Dulles, with the "big picture" in mind, would send another $785 million to Vietnam in 1953 alone.[31]

Indeed, this gap between civilian and military views on Vietnam would become crystal clear during the Dien Bien Phu crisis. The besieged French made overtures to the United States for air support, though not, as rumors then and since have maintained, for atomic weapons. Secretary of State Dulles, Chair of the JCS Admiral Radford, and others urged Eisenhower to meet the French request. The military emphatically said "No!" Admiral A. C. Davis, a Pentagon official, feared American leaders would dupe themselves into making a "limited" commitment to Dien Bien Phu even though, as he put it, "one cannot go over Niagara Falls in a barrel only slightly." Marine Commandant Lemuel Shepherd worried that US involvement would "greatly increase . . . [the] risk of general war" in Asia. Among officers, no-one attacked the idea of intervention more vigorously than General Matthew B. Ridgway. Ridgway was a genuine American hero, having parachuted on D-Day, commanded UN troops in Korea after

Douglas MacArthur was fired, and served as Army Chief of Staff from 1953 to 1955. Ridgway and his planning chief, General James Gavin, believed that the United States had no vital interests in Indochina, that American units were "too ponderous" for guerrilla warfare in the jungles, that war in Vietnam would be financially costly, that Vietnam lacked the logistics capacity – ports, roads, communications – needed for war, and that the United States would suffer over 25,000 casualties per month. The JCS, except for Radford, agreed with Ridgway, understanding that any initial commitment to Vietnam would, inevitably, "expand considerably even though initial efforts were indecisive"; and in due time, Vietnam would be an American war.[32] With the military so deeply opposed to intervention, and the British discouraging Eisenhower as well, the president did not commit troops to save Dien Bien Phu in the spring of 1954, and so the French fell. Writing later, Ridgway would cite this as one of his proudest moments, calling American plans to intervene a "hare-brained tactical scheme" and including American non-intervention in "that list of tragic accidents that fortunately never happened."[33] But Ridgway's triumph was temporary, for the United States let France fall but did not allow Ho to claim victory and move on. In fact, for the Americans, the war was just beginning.

Defeat in Victory

Giap had pressed his attack on Dien Bien Phu in April in large measure to have his troops in strong positions when a conference on East–West affairs opened in Geneva in the first week of May. The conference, long scheduled, would surely take up the Vietnamese situation and, DRVN leaders hoped, validate the Viet Minh victory. And, with dramatic timing, Dien Bien Phu fell just as the proceedings began. Ho and Giap, however, emerged from Geneva with their glass only half full. The United States, represented by Dulles, remained hostile to the very idea of negotiating with Communists such as the DRVN or PRC and so refused to recognize Ho as the leader of a unified Vietnam. Vietnam's allies did not serve it much better. Zhou Enlai, the Chinese representative, did not back Ho either. To the Chinese, Vietnam was not a principal concern – they were much more concerned with international recognition and gaining Taiwan's seat at the United Nations – and traditional mistrust between the two countries was still strong. Thus, Ho, with dedicated enemies and no effective allies, had to accept compromise at Geneva: rather than unifying Vietnam under his rule, he acquiesced in the temporary partition of his country at the seventeenth parallel, in Annam, with the DRVN recognized north of the demarcation line and some type of anti-Communist entity to be established south of it. In 1956, according to the Geneva settlement, elections would be held to unify Vietnam and elect a president. The Viet Minh, feeling betrayed and isolated, was furious, but Ho counselled patience once more. Declaring that Geneva was a "great victory," he urged the Vietnamese to be "capable of enduring the present. Doing so will bring them great honor."[34] With little outside support, but great confidence in victory in 1956, Ho could do little else.

Indeed, American officials recognized the Viet Minh's strength too. Military leaders, the Department of State, and the White House all conceded that Ho would win 80 to 90 percent of the vote in any free election. The JCS, for instance, was aware that any settlement "based on free elections would be attended by the almost certain loss of [Indochina] to Communist control."[35] Rather than accept the Viet Minh as elected representatives of an internationally recognized DRVN, the United States assumed the French role in Vietnam and created the conditions for the Second Indochina War. Within a year after the Viet Minh victory at Dien Bien Phu, the United States would, most importantly, essentially invent a nation, the Republic of Vietnam (RVN), below the seventeenth parallel. It would, moreover, establish a military training mission to Vietnam and a regional anti-Communist force, the Southeast Asia Treaty Organization (SEATO). With these decisions, the United States created a rival government to the DRVN and backed it with American arms and dollars. In 1956, the RVN, with US encouragement, canceled the Geneva-scheduled elections and thus left Ho and his supporters in the south with little choice but to again wage a war for liberation, unification, and Vietnamese socialism.

Decades later, as we study Vietnam, the events of 1954–5 are still decisive. Because of the Viet Minh's popularity and nationalist credentials, there was no real opposition to Ho inside Vietnam. Thus the United States had to establish and nurture the RVN with little indigenous support. Like the French, the Americans had to find and put in power Vietnamese officials, who would remain tainted as US puppets throughout the next generation. As a result, the RVN could never be seen as a legitimate alternative to Ho. The Vietnamese people, with their legacy of conquering the Chinese, Mongols, Japanese, and French, were not about to accept the rule of Americans and their clients. But the United States would try. In June 1954, Americans persuaded Bao Dai to appoint a Vietnamese elite named Ngo Dinh Diem to be Prime Minister. In so far as he hated the French, Diem was a nationalist, but he had little knowledge of Vietnamese society and no concern for the Vietnamese people. He had spent the previous decade in a monastery in the United States where, quite unlike Bao Dai, he practiced sobriety and celibacy. He did, however, have influential friends, including Cold War icons such as Francis Cardinal Spellman and Senators Mike Mansfield and John F. Kennedy. So when it came time for the Americans to find a leader for the RVN, they looked no further than Diem.

At the same time, the United States took steps to protect the RVN and other countries against the DRVN and other Asian Communists by sending a training group to the RVN and establishing SEATO. The training mission, the Military Assistance Advisory Group (MAAG), originally consisted of a few hundred American advisers whose duty was to help reorganize and improve the Vietnamese army so that it could eventually resist outside forces, namely the DRVN, without US help. More broadly, the SEATO, comprising anti-Communist nations in Southeast Asia, would prevent Ho, Mao, or others from exporting Communism throughout the region. American military leaders, again, resisted this expansion of their role in Vietnam. Air Force General and psychological warfare expert Edward Lansdale, a strong supporter of Diem, nonetheless admitted that the Viet Minh had "exemplary relations" with Vietnamese villagers, while the southern soldiers were only "adept at cowing a population into feeding them [and] providing them with girls." Army officers reported that Ho and Giap had about 340,000 troops at their disposal, with nearly 100,000 *below* the seventeenth parallel. And General J. Lawton Collins, whom Eisenhower sent to Saigon as his personal representative, consistently advised the White House to consider abandoning the unpopular and repressive Diem regime. Likewise, Ridgway and others warned that it was "hopeless" to expect the training mission to succeed in the absence of popular government and political stability in the south, while General Gavin feared that American troops would get stuck in the middle of a "civil war" in Vietnam. The JCS meanwhile pointed out that a training program for the RVN would cost almost a half billion dollars, a steep price for an area of "low priority" such as Vietnam.[36] Eisenhower and Dulles dismissed such critiques, though, and, after Diem survived an overthrow attempt in early 1955, were set to put American money, soldiers, and credibility on the line to preserve the RVN.

"The Mandarin in the Sharkskin Suit" . . .

The American commitment to Diem was momentous, for not only did the United States become the guarantor of the RVN but, in large measure, of Diem himself. By sending money to the regime – $322 million in 1954–5 alone – canceling the elections, and not holding Diem accountable for any political reform, Americans sent a clear signal that the partition at the seventeenth parallel could become permanent and that they would not abandon their new client. Diem, who had no commitment to democracy to begin with, thus had free reign to run the RVN as a personal fiefdom – and he did. To give himself an air of legitimacy, Diem held elections in 1955 that would have embarrassed a Chicago alderman, winning more votes than eligible voters in some areas and 98 percent of the vote in the entire RVN. The American ambassador had to admit that the ballot was "a travesty of democratic procedures."[37] In office, Diem established the *Can Lao*, or Personalist, Party as an appendage of the Ngo family, not as a governing institution. His brother and sister-in-law, Ngo Dinh Nhu and Madame Nhu, were the power behind the throne – he as secretary of the interior, and she, the stereotypical Asian "dragon lady," as the head of the Vietnamese Women's Movement. Madame Nhu's father was in the cabinet also, and her uncle was Diem's foreign minister, while another relative was minister of education. Diem's brother Ngo Dinh Canh ran the northern provinces around Hué without any official title, and another brother, Bishop Ngo Dinh Thuc, was head of the Vietnamese Catholic Church. Although less than 10 percent of Vietnam was Catholic, disciples of Rome had huge power inside this Buddhist country, a major point of conflict already and one that would worsen in the coming years.

To solidify his power further, Diem and Nhu fired about 6,000 army officers and replaced them with more loyal, if less qualified, soldiers, while forcing military personnel to join the Can Lao Party. The army also assumed civil police functions, and officers took over civil administration duties. Under the Ngos the civil order was steadily militarized, and the army's responsibility was not to fight the Communists but to protect the first family. Thus secure, the Ngos went after their enemies, both real and imagined. Diem closed newspapers, made it illegal to criticize his government, and made it a capital offense to be a "Communist." By 1958, he had jailed over 40,000 political prisoners and executed over 12,000 dissidents. By 1961, those numbers had tripled. The United States apparently had little trouble with the Ngos' behavior: Washington supplied the RVN with 85 percent of its military budget and two-thirds of its overall budget. Despite American rhetoric about building a better life for the Vietnamese people, 78 percent of all American monies were used by Diem for military purposes, but that meant that it was being utilized to keep the regime in power, not to fight the enemy.

The United States also accepted Diem's regressive land policies. As always, property ownership was the crucial political issue in Vietnam. In 1954, after the victory over France, the Viet Minh began to seize lands held by the French and Vietnamese collaborators and to redistribute over 600,000 hectares of it to landless peasants. Once in power, Diem began to reverse those agrarian programs and took personal control of 650,000 hectares, much of it by denying the titles of peasants or by seizing it in place of tax payments. He then gave out about 250,000 hectares to loyal military officials and Catholic cronies, while keeping the rest, and the best, for his family. By the later 1950s, the land situation for southern peasants was not appreciably different than it had been in the French period. Diem at the same time put friends and supporters in charge of all the village councils, increased taxes, and intimidated and arrested those criticizing his land policies. In May 1959, in Law 10/59, he authorized his military-political forces to arrest any "subversives," which was a blank check for roving bands of armed forces and Can Lao zealots to arrest, try, convict, and execute anyone suspected of disloyalty. Such oppression worked in one important respect, however; the Viet Minh in the south was on the ropes, its membership in hiding, in prison, or dead. American support of Diem seemed to be paying off. Little wonder, then, that *Time* magazine called him "The Mandarin in the Sharkskin Suit" who was saving Southeast Asia from the Communists.

. . . and "Uncle Ho"

The later 1950s were a dark time for Ho and the Viet Minh. While trying to organize society and the economy in the north, they also suffered through the Diemist repression in the south. The triumph of Dien Bien Phu had been replaced by the reality of reconstruction and continued struggle. The promise of elections and reunification in 1956 was unfulfilled, and Ho and his associates on both sides of the seventeenth parallel had no alternative but to accept it. With western, namely American, pressure against the DRVN and internal problems to confront, Ho faced a major challenge in any event. Most of the fighting against the French had taken place in Tonkin, so the north had been terribly damaged and faced acute food shortages, especially since 60 percent of the rice crop – the staple of the Vietnamese diet – was produced in the south. To alleviate food shortages and help rebuild the north, Ho even made overtures to the RVN about economic integration, but they were dismissed, helping drive the DRVN closer to the PRC and the Soviet Union.

Internally, the reconstituted Communist movement – the *Lao Dong*, or Worker's Party – took control in Hanoi, nationalizing banks and some large businesses but mixing the economy by maintaining private manufacturing and trade firms. In the agricultural sector, Ho tried to continue the reforms he had attempted in 1946 and 1954 by redistributing land to peasants. The government transferred over two million hectares of land to the people, turning about half of northern families into property owners, an exponential increase over the French years. To keep the support of "middle" or "rich" peasants, Ho allowed many of them to retain their holdings while channeling anger toward the "local despots," the big landlords. Unfortunately, local officials often became overzealous in enacting land reform and assaulted many peasants who held land but supported the government. In various areas, including Ho's home province of Nghe An, peasants protested the land takings. Lao Dong officials turned on the protestors, killing several hundreds of them (but by no means the half million Richard Nixon would later claim as justification for the US war). Ho, realizing he had overreacted, chastised the peasants for rising up but also dismissed those officials, including his old friend and Communist leader Truong Chinh, responsible for the crackdown.[38] Though a disaster, the episode of the assault on the peasant protestors offered a strong contrast to the Diem regime's behavior. While the Ngos boasted of arresting and executing their enemies, the DRVN recognized its mistakes and moved forward. Even after a tragic blunder, the DRVN's leader could remain "Uncle Ho" to his people.

Events below the seventeenth parallel, however, were not as easily handled. Diem's attacks on Viet Minh cadre and political supporters had badly destabilized the resistance in the south and damaged its morale. Ho and Lao Dong officials advised southern activists to lay low, agitate for elections, and develop political organizations. Ho wanted to "combat the idea of violent, reckless, and dangerous armed struggle," but many of the anti-Diem groups in the RVN wanted to act with force. Some ignored Ho's orders and formed secret cells, established bases, and even conducted ambushes, sabotaged facilities, and killed southern officials. By 1959, with the southern situation deteriorating and Hanoi facing pressure from its loyalists in the RVN, Ho and the Communist Central Committee endorsed "violent struggle" as well as political action. About 5,000 "regroupees," southern party members who had trained in the north, returned to the RVN and the DRVN began to send military equipment and supplies into the south, by foot or by bicycle at first. While Hanoi remained hesitant to take on Diem, the southern resistance began to more openly urge armed struggle. By 1960, Ho and his lieutenants were lagging behind the southern rebels, but being forced into a more militant approach to liberate the south and unify the country.

3

Destroying the Country to Save It: The American War on Vietnam, 1960–1968

In the later 1960s and 1970s the Johnson and Nixon administrations would often justify the American war on Vietnam as an effort to defend an ally, the RVN, from an outside aggressor, the DRVN. The northern Vietnamese, they claimed, had "invaded" the country below the seventeenth parallel, thereby forcing the United States to intervene with advisers, material, and eventually combat troops. But, for several reasons, that justification falls short. Vietnam was historically one nation, albeit "temporarily" divided at Geneva; the RVN was a fictive state, conceived and carried by the United States; and perhaps most importantly, the opposition to Diem arose in the south *despite* Ho's advice to be cautious and patient. Later claims that the north invaded the south notwithstanding, it was in fact southerners who led the struggle against the RVN.

Revolution from the Bottom Up

In 1954, as part of the Geneva settlement, Vietnamese on both sides of the partition line were allowed to travel north- or southward. Alarmed by government and church propaganda and afraid of Ho's socialist doctrine, about a million Vietnamese, especially Catholics, moved from the north to the RVN. A smaller yet still significant number of Viet Minh supporters moved to the DRVN. The southern Catholics,

American officials hoped, would provide popular support for Diem's state; the Viet Minh in the north hoped to settle down and possibly return to the south after the 1956 reunification. In both cases, they were disappointed. The Diem regime never developed any popular appeal, while many in the north finally did move below the seventeenth parallel, but as soldiers returning to take on the RVN. Thus, when the war began in earnest in 1960–1, the RVN would have little native backing, while Viet Minh forces *in the south*, either those who had remained there or returnees, would fight against the southern military, now known as the Army of the Republic of Vietnam, or *ARVN*. In fact, Ho continued to oppose war in Vietnam.

Beginning in mid-1959 and continuing throughout the year, southern insurgents, alarmed by Diem's repression and especially Law 10/59, began a series of "spontaneous uprisings." In Quang Ngai, a coastal city in the northern RVN, about 16,000 local activists seized 16 villages in Tra Bong district and established a larger liberated zone of about 50 villages. By the end of the year, villagers and Viet Minh support personnel, with minimal and sometimes no involvement from Hanoi, had rebelled in various places throughout the central highlands and Mekong areas. In January 1960, uprisings began in Ben Tre, in the delta just outside Saigon. The Viet Minh had been strong there in the French period and had redistributed land to the peasantry, only to see the old French and Mandarin landlords return after 1954 and confiscate land from the new owners. Boiling with resentment, villagers and Viet Minh self-defense forces struck and liberated dozens of villages in Ben Tre. As Madame Nguyen Thi Dinh, a Communist insurgent, described it, "it was a night of terrifying thunder and lightning striking the enemy on their heads. Attacked by surprise, they were scared out of their wits and stayed put in the posts."[1] The ARVN ultimately cracked down at Ben Tre, but the rebellions continued through early 1960. Indeed, various southerners met to consider forming a united front against Diem as the uprisings had included all groups in Vietnamese society – landholders, civil servants, and intellectuals, as well as Communists, workers, and peasants. But the northern leadership in Hanoi remained conservative and even critical of southern insurgents who, they believed, acted prematurely and whose tactics often bordered on terrorism against those who might be persuaded to join the cause. The "Committee for the South," organized in Hanoi and led by Le Duan, believed that reunification could be achieved peacefully and insisted that "for the moment, our emphasis must remain on organizing our forces, propagandizing the masses, and preparing for the future general uprising."[2]

The people were moving ahead of the northern leadership, however. While southern insurgency leaders had recognized the need for a political base, they were also deeply damaged by the Diemist attacks and decided to organize themselves for armed struggle. Thus, on 20 December 1960, at a meeting in Tay Ninh Province in northwest Saigon on the Cambodian border, representatives of various southern Vietnamese political, social, religious, and ethnic groups established the *National Liberation Front*, or NLF. Almost all the delegates at Tay Ninh were native southerners, although a handful of old Viet Minh cadre were there as well. All agreed, as the founding communiqué put it, that "the immediate task of the revolution in the South is to achieve the unity of the whole people, to fight resolutely against the aggressive and war-mongering US imperialists, to overthrow the dictatorial ruling Ngo Dinh Diem clique, lackeys of the US imperialists, to form a national democratic coalition in south Viet Nam, to win national independence and to achieve national reunification."[3] By linking together the forces of imperialism (the United States) and feudalism (the Diem regime), as well as calling for a broad political spectrum and unification, the NLF could retain popular backing and emphasize the fundamentally nationalist, not Communist, nature of the struggle. To that end, the NLF both tried to lower rents and taxes for peasants while allowing all but the worst landlords and cronies of the Ngos to retain their property. The Front thus grew out of conditions in the south between 1954 and 1960 and, if anything, Ngo Dinh Diem was as responsible for its creation as Ho Chi Minh.

Kennedy and Vietnam: Hollywood versus Reality

The establishment of the NLF amounted to a vital challenge to the Diem regime, one that, without popular support, the RVN would not be able to meet. Just weeks after the Front was born, however, the new US president essentially pledged to meet such challenges for them. John Fitzgerald Kennedy (JFK) of Massachusetts – young, handsome, and vigorous – took the oath of office on 20 January 1961 promising to "pay any price, bear any burden, meet any hardship, support any friend, oppose any foe, to assure the survival and success of liberty." Ironically, outgoing President Eisenhower, in his farewell address, had warned against the growing militarism in American society and such bellicose rhetoric, but JFK sent an opposite message. Though Kennedy had not specifically referred to Vietnam in his speech, the Diem regime could feel comfortable that their old friend would not let them down. In 1956, as a senator, Kennedy had called the RVN "the cornerstone of the free world in Asia"; it was, he admitted, "our offspring, we cannot abandon it."[4] As president, he would not.

In 1991, millions of Americans plunked down seven or eight dollars to see Oliver Stone's epic film *JFK*. The young president, Stone suggested, had seen the futility of the Cold War and was ready to withdraw from Vietnam when the CIA, the military, and other representatives of the military-industrial complex, fearing that his new-found pacifism was bad for business, had him assassinated. Such ideas may be a conspiracy theorist's dream, but historically they are nightmarish. In truth, JFK, in less than three years, committed American treasure, men, and credibility to the RVN and dramatically enlarged the American role there. By 22 November 1963, the United States, rather than pulling out, was deeply involved in the civil war in Vietnam. Far from being a dove, Kennedy was the driving force behind the American intervention in Indochina.

Vietnam had not been crucial to JFK as he entered the White House; in fact, Eisenhower had warned him that events in Laos would be more difficult in 1961. But, just months into his presidency, Kennedy was beset with challenges and failure. In Laos, he had to agree to the formation of a government which included the Communist Pathet Lao. Worse, in Cuba the US-backed Bay of Pigs invasion, of Cuban exiles determined to overthrow Castro, was a fiasco. The leader of the Soviet Union, Nikita Khrushchev, added to Kennedy's woes, pledging support for wars of liberation in the Third World, refusing to remove the Berlin Wall, and treating the American president with disdain at a summer meeting in Vienna. Kennedy thus believed that he had to make a stand somewhere – "that son of a bitch [Khrushchev] won't pay any attention to words, he has to see you move," he told reporters – so why not Vietnam? Walt Whitman Rostow, one of his closest advisers, suggested that "clean-cut success in Vietnam" could erase the stain of disaster from the Bay of Pigs. In Saigon, the head of the American MAAG, General Lionel McGarr, likewise noted the White House's "strong determination" to stop the "deterioration of US prestige" in April 1961.[5]

Thus JFK, if not desperate then at least anxious for a Cold War success, began to increase significantly the US commitment to the RVN and eventually to conduct an aggressive war there. In January 1961, he authorized the Counterinsurgency Plan for southern Vietnam, which called for training the southern army in anti-guerrilla tactics, not just conventional warfare. He then approved expanding the ARVN by 20,000 troops, to 170,000, and then by another 30,000, while enlarging the Civil Guard from 32,000 to 68,000 troops. To pay for these reinforcements, the White House sent Diem an additional $42 million in 1961, on top of the $225 million per year he was receiving already. And in May, Kennedy sent Vice-President Lyndon Baines Johnson (LBJ) to Vietnam as a public relations measure. While in Saigon, Johnson told the media that Diem was "the Winston Churchill of Southeast Asia," though he privately admitted later that "shit, man, he's the only boy we got out there."[6]

Recognition of Diem's repression and America's limited choices did not deter the White House. Indeed, JFK refused to even talk with Ho Chi Minh or the NLF, fearing that negotiations would lead to "a major crisis of nerve" in Vietnam. To the president, American *credibility* – appearing strong against Communist advance – would thus be a major factor driving his Indochina policy, and he would not back down. Nor would his Secretary of Defense, Robert Strange McNamara, who informed military officials that the administration "had made the decision to pursue the Vietnam affair with vigor and that all reasonable amounts of resources could be placed at the disposal of the commanders in the area."[7] And so, in 1962, it was done. In January, a new commander, Paul D. Harkins, arrived in Vietnam convinced that America's technological superiority would reverse conditions there. The war was going badly, with the NLF's political influence growing and the armed wing of the insurgency, the *Viet Cong*, or VC, holding the military initiative. To Harkins, and the White House, American tanks and aircraft could be used to flush out the VC and destroy them. In 1962, then, JFK deployed Army helicopter companies, fixed-wing aircraft, a troop carrier squadron, reconnaissance planes, air controllers, crop defoliants to destroy the VC's jungle cover, Navy mine sweepers, CS gas, and napalm – a gasoline gel that seared human flesh. He also authorized the development of "strategic hamlets" in the RVN – a disastrous program in which Vietnamese peasants were removed from their homes and possessions and relocated to allegedly safe hamlets where they would be protected from the NLF, but which in fact alienated even more villagers from the government and helped VC recruiting efforts. At the same time, the number of US "Advisers" in Vietnam, 800 in January 1961, rose to 3,400 in April 1962 and over 11,000 by the end of the year, and would go up again to 16,700 by the time of Kennedy's assassination. The ARVN grew again too, to 219,000, while the Civil Guard increased to 77,000. That level of commitment and the introduction of American firepower had the desired impact. The VC fled in horror as US-provided weapons and ammunition rained down on them. As Harkins put it, the napalm "really puts the fear of God into the Viet Cong . . . and that is what counts." McNamara was similarly pleased with the "tremendous progress" in 1962, and the

American commander was assuring him that "there is no doubt we are on the winning side."[8] The administration was so flush with success and optimistic that the war would be over quickly, it even approved the withdrawal of 1,000 American troops. While it may not have been as pleasing as Marilyn Monroe's seductive rendition of "Happy Birthday Mr President" at Madison Square Garden, events in Vietnam surely put a smile on Kennedy's face in 1962.

Breakdown 1963

The optimism of 1962 was short-lived. On 2 January 1963, the VC routed the ARVN, even though the latter had a 4 to 1 troop advantage, artillery, armor, and helicopters, at the village of *Ap Bac*, 35 miles southwest of Saigon in the Mekong. The enemy struck, eluded the southern army, and struck again, killing three Americans and downing five helicopters in the process. ARVN commanders, under orders from Diem not to lose troops, did not force their men to fight and so allowed the VC to take the initiative and then escape from Ap Bac. For the NLF, Ap Bac marked a turnaround from the previous year, and its prospects would improve throughout the next twelve months, while Diem's took a corresponding downturn, militarily and politically. For the RVN, the biggest crisis in 1963 was religious turmoil. The Ngo family had favored Catholics in administrative and military matters since 1954, and began to repress the majority *Buddhists* – whom they saw, with reason, as a political enemy – more intensely in the spring, forbidding them from celebrating Buddha's birthday and even sending troops into their temples to attack and kill the faithful.

Then, on 10 June, a monk named Quang Duc sat down in the middle of a busy Saigon street, doused himself with gasoline, and lit himself on fire to protest the Diemist repression of his people. The world's media, tipped off by the Buddhists, were there and Quang Duc's story and photo were front page news worldwide. Madame Nhu, ever tactful, referred to the immolation as a "Buddhist barbecue" and offered to supply fuel for the next one. For his part, Diem continued to strike at the Buddhists. After nearly a decade of supporting the RVN and the Ngos, it was finally clear to the United States that Diem and his brother were beyond rehabilitation. Thus America, which had followed a policy of "sink or swim with Ngo Dinh Diem," finally accepted his overthrow on 1 November 1963 in a coup led by ARVN officers in which Diem and Nhu were both killed. Publicly, the Buddhist situation had become, so to speak, incendiary, and it was impossible to credibly claim that America was fighting for "democracy" in Vietnam so long as the Ngos were in power.

There was, however, a private yet probably more important reason behind the US abandonment of Diem. His brother Nhu, also aware that the regime's days were numbered, began to make overtures to the NLF about a negotiated settlement and the establishment of a coalition, neutral government in the south, with the Ngos and the Front both included. Killing Buddhists may have been awfully distasteful, but going behind American backs to discuss an end to the civil war was unforgivable. Afraid that peace might break out short of victory, Kennedy reiterated the American commitment to Vietnam in late 1963. In interviews with TV anchormen Chet Huntley and Walter Cronkite shortly before his death, JFK insisted that Vietnam was "a very important struggle" and that withdrawal "only makes it easy for the Communists. I think we should stay."[9] Despite recognizing the laundry list of military and political shortcomings and barriers to success in the RVN, and sending 16,000 advisers and billions of dollars to that point with little noticeable improvement, JFK was not retreating from his commitment in Vietnam. Contrary to apologists like Oliver Stone, Arthur Schlesinger, John Newman, and others who claim that he would have pulled out of Vietnam after the 1964 elections, Kennedy has to be judged on his actual deeds, and his record was one of constant reinforcement and escalation. As the noted historian Thomas Paterson observed, "he had his chance, and he failed."[10]

"No More Coup Shit"

Lyndon Johnson of Texas became president in November 1963, dedicated to "seeing things through in Vietnam." At his first meeting with diplomatic and military officials he told them to "tell those generals in Saigon that Lyndon Johnson intends to stand by our word."[11] To LBJ, a product of World War II and a congressman raised on the Cold War, there was really no thought of pulling away from Vietnam. Indeed, America's biggest problem remained the absence of a legitimate government in the south to take on the NLF. If anything, instability and chaos in the RVN *worsened* after Diem's removal. The new president, Duong Van "Big" Minh, lost US support when he, like the Ngos, considered a negotiated, neutralist settlement with the NLF. As George Ball, a State Department official, observed, "nothing is further from [our] mind than 'neutral solution for Vietnam.' We intend to win."[12]

For his heresy, "Big" Minh too was deposed. In another coup, directed by American officials, General Nguyen Khanh came to power in January 1964. Minh, however, remained in the country and he and Khanh continued to feud, so Khanh was overthrown in the spring, returned in the summer, and was ousted again in September. At that point, Tran Van Huong became president, only to be removed under Buddhist pressure in December and replaced by Phan Huy Quat, who in turn was replaced by a government led by both Huong and Khanh in January 1965. The ARVN was overthrowing presidents and changing governments the way George Steinbrenner hired and fired Yankee managers – between the Diem coup and February 1965, there were over a dozen different governments in the RVN, with six between September 1964 and the following February alone. Amid such disarray, the ambassador in Saigon, General Maxwell D. Taylor, found it "impossible to foresee a stable and effective government under any name in anything like the near future." LBJ, typically, was more blunt: "no more of this coup shit," he ordered his aides.[13]

Ever since putting Ngo Dinh Diem in power, the United

States had been looking for a popular and effective government in southern Vietnam, but was no closer in 1964 than a decade earlier. Still, this did not deter the American mission in Vietnam. For reasons of credibility and politics, the United States would stay the course in Indochina. As John McNaughton, a Pentagon official, described it, America had to intervene in Vietnam to prove its strength and conviction to allies and potential enemies alike. Only 10 percent of the reason for involvement, he believed, was to help the people of Vietnam have a better life. To the president, the lessons of Harry Truman – who was blamed for "losing" China at the time of Mao's victory – and the rise of McCarthyism were always present. If Ho won in Vietnam, LBJ feared a "mean and destructive debate . . . that would shatter my presidency, kill my administration, and damage our democracy." Apparently in seriousness, he added that Truman's problems with China "were chickenshit compared with what might happen if we lost Vietnam."[14] And so Johnson escalated.

A Streetcar Named Pleiku: Escalation and Americanization

Throughout 1964, the president sent more military personnel and arms to the RVN, and authorized a series of covert measures – called 34-A operations and DeSoto patrols – to undermine the DRVN. In August, two American destroyers, the *Maddox* and the *C. Turner Joy*, were in DRVN territorial waters as part of the 34-A operations when they were allegedly attacked by north Vietnamese torpedo boats in the *Gulf of Tonkin*. The attacks were never substantiated – Johnson himself laughed, "hell, those dumb stupid sailors were just shooting at flying fish" – but the episode gave LBJ a convenient excuse to begin air strikes above the seventeenth parallel and to ask Congress for authority to "take all necessary measures" to defend the RVN. The so-called Gulf of Tonkin Resolution then passed 416–0 in the House of Representatives and 88–2 in the Senate (with Ernest Gruening of Alaska and Wayne

Morse of Oregon dissenting). The resolution was a blank check for the president to wage war in Vietnam, or, as he put it, "it was like Grandma's nightshirt, it covered everything."[15] The Tonkin episode was indeed timely, for conditions in Vietnam were deteriorating. Despite receiving $2 million *a day* in American aid, the RVN was still in chaos, and the ARVN's desertion rates were rising as morale was sinking. Meanwhile, the NLF and VC were consistently impressive. The enemy, by McNamara's admission, controlled over 40 percent of all RVN territory, and had majority control in over 50 percent of all southern provinces, with over 90 percent control in five.[16]

The Defense Secretary and National Security Adviser McGeorge Bundy, duly alarmed, thus visited the president on 27 January 1965 to tell him that *"our current policy can lead only to disastrous defeat"* and to recommend that he "use our military power" to take on the NLF.[17] Johnson agreed and in mid-February began to ratchet up the war, at first through the air. The immediate cause of this new escalation came when the VC mortared a US army barracks at Pleiku in the central highlands, killing nine Americans, wounding 109 others, and damaging or destroying 22 aircraft. The president thus began *Operation Rolling Thunder*, a series of sustained air attacks against the DRVN. Assuming that Ho was controlling the insurgency in the south, LBJ believed that Rolling Thunder would convince the north Vietnamese to stop the rebellion against the RVN. "Now I have Ho Chi Minh's pecker in my pocket," the president even boasted. Rolling Thunder began ostensibly in retaliation for the Pleiku attacks, but that was simply a rationale, an expedient excuse, for a policy decision that was already in the works. As Bundy, who was visiting the army base at the time of the VC strikes, admitted, "Pleikus are like streetcars" – if you miss one, another will come along shortly.[18]

In time, Rolling Thunder would become the most massive air campaign in the history of warfare. Its impact never lived up to the hype, however, as the bombings did not affect the DRVN's ability to support the insurgency or its resolve to liberate Vietnam on both sides of the seventeenth parallel. The

Army's Chief of Staff, General Harold K. Johnson, later observed that "if anything came out of Vietnam, it was that airpower couldn't do the job."[19] It was thus clear in early 1965 that NLF victory was imminent short of a dramatic American response. So, on 8 March, American Marines landed at Da Nang, the first US troops to enter Vietnam with a stated combat mission. By April, the United States had 33,000 troops in the RVN, with another 20,000 on the way, and they were engaging in offensive operations against the VC. Just months later, with conditions no better, Harkins's replacement as commander, General William Westmoreland, asked for an additional 44 battalions (125,000 troops) and authority to conduct operations in the RVN with even fewer restrictions. After weeks of agonizing debate, during which McNamara and the military made it clear that the situation in Vietnam was not promising, LBJ, on 28 July, approved the deployment of 50,000 troops to Vietnam, increased monthly draft calls to 35,000, and promised more soldiers to Westmoreland "as requested." That decision essentially *Americanized* the war in Vietnam. Johnson had signaled that the United States was ready to take over the responsibility of fighting the VC from the ARVN. At the same time, however, LBJ refused to activate the National Guard, to put the economy on a war footing, or to commit as many troops as the military had wanted. American officials, the historian Larry Berman has observed, had thus "decided to lose the war slowly."[20] But not everyone was so pessimistic. Shortly after the July decisions, LBJ received a telegram from the Hell's Angels Motorcycle Gang offering to go to Vietnam to kill Communists. At least someone wanted to.

Hell No, We Won't Go

US military officials were ambivalent about the Americanization of the war in July 1965, in large measure because they remained opposed to war in Vietnam, as they had since the 1950s. Indeed, Ridgway's stand against intervention at Dien Bien Phu was fairly representative of the armed forces approach to Vietnam in the next decade as well. In 1960, a good number of officers, including Generals Maxwell Taylor and James Gavin, had publicly supported JFK's candidacy, and in return the president and McNamara had substantially increased defense budgets once in office. The brass certainly appreciated the money, but did not share Kennedy's enthusiasm for involvement in Vietnam. The heads of the Air Force and Navy, which would fight at a distance and take far fewer casualties, were willing to consider a military role in Indochina, but they were not a majority. More typically, Marine Commandant David Shoup rejected calls for intervention while the Army Chief of Staff, General George Decker, thought that "there was no good place to fight" in Southeast Asia. The commander of US forces in the Pacific, Admiral Harry D. Felt, was also "strongly opposed" to troop deployments, especially because he anticipated that the ARVN would fight even less if American troops were there to bail them out. Felt, like most officers, believed that the United States should limit its role to training and supplying the south Vietnamese military to take on the VC by themselves. Perhaps no officer received as much publicity for his criticism as Colonel John Paul Vann, whose leaks to the *New York Times* revealed that the ARVN was avoiding battle and that the heavy use of American firepower and air strikes was killing huge numbers of civilian villagers – the very people that the Americans were trying to "save" – throughout the south. As one Army report from 1962 concluded, "the military and political situation in South Vietnam can be aptly described by four words, 'it is a mess.'"[21]

General Wallace M. Greene, Jr, Shoup's replacement as Marine Commandant, was just as candid. "We're up to our knees in the quagmire" already, he said in 1963, and "frankly . . . we do not want to get any more involved in South Vietnam." He then warned fellow Marine officers, "you see what happened to the French? Well, maybe the same thing is going to happen to us." Throughout 1964 and 1965, as the Johnson administration repeatedly escalated the war in Vietnam, the military remained unconvinced of the need for or value of intervention. Indeed, both Generals Taylor and Westmoreland, the ambassador and commander who are remembered as hawks on Vietnam, strongly opposed the introduction of combat troops in the crucial 1964–5 period. To Taylor, it was neither "reasonable or feasible" to expect Caucasian American soldiers to take on the duties of Asian guerrilla warfare. As soon as American troops entered the RVN, the Vietnamese would "seek to unload other ground force tasks upon us" and would perform even "worse in a mood of relaxation at passing the Viet Cong burden to the US." Taylor even went so far as to suggest that LBJ reduce the US role to sending in advisers, or maybe even "disengage and let the [RVN] stand alone."[22]

Westmoreland was likewise reluctant to fight in Vietnam. In September 1964, the commander "did not contemplate" putting US troops into combat; that "would be a mistake," he told Taylor, because "it is the Vietnamese's war." In December, again insisting that "a purely military solution is not possible," Westmoreland did not even mention using ground troops in his reports to Washington. In probably his most prophetic analysis, in January 1965, just ten weeks before the Marine landings at Da Nang, he and his staff urged a continuation of the flawed advisory system, but no combat troops. The United States, they recognized, had spent vast amounts of time and money to develop the ARVN, with little luck, and "if that effort has not succeeded, there is even less reason to think that US combat forces would have the desired effect." The involvement of American troops in the RVN, the military staff in Saigon concluded, quite amazingly, "would at best buy time and would lead to ever increasing commitments until, like the French, we would be occupying an essentially hostile foreign country."[23] LBJ was not pessimistic, however, so the military followed the civilian charge into a major war in Vietnam. Perhaps had Taylor made a stand as Ridgway had in 1954, the president would have been more reluctant, but the ambassador and Westmoreland were good soldiers and accepted new and increasing commitments to the RVN. In fact, LBJ was so dedicated to "victory" in Indochina that, in truth, it was doubtful that anyone could have stopped him.

As the president himself said in April 1965, "we will not be defeated. We will not grow tired. We will not withdraw . . . We must stay in Southeast Asia."[24] With the Commander-in-Chief thus focused on winning in Vietnam, for reasons of anti-Communism and credibility, the military fell in line. But America's problems were, in a very real sense, just beginning.

Home Front Vietnam

The major barrier to success would remain the relative strengths of the enemy and the weaknesses of the ally. Despite later claims of fighting with "hands tied behind their backs," the American military always possessed resources vastly superior to those of the VC. The NLF, however, had popular backing and political appeal; the RVN did not. Ho's strategic skills, developed in the French period, matured throughout the Second Indochina War. He always realized, unlike Diem and his successors, that the key to victory was gaining the support of the mass of peasants and workers of Vietnam. As Mao had described it, the people were "the water" and the guerrillas were "the fish." Without popular support, then, the NLF would drown. Ho and the southern resistance were thus prepared to tread and float for as long as it took to gain liberation, per their doctrine of protracted war. At the birth of the NLF, it wisely established an organizational structure to take advantage of the Vietnamese people's desires for independence and justice. The VC was organized at three levels: local, self-defense forces who were farmers by day and fighters by night; guerrilla, or Regional, forces which were better armed and under district command; and Main Force units, organized into battalions and under the central control of Hanoi's authorities in the RVN.

But, still, the NLF insisted that politics, not war, was the key to victory. Ho always hoped to win without US intervention and wanted to topple Diem without large-scale force, so that America would not be prompted to invade and "save" the RVN. Toward that end, the NLF established

various support groups of youth, intellectuals, urban workers, and others to showcase the widespread appeal of its cause
and the overwhelming rejection of the Diemist state. The largest of these groups was the Farmer's Liberation Association,
with 1.8 million members by 1963, which consisted of poor
peasants attracted to the "land to the tiller" promises of the
Revolution. Another vital organization was the Women's Liberation Association, to harness the power of Vietnamese females in the fight for independence. In the war against the
French, women had vital roles as spies, propaganda activists,
transport workers, and guerrillas. Ho, contrary to patriarchal
Confucian doctrine, stressed the equality of females. "Women
are not only equal to men in society," the NLF stressed, "they
are also equal to their husbands. We will abolish inequality
between husbands and wives . . . Family property is common
property . . . Women are equal to men in standing for elections . . . women are to receive the same pay as men."[25] Compared to the mere symbolism of Madame Nhu's women's
movement in the RVN, or even to the role of women in the
United States, such rhetoric quite clearly appealed to the
women of the NLF.

Indeed, the NLF's popularity ran quite deep. As one peasant observed, "The Liberation had answers for all the most
important problems that we all knew . . . [T]hey would give
land to the poor people . . . They would spend taxes only for
the people, and would collect them without corruption. They
also said they would help the poor, and this was something
that made them very popular, because many people in the
village were very poor."[26] While land and taxes remained crucial wedge issues in recruiting for the NLF, many joined out
of a sense of patriotism and disgust with Diem, whom they
saw as a US puppet. Others feared VC reprisal, for the guerrillas were not averse to attacking or even executing "local
tyrants," big landholders who remained loyal to the RVN.
Once enlisted in the NLF, the Vietnamese were trained in *khiem
thao*, or self-criticism, sessions in which they were taught the
basic beliefs of the Revolution. From there they joined small
groups, or cells, with three to ten members, so that they could

develop a sense of camaraderie and purpose, and they had daily indoctrination sessions. The broad appeal of the NLF, combined with the personal attention paid to recruits, made for a highly effective and dedicated politico-military organization, one which the RVN could never come close to creating.[27]

Thus, by 1963, as the Buddhist crisis erupted, the NLF/VC had a huge political advantage and was, in fact, quite reluctant to see the Ngos removed, as Diem and his brother had alienated the mass of southerners. But the instability of 1964–5 continued to work in the Revolution's favor. The VC actually slowed down its military activity to let the RVN self-destruct even more, and by the early months of 1965, NLF victory was imminent. The Americans too recognized that and thus intervened in mass, but the US presence did not deter Ho. "Johnson and his clique should realize this," he warned. "They may bring in 500,000 troops, 1 million, or even more to step up their war of aggression in South Viet-Nam. They may use thousands of aircraft for intensified attacks against North Viet-Nam. But never will they break the iron will of the heroic Vietnamese people to fight against US aggression, for national salvation . . . The war may last ten, twenty years, or longer . . . but the Vietnamese people will not be intimidated. Nothing is more precious than independence and freedom."[28]

In the south, a new regime led by Generals Nguyen Cao Ky and Nguyen Van Thieu emerged in mid-1965. Ky and Thieu would both serve as leaders of the RVN until the end of the war in 1975, thus bringing stability after the merry-go-round of governments after Diem's death. While they received huge amounts of American aid and could be quite colorful – Ky's usual attire consisted of a white silk jump suit and purple scarf – they could never match the levels of support or effective organization of the NLF. Nor was the southern military, the ARVN, a vigorous fighting force. Barely 10 percent of young men drafted ever reported for military service and, by early 1965, over 110,000 troops had deserted, a huge increase over previous years and a trend that would grow in the future. At the same time, allegations of corruption, bribes, and kickbacks among government officials were rampant and haunted the RVN for the entire war. In addition, Ky and Navy officials were rumored to have a large stake in the lucrative Southeast Asia opium and heroin trades. Tensions between Catholics and Buddhists had worsened as well. In 1966, nine Buddhist leaders had immolated themselves to protest government policies. Then, Ky fired one of his commanders, General Nguyen Chanh Thi, provoking Buddhist troops loyal to Thi to take arms against other ARVN units. Finally, American troops had to intervene on behalf of Ky to stop the ARVN rebellion. Victor Krulak, a Marine general, was so disgusted by the episode that he wrote to a Navy official that "despite all our assertions to the contrary, the South Vietnamese are not – and never have been – a nation."[29] Krulak's confession was quite revealing, and disturbing. Since the United States had entered Vietnam, American officials had claimed that their responsibility was to build up the government and military in the south to exist on their own and fight the VC. Despite billions of dollars in aid and over 300,000 American soldiers in the country by 1966, success was as far off as ever.

Strategy for Defeat

Despite the political cesspool in the RVN and the proven endurance of the VC, the Americans continued to wage war throughout Vietnam, by air over the DRVN and by air and on the ground in the south. As commander, Westmoreland pursued a strategy of *attrition*: using America's huge advantage in weaponry to erode the VC to the point that southern recruiting and northern replacement could not make up for their losses. When that "crossover point" – more VC losses than recruits and replacements – was reached, US success would be imminent. Westmoreland, during the war and since, has been stridently criticized for adopting that strategy, but attrition actually worked quite well – for the enemy. The VC in the south and Giap's conventional forces in the north, the

PAVN, were far more capable of suffering big losses in manpower, replacing them, and keeping on fighting.

The Americans never quite understood or accepted this. Defense Secretary McNamara, the architect of the war, so firmly believed in technology, computers, and systems analysis that he could not conceive of the enemy holding out in the face of huge "body counts" caused by the lavish use of artillery and airpower. Indeed, in response to one aide who was pessimistic about Vietnam, McNamara yelled "where is your data? Give me something I can put in the computer. Don't give me your poetry."[30] Based on this mindset, the Americans in Vietnam began conducting "search and destroy" operations in which they would deforest areas with herbicides, level villages with bombardments, and resettle the population. Such tactics did in fact seriously damage the enemy, causing tremendous numbers of VC wounded and killed throughout the war, but did not bring victory. The VC always found a way to withstand the attacks and replace their losses. For instance, in a battle somewhat symbolic of the entire war, in November 1965, US forces attached to the 7th Cavalry met PAVN troops in the *Ia Drang Valley* in the central highlands near the Cambodian border. In this conventional, set-piece battle the Americans killed perhaps 2,000 to 2,500 of the enemy, while losing about 300 US soldiers. To Westmoreland, this proved the validity of attrition as American weaponry had been used to rout the enemy. But the PAVN did not see Ia Drang as a defeat. As General Chu Huy Man, one of its commanders there, noted, the PAVN wanted to provoke the Americans into a battle in order to learn how to fight them – "We wanted to lure the tiger out of the mountain," he explained. Moreover, the PAVN retreat was not a concession but rather part of the plan: "We did not have any plans to liberate the land," General Man related, "only to destroy troops."[31] General Giap had learned valuable lessons from Ia Drang as well, and thereafter avoided such big-unit engagements unless on terms preferable to the PAVN.

Westmoreland learned otherwise, however, and continued his war of attrition. Thus, in battles similar to Ia Drang,

American units caused serious losses to the enemy in Operations Attleboro, Cedar Falls, and Junction City in 1966 and early 1967, but without long-term impact. In Cedar Falls, for instance, American infantry, armored, and airborne units wanted to clear the "Iron Triangle" outside of Saigon of VC using a "hammer and anvil" tactic in which American units at one end of the war zone would drive the enemy into other units deployed on the other edge of the battlefield. The VC lost about 750 soldiers and had a huge complex of tunnels destroyed during the operation, but the victory was temporary at best. Before the operation, US forces had to clear civilians out of the Iron Triangle so that they could establish a "free-fire zone" in which *all* Vietnamese were considered VC and potential targets of American firepower. By displacing and attacking the villagers in the area, the Americans alienated the very people they were there to help. Then, just six months after Cedar Falls, the VC returned in full strength, with even more support from the local population than before. Even Westmoreland's hawkish deputy, General William DePuy, admitted that in such battles the VC "just backed off and waited . . . They were more elusive. They controlled the battle better. They were the ones who decided whether there should be a fight."[32]

The enemy was retaining its strength and deciding the nature of battle throughout 1966 and 1967. Despite massive air strikes on the Ho Chi Minh Trail – a supply route running from the DRVN, through Laos and Cambodia, and into the RVN – the enemy was monthly infiltrating nearly 10,000 men into the south, while recruiting about 3,000 in the RVN. Westmoreland's Intelligence Chief, General George McChristian, added that the enemy could infiltrate 175,000 new troops into the RVN, for a net gain in manpower of 65,000 for 1967. Such VC strength, on top of continued ARVN inactivity – south Vietnamese units only made contact with the enemy in 40 percent of engagements – led Westmoreland time and again to ask for more troops. With 470,000 American soldiers already in Vietnam in 1967, the commander requested 200,000 more, a request which LBJ met only partially, with 40,000 reinforcements. The commander needed additional men merely to keep up with the enemy. Between September 1966 and January 1967, the VC had initiated 87 engagements in Vietnam, numbers far in excess of the originally estimated five. The new figures shocked JCS Chair Earle Wheeler, who warned Westmoreland that "I cannot go to the President and tell him that contrary to my reports . . . we are not sure who has the initiative in South Vietnam." Duly alarmed, Wheeler ordered Westmoreland to suppress the figures, for if they appeared in the media "they would, literally, blow the lid off of Washington."[33]

Westmoreland did not release the statistics, but neither did he reconsider his strategy. With elections a year off, the commander understood that LBJ wanted progress in Vietnam so that the war would not wreck his re-election campaign. So, with few options and little imagination, he kept asking for more troops. At the same time, he understood that reinforcements would have limited value. "Killing guerrillas is like killing termites with a screw driver," he explained to the president, "where you have to kill them one by one and they're inclined to multiply as rapidly as you kill them."[34] While continuing the war with 470,000 troops would set up a "meat grinder," Westmoreland and Wheeler could not guarantee success with even 200,000 more. Worse, as LBJ saw it, such reinforcements might provoke China to intervene in Vietnam as it had done in Korea, or the Soviet Union to commit aggression elsewhere while America was tied down in Vietnam. So Westmoreland, despite his admissions of trouble ahead, knew that the president wanted to hear good news. Accordingly, he claimed that US and ARVN troops had met the "crossover point" in south Vietnam in the spring, and during a November public relations trip to Washington, he optimistically reported that the war was going well and that he could see "light at the end of the tunnel." Westmoreland's Army boss, Harold K. Johnson, was happy to hear such a bright forecast but anxious about the war all the same, hoping that the commander "has not dug a hole for himself with regard to his prognostications. The platform of false prophets is crowded."[35]

A Grindstone on Our Backs

Harold K. Johnson's caution was not unusual. Beginning in the 1950s, there had been serious interservice division over the nature of the war in Vietnam. Although American advisers were training the south Vietnamese for a conventional war, a good number of US generals thought that guerrilla warfare should be emphasized. After American combat troops entered Vietnam in 1965, many ranking officers had continued criticizing the war, especially the way Westmoreland was conducting it. At no time did the armed services ever have the unity of purpose so necessary to the successful conduct of warfare. Within the military, no-one attacked the war and Westmoreland as fiercely as did the Marines. Commandant Wallace M. Greene, Jr, Pacific Commander Victor H. Krulak, and other Marine leaders were appalled at the manner in which the war was being fought. They believed that the strategy of attrition and awesome use of firepower against south Vietnamese peasants and villages was counterproductive and had to be stopped. The Marines instead advocated an emphasis on *pacification* – also known at various times as counterinsurgency, enclaves, rural development, or nation-building. They believed that American forces should operate at the village level, providing security, health care, and economic development for the Vietnamese people. Once American forces "pacified" a hamlet, they would move out, like an oil blot slowly spreading, to another village and provide the same services. In this way, they would win the "hearts and minds" of the villagers, who would then turn against the VC. Attrition, however, was not only alienating the people – "grab 'em by their balls and their hearts and minds will follow" was a common slogan among US troops – but could not succeed as a military policy either.

According to General Krulak, American forces could never erode the enemy to the point where it would give up. If losses in the south became too heavy, Hanoi had over 2.5 million young men in the north it could send into battle below the seventeenth parallel, and, should the Chinese intervene as they had done in the Korean War, another 100 million. Thus the Marine commander considered Westmoreland's strategy "wasteful of American lives [and] promising a protracted, strength-sapping battle with small likelihood of a successful outcome." Even if US troops killed ten VC for every one of their own lost, it would still require a tremendous sacrifice in American blood. At 1965–6 rates, Krulak estimated, it would cost 175,000 lives just to reduce the enemy's pool of young men by 20 percent. Manpower was Ho's "greatest strength," he concluded, and "we have no license and less reason to join battle with him on that ground."[36]

General Greene agreed. The United States "could kill all [the] PAVN & VC [in the south] and still lose the war," he warned, unless a real effort at pacification was made because the enemy could replace its losses and retain the loyalty or fear of the people. To the Commandant, attrition was like "a grindstone that's being turned by the Communist side, and we're backing into it and having our skin taken off of . . . our entire body because they've got enough [men] to keep the old stone going." In the end, the VC's casualty rate "may be fifty times what ours is" but they would win anyway because of "their capability to wage a war of attrition." Body counts, the Marines believed, might look good on paper but brought no clear success. "This is not a strategy for victory," Krulak emphasized.[37]

The Marines were not alone in criticizing Westmoreland and attrition. In 1966 Army Chief Harold K. Johnson directed his staff officers to analyze American strategy, and so they produced the "Program for the Pacification and Long-Term Development of South Vietnam," or *PROVN*, report. This study "forthrightly attacked the search-and-destroy" concept that Westmoreland was using, according to one Army general. The PROVN report conceded the NLF's political appeal and the VC's military skills, as well as the ARVN's corruption and inefficiency. As a result, the officers who prepared the study could only conclude that "the situation in South Vietnam has seriously deteriorated [and] 1966 may well be the last chance to achieve eventual success." To improve conditions, however, the United States would have to shift to a strategy of pacification. The village level "was where the war must be fought [and] won" and all American and ARVN resources should be focused on that, not on the escalating use of heavy weapons and air strikes. Westmoreland and others in power, however, simply ignored or dismissed the PROVN findings. Dissenters were not easily accepted in the military, even the Army Chief of Staff.[38]

And perhaps no-one was as unwelcome as John Paul Vann. Though a promising adviser in Vietnam in the early 1960s, the colonel's military career was sidetracked when he was charged with the statutory rape of a 15-year-old babysitter. He avoided conviction by beating a lie detector test, but his rise to general was derailed. In the later 1960s, Vann returned to Vietnam as a civilian adviser, and he continued to attack the heavy use of firepower and the ARVN's reluctance to fight. Like the Marines and PROVN officers, Vann complained of the "widespread use of air and artillery as a substitute for getting into the countryside." The emphasis on attrition, he added, had led to the destruction of villages and alienation of the local population and made political reform impossible. As conditions worsened, Vann developed a dark sense of humor about Vietnam: in 1967, National Security Adviser Walt Rostow asked him if he thought the war would be over within six months, and Vann replied, "oh hell no, Mr. Rostow. I'm a born optimist. I think we can hold out longer than that."[39] American troops would remain in Vietnam for many more years, but by 1968 it would be clear that they would not win there.

A Whole New Ball Game

The "light at the end of the tunnel," Westmoreland's critics later joked, was a train headed toward the general. And at the end of January 1968, it thundered through Vietnam. Taking advantage of a Tet New Year cease-fire, the VC and northern army struck virtually every military and political center of importance, even invading the US embassy grounds. Within sixty days, Tet would bring down the president, finally force a reassessment of the war at the highest levels, and bring to a climax one of the gravest contemporary crises in US history. Tet, as it were, became the US obituary in Vietnam.

Since 1968, the Tet Offensive has attained mythic status, with analysts of virtually every ideological stripe agreeing that Tet was – as Westmoreland and Johnson publicly claimed at the time – a great US military victory, but political and psychological defeat. Such observations, however, neglect the military's own outlook on the war in February and March 1968. Indeed, throughout the Tet crisis, military officials in Washington and Saigon as well as political leaders recognized America's perhaps intractable dilemma in Vietnam. Just days after the attacks began, Westmoreland reported to Wheeler that, "from a realistic point of view, we must accept the fact that the enemy has dealt [South Vietnam] a severe blow," bringing the war to the people, inflicting heavy casualties and damage, and disrupting the economy. The Commander did end on an upbeat note, though, claiming that the enemy's own huge losses and failure to overthrow the southern government constituted the failure of the offensive. But he also recognized that the enemy's objectives "were primarily psychological and political." A week later Westmoreland would candidly explain, "we are now in a new ballgame where we face a determined, highly disciplined enemy, fully mobilized to achieve a quick victory." Such reports would continue throughout February 1968, leading an obviously alarmed Lyndon Johnson to despatch Wheeler to Saigon at the end of the month.[40]

After the war, the JCS Chair would claim that Tet was a military defeat for the VC and DRVN but had become "a propaganda victory for [them] here in the United States, [which] I attribute primarily to the press coverage at that time and to the dissident groups here in the United States." Among newsmen, the respected CBS anchor Walter Cronkite came in for special criticism, for on 27 February – ironically the same day that Wheeler returned from Vietnam and reported to LBJ

– he urged the United States to disengage from Vietnam. The attack on the media, however, was "incomplete and self-serving," as Secretary of Defense Clark Clifford saw it, for Wheeler himself recognized and admitted the grave problems that Tet had caused.[41] In his well-documented report, the JCS Chair found the enemy strong and capable of continuing its attacks. The ARVN meanwhile had lost about one-quarter of its pre-Tet strength. The pacification program had been badly undermined. And the government's effectiveness was obviously in question, especially as it confronted the massive problems of refugees and reconstruction. "In short," Wheeler concluded, "it was a very near thing." Harold K. Johnson did not resort to euphemism. "We suffered a loss," he cabled Westmoreland, "there can be no doubt about it." Clearly then, later claims that Tet was a great US victory are essentially moot. American leaders in early 1968 did not have time for the dust to settle in Vietnam for a thorough analysis of the situation. With a barrage of candid and often pessimistic reports pelting Washington from Saigon, policymakers could do little more than seek an effective way to cut their losses in Vietnam.

And so they did. In early March, Clifford, who had just replaced McNamara, would reassess the war; Johnson's informal advisers, the so-called Wise Men, would finally urge de-escalation; and US military leaders would continue to provide candid evaluations of the enemy's capabilities and America's problems. By the end of March, the president would lament that *"everybody is recommending surrender."* But it was Johnson himself who surrendered, withdrawing from the 1968 presidential campaign at the end of a 31 March national address. Finally forced by the shock of Tet to confront his failure to determine a consistent policy on Vietnam, the president knew that time had run out on both his political career and the US experience in Vietnam.

Johnson's decision came amid one of the more intense and tragic periods in modern history. Besides Tet, Senators Eugene McCarthy and Robert F. Kennedy had announced their candidacies for the White House, helping prompt LBJ's withdrawal from the race. In mid-March, European nations, alarmed by events in Vietnam and fearful of more escalation, began to exchange billions of American dollars for gold, leaving the United States with a serious shortage of hard currency and thereby triggering a world financial crisis that, LBJ and Wall Street feared, could lead to an economic crisis on a par with 1929. On 4 April, Martin Luther King was assassinated in Memphis, setting off uprisings in many major urban areas. Two months later, Robert Kennedy was killed after winning the California primary, ending the dream of a new Camelot and giving Vice-President Hubert Humphrey a clear path to the Democratic nomination, though his candidacy was ruined by police-incited riots at the Democratic convention in Chicago that August. In 1968, the so-called American century – a celebration of unrivaled US power after World War II – had come to an end.

Who's to Blame?

Tet signaled the failure of the American war on Vietnam. By conducting the nationwide offensive, the enemy had exposed the false promises of success that the Johnson administration had been putting forth so often and for so long. When, in February, Westmoreland and Wheeler asked the president for a massive reinforcement of about 200,000 more troops and the activation of 280,000 reserves, he rejected the request. LBJ too now realized that additional soldiers and more firepower would not affect the outcome in Vietnam. Even when the military's reports out of Vietnam had been optimistic about future progress, such massive reinforcement was never realistically likely; amid the crisis of Tet, it was impossible. Westmoreland himself later admitted that he and the JCS Chair "both knew the grave political and economic implications of a major call-up of reserves." Nonetheless the military asked for a remarkable escalation of the war at the very moment it had descended to its nadir.

Within the context of civil–military relations during the Vietnam War, however, the reinforcement request had a certain logic. It was consistent with long-term White House and military patterns of behavior toward the war. By February and March 1968, military and civilian leaders understood that reinforcement, especially in such vast numbers, was not politically feasible or affordable – McNamara estimated that the Westmoreland request would cost an additional $20–25 billion in the next two fiscal years. But the military, rather than change course after Tet, sent notice that it would continue its now-discredited war of attrition. In so doing, however, the service leaders forced Lyndon Johnson to finally take decisive action regarding Vietnam and bear responsibility for future failure.

The military realized that the request for more forces would cause a political firestorm. The Army's Pacific Commander, General Dwight Beach, when notified of Westmoreland's proposals, "had commented that it would shock" government officials. Indeed, the military had reason to expect such a reaction from Washington. Not only had the White House rejected Westmoreland's previous proposals for such escalation, but the president himself, on 2 February, had told reporters that he saw no reason to expand troop levels beyond the 525,000 then deployed to Vietnam. Johnson was also worried that the crisis of Tet might be politically devastating. At a meeting with his advisers, he charged that "all of you have counseled, advised, consulted and then – as usual – placed the monkey on my back again . . . I do not like what I am smelling from those cables from Vietnam."

Johnson's outburst may have been disingenuous but it was well-founded. The monkey in fact belonged squarely on his back, but it was true that his advisers had developed even more grave reservations about the Vietnam War as a result of Tet. Thus, the president feared that the military might be able to exploit White House division over Vietnam. "I don't want them [US military leaders] to ask for something," Johnson worried aloud, "not get it, and have all the blame placed on me." Although not expecting such a huge reinforcement request, it was thus clear that the president understood the political implications of any future moves regarding Vietnam. Ambassador to Saigon Ellsworth Bunker understood as well, warning

Westmoreland against asking for so many additional forces because reinforcement was now "politically impossible," even if Johnson had wanted it, which was also more unlikely than ever. LBJ's rejection of the request for more resources, then, was not a surprise, but it did enable the military to charge that they were forced to fight "with one hand tied behind their back."

Such feuding, maneuvering, and attempts to shift blame between civilian leaders and officers reached its peak during the Tet crisis, but had a long history up to that point as well. From the earliest days of the American intervention, the brass recognized the possibility, if not likelihood, of failure in Vietnam and were worried that they would be blamed for any shortcomings there. As early as 1961, General McGarr concluded with striking honesty that "as I am jealous of the professional good name of our Army, I do not wish it to be placed in the position of fighting a losing battle and being charged with the loss." In 1965, as combat forces arrived in Vietnam, the Pacific Commander, Admiral U. S. G. Sharp, warned Westmoreland of "grave political implications" if US troops "are committed for the first time and suffer a defeat." Admiral David McDonald, the Chief of Naval Operations, likewise feared that, after American defeat, "the only group left answerable for the war would be the military." In 1967, Harold K. Johnson, expecting the worst, warned fellow officers that the military was going to "take the fall" for the impending disaster.[42] By 1968, then, victory was less likely than ever so the chiefs, fearing blame for failure, more directly than ever tried to pin the White House with responsibility for the war, to make it clear that LBJ was making them fight short-handed. By turning down the request for reinforcement, the president essentially gave the military an alibi for the failure it had seen coming more than a decade earlier.

Charlie Meets GI Joe

While civilians and generals in Washington DC fought a political war over responsibility *for* Vietnam, young men fought a real war *in* Vietnam. There was, however, a marked difference between the opposing armies there. While soldiers on both sides displayed military skills and courage, the Viet Cong – or "Charlie," as nicknamed by the Americans – and PAVN maintained discipline and morale throughout the war. American troops, on the other hand, were not committed to their cause like the enemy, and drug use, racial conflict, discipline problems, and anti-war activity were common experiences for the "grunt," the common field soldier, in Vietnam.

The enemy in the south was well armed – using both Soviet-made AK-47s and American M-14s and M-16s captured from the ARVN or purchased on the black market – and usually well rested. The bigger VC units fought infrequently, only a couple of times a year, so that they could maintain strength and discipline. For those engaging the Americans and ARVN more often, the NLF continued to conduct *khiem thao* sessions to keep up their morale. Both northern and VC soldiers seemed willing to die for their cause as well. As one private, echoing the messages of Phan Boi Chau, Ho, and other Vietnamese heroes, told the journalist Stanley Karnow, "I know that I might be killed, but I was committed to the sacred salvation of the nation." Tactically, the VC did well too. Often, the guerrillas would "cling to the enemy's belt," meaning that they would stay so close to the Americans that any artillery or air strike would endanger US troops as much as the Vietnamese.[43] Soldiers in the north endured and succeeded despite huge losses as well. As the war wore on and Rolling Thunder intensified, North Vietnam developed one of the better air defense systems in the world. Using surface-to-air missiles (SAMs) from the Soviet Union, anti-aircraft guns, and, eventually, fighter jets, they caused huge losses for the US Air Force. To protect the civilian population, the government built over 30,000 miles of trenches and 20 million bomb shelters. By 1968, most of the northern population had experienced an American air attack within kilometers of their homes.

American soldiers, 8,000 miles from home and fighting for nebulous reasons in Asian jungles, could not have been as dedicated as the VC, fighting for its homeland, to begin with, and as the war dragged on inconclusively, their morale declined. The typical American soldier was young – late teens or early twenties – and poor. Christian Appy, who has analyzed the socio-economic backgrounds of American soldiers most closely, explained that "the institutions most responsible for channeling men into the military – the draft, the schools, and the job market – directed working-class children to the armed forces and their wealthier peers toward college."[44] For those with education or connections – Dan Quayle, Bill Clinton, Pat Buchanan, and thousands of others – it was relatively easy to avoid service by getting deferments or joining the Reserves. Those who could not pull strings, however, often served in Vietnam, and, once there, came to believe that the stated reasons for the war – anti-Communism and bringing "democracy" to the Vietnamese – were lies; their disillusionment, as well as antagonism from the local population, grew and led to a breakdown in the military order.

While the army's worst crises with drugs, racial tension, and discipline would occur after Tet, such problems were already apparent when American forces entered Vietnam in the earlier 1960s. The widespread use of drugs that had been common at home was, if anything, even worse in Vietnam. With RVN leaders and Laotian generals working with the CIA involved in the local drug traffic, and the United States thus reluctant to pressure them to end it, marijuana, opium, and heroin, among others, were available and cheap. Units often were divided between "juicers," who preferred alcohol, and "heads," those who took drugs and listened to the likes of Jimi Hendrix, Janis Joplin, The Doors, or Jefferson Airplane. As the war progressed, American soldiers used drugs to express their disgust with the situation there. Dave Cline, an infantryman, explained that the nature of the fighting – bombing villages and killing peasants – became so repugnant that he "was involved with smoking marijuana. At the time that was like the symbolism of the antiwar movement in the service."[45]

In addition to growing drug use, racial conflict began to plague the armed forces. Many black soldiers saw the contradiction, or hypocrisy, of being sent to Vietnam to fight for "democracy" while many American political leaders were fighting against civil rights at home. Leslie Whitfield, an African-American soldier, wondered "why can we be . . . fighting for this country . . . and then go back and we can't take advantage of opportunities that were offered us by the Constitution?" Such sentiment became more common and black soldiers began to identify with each other along racial lines, wearing black arm bands, offering black power salutes, and giving the "dap" to other "bloods" in their unit. At the same time, racial tension between black and white soldiers was growing worse. Some units experienced *de facto* segregation as African-American and Caucasian troops would not communicate with each other. In the same way, Chicano and Puerto Rican soldiers began to identify and associate with each other. Miguel Lemus, who served in Vietnam in 1967, explained that "in my company we had to protect each other 'cause no one else was going to protect us."[46] Racial conflict in Vietnam was sharpened as various groups at home such as "black power" or "la raza" activists began to speak about and educate young men on the connection between race, discrimination at home, and service in Vietnam. By 1967, incoming black and Chicano soldiers could not avoid noticing the similarities between social conditions among the Vietnamese and the situation in America being highlighted by Martin Luther King, Cesar Chávez, and others. And when the World Heavyweight Champion, Muhammad Ali, was stripped of his title for refusing induction into the army in 1967 – saying "no Viet Cong ever called me 'Nigger'" – racial antagonism jumped noticeably. In April 1968, at the time of King's assassination, several units verged on civil war when Caucasian soldiers flew rebel flags to taunt the African-American troops.[47]

With drugs and racial division prevalent, a breakdown in military discipline was inevitable. Again, the problem would become much worse in the later years of the war, but was present from 1965 onward. Both active-duty servicemen and veterans actively criticized and opposed the war from the earliest days of intervention. In September 1965, Master Sergeant Donald Duncan, a Green Beret, gained national exposure when he publicly quit Vietnam, charging that American forces were using torture tactics there and that "the whole thing was a lie. We weren't preserving freedom in South Vietnam. There was no freedom to preserve."[48] Duncan may have gained notoriety, but many other soldiers dissented from the war as well. In 1965, a Special Forces officer, Richard Steinke, refused to go into combat to protect US actions in Vietnam; Adam Weber, an infantryman, was sent to jail for a year for refusing to fight; and in 1966, the "Fort Hood Three" – David Samos, Dennis Mora, and James Johnson – were court-martialed after rejecting orders to serve in Vietnam. As they announced, "we have decided to take a stand against this war, which we consider immoral, illegal and unjust." William Harvey, an African-American Marine who was a Muslim, spent two years in military prison for his activity against the war. To Harvey, the US role in Vietnam was strikingly similar to American society's treatment of blacks. "I feel that the black man's attitude is that the war is one of genocide toward the colored people of the world in general," he charged.[49]

Such sentiments increased over time and soldiers and veterans began to organize and express their disdain for the war. In early 1966, about one hundred veterans marched on the White House, with many turning in their service medals and discharge papers to protest the growing war in Vietnam. Antiwar celebrities such as Jane Fonda, Donald Sutherland, Holly Near, and others played at GI "coffee houses" on various bases throughout the country, agitating and organizing against the war. An Army doctor, Howard Levy, became a national figure when he was court-martialed for refusing to train Special Forces soldiers, who to him were "murderers of women and children." More broadly, in 1966 and 1967 military personnel formed, among other groups, the Veterans for Peace, Veterans and Reservists to End the War in Vietnam, GIs United Against the War, the American Serviceman's Union (ASU), Resist Inside the Army (RITA), and, most notably, the Vietnam Veterans Against the War (VVAW).

Such organized anti-war activity within the military translated into serious discipline problems. "Fraggings," intentional attacks on a unit's officers via fragmentation grenade or other weaponry, became common and were especially directed against commanders who were "gung ho" on fighting the VC. Many soldiers preferred "search and evade" operations, where they would go on patrol and make a point of staying away from the enemy, or shooting their rifles into the air and reporting it as an engagement. As one Marine Captain explained, he and the local VC commander had an "unwritten, informal agreement" to avoid contact with each other in the field. For many soldiers, evasion was not enough and a significant number simply bolted. According to Richard Moser's figures, Army AWOL rates rose nearly 40 percent – from 57 to 78 per thousand – between 1966 and 1967, while desertion rates grew almost 50 percent – from 15 to 21.4 per thousand – in the same period. The Marine desertion problem was worse, increasing from 16 to 27 per thousand. By mid-1967, over 40,000 servicemen, or about 10 percent of the troop total in Vietnam, were classified as deserters and had committed over 500,000 "incidents of desertion." While the American numbers were smaller than the ARVN's, there can be no doubt that the level of desertions and dissatisfaction with the war was substantially higher among US troops than the enemy, making an already difficult mission in Vietnam even harder.

One, Two, Three, Four, We Don't Want Your Bloody War

Such dissent within the military emerged in conjunction with the anti-war movement at home, which grew exponentially in the later 1960s. Despite the number of anti-war protestors, though, the movement against the war in Vietnam never represented a majority of Americans, and its impact is still open to debate today. The movement began on college campuses and in pacifist churches and ultimately spread to business groups, the political arena, and mainstream America. While the media often portrayed the anti-war protests as dominated by hippies and Communists, the typical demonstrator was probably a middle-class Caucasian American with strong political or moral reservations about the war. The Johnson, and even more so the Nixon, administrations were concerned with the growth of the movement, but it is not clear just what effect it had on the war in Indochina. Many participants in and critics of the Vietnam-era peace protests tend to either credit or blame the public's opposition to the war for the US failure there, but it was the VC, not the media or "Mustang Maoists" on the campuses, that caused America's undoing.

The anti-Vietnam War movement had various sources, especially in the "Ban the Bomb" campaign of the 1950s and 1960s, among the "Beats" in cafés, and in the Students for a Democratic Society (SDS) organization in the early 1960s. Nuclear disarmament advocates such as Bertrand Russell, Benjamin Spock, and A. J. Muste became stalwarts of the Vietnam peace movement as well, while SDS organized the first large-scale resistance to the war. In 1964, after the Tonkin incident, SDS issued a call for a national demonstration against the war in Washington in April 1965. Expecting a meager turnout, protest leaders were shocked when about 25,000 showed up to criticize the war. At around the same time, over 3,000 students participated in the first "*teach-in*" – a series of debates and lectures about Vietnam with supporters and critics of the war – at the University of Michigan in Ann Arbor, and in May 1965, 122 colleges and universities were linked by telephone to Washington, DC and took part in the biggest teach-in to that point. Many young men began to protest more stridently, burning their draft cards or committing acts of civil disobedience against selective service offices or other government installations. For instance, protestors in Oakland blocked trains carrying troops to induction centers. Tragically, in early 1965, an 82-year-old Holocaust survivor in Detroit, Alice Herz, immolated herself to protest the war. In time, at least six others – Norman Morrison, Roger LaPorte, J. D. Copping, Hiroko Hayashi, Florence Beaumont, and J. D. Winne – would burn themselves to death as well, with Morrison immolating himself in view of Robert McNamara's Pentagon office window.

Though few demonstrators made the ultimate sacrifice like Herz, the movement grew rapidly. Political, academic, and cultural figures such as Leonard Bernstein, Gregory Peck, Allen Ginsberg, William Appleman Williams, Noam Chomsky, and countless others began to speak out against the war. SDS leaders like Tom Hayden, Paul Potter, and Carl Oglesby became national anti-war leaders with their work in the resistance. But the movement was showing signs of strain too, and those would worsen over time. In November 1965, the anti-nuclear group SANE called a march on Washington to express "responsible criticism" of the war, but it was SDS President Oglesby who roused the crowd with his fiery oratory about not only the war but the system of "corporate liberalism" that drove America into Vietnam.[50] Such rhetoric turned off old-line liberals like Irving Howe, Michael Harrington, and Norman Thomas, giving the early movement somewhat of a leftist cast. To many older activists, SDS and other youth groups were not just anti-war but pro-VC, a charge raised more frequently as peace activists like Hayden, Staughton Lynd, Herbert Apthecker, Joan Baez, and Jane Fonda traveled to the DRVN to protest the war and as young people marched on the White House chanting "Ho, Ho, Ho Chi Minh, NLF is gonna win" or, more sharply, "Hey, Hey, LBJ, How Many Kids Did You Kill Today?"

Despite tensions, the anti-war campaign accelerated from 1966 to 1968. In early 1966, many Establishment leaders began to take on the war as well. In February, the chair of the Senate Committee on Foreign Relations, J. William Fulbright, conducted hearings at which General James Gavin and diplomat George Frost Kennan strongly criticized US involvement in Vietnam. Ex-Commandant David Shoup went further, excoriating the war publicly in a 1966 speech, asserting that "if we had and would keep our dirty, bloody, dollar-crooked fingers" out of Vietnamese affairs, the people there will determine their own fate, not have one "crammed down their throats by Americans."[51] Hans Morgenthau, a respected political scientist, began to speak out also, as did other academics such as George McT. Kahin, Howard Zinn, and Gabriel Kolko.

Among intellectuals, none matched the impact of MIT linguist Noam Chomsky, whose articles in the *New York Review of Books, Ramparts,* and elsewhere placed the war within the larger contexts of the Cold War, capitalism, and American political culture. In the most important essay of the Vietnam generation, "The Responsibility of Intellectuals," Chomsky in particular attacked political and academic apologists for the war. "Intellectuals are in a position to expose the lies of governments, to analyze actions according to their causes and motives and often hidden intentions," he explained, and it was "the responsibility of intellectuals to speak the truth and to expose lies." For the most part, however, America's educated elite bought into the war and supported it, while even critics saw it as principally a mistake or an aberration rather than a systemic condition. Chomsky thus concluded: "The question 'What have I done?' is one that we may well ask ourselves, as we read, each day, of fresh atrocities in Vietnam – as we create, or mouth, or tolerate the deceptions that will be used to justify the next defense of freedom."[52] Others did "speak truth to power," as a favorite slogan of the day suggested. David Dellinger and David McReynolds, peace veterans, tirelessly organized against the war, while Philip and Daniel Berrigan, Jesuit priests, counseled young men on avoiding military service and were arrested and convicted for destroying selective service records at a government office in Catonsville, Maryland. Even the well-known political scientist Hans Morgenthau, once a favorite of the Washington establishment, chastised the intellectual community for its acquiescence in the war. Accusing them of "political opportunism" and caving in to government pressure, Morgenthau lamented that "the intellectuals of America have indeed been raped; but many of them have looked forward to the experience and are enjoying it."[53]

The heart of the movement, however, was still in the streets. Demonstrations in most major cities continued throughout 1966 and 1967, and included millions of Americans of all age groups, religions, and classes. In April 1967, between 125,000 and 400,000 (depending on whether the police or the demonstrators were counting) people protested the war in New York, while at least 75,000 took to the streets for the same purpose in San Francisco. While gaining strength, the movement was also evolving, offering a harsh political condemnation of Vietnam but with some segments creating a sense of the absurd as well. In October 1967 in Washington, for instance, over 100,000 demonstrators listened to intellectual attacks on the war, burned their draft cards, or tried to levitate the Pentagon by chanting and meditating – and many participants to this day claim they saw the building leave the ground. Abbie Hoffman and Jerry Rubin became media stars – part Karl Marx and part Groucho Marx – as they brought guerrilla theater to the movement. Rubin once appeared before a government committee dressed as George Washington, with silk stockings and powdered wig, and he and Hoffman went to Wall Street and threw dollar bills onto the floor of the New York Stock Exchange, causing a wild scramble for money among the traders in the pit. In 1968, Hoffman, Rubin, Allen Ginsberg, folk-protest singer Phil Ochs, and rock groups Country Joe and the Fish and The Fugs were founders of the Youth International Party, better known as the yippies. Though a small minority in the peace movement, the yippies received tremendous media coverage, especially for their plans to disrupt the 1968 Democratic convention in Chicago with dancing bears and a pig – named "Pigasus" – that they would nominate for president and then eat. Among the yippies' demands besides an end to the war in Vietnam were the legalization of all drugs, the abolition of money, the disarmament of police, and free love in the streets.

The attention focused on the yippies, though sensational, did not reflect mainstream opposition to the war. After Tet, the government's reasons for fighting in Vietnam had been exposed as unwarranted optimism or lies. Many liberals who had still supported Johnson felt betrayed by the administration and, maybe most importantly, Wall Street turned against the war amid the dollar–gold crisis. Walter Wriston, the president of Citibank, told a group of financial leaders that it would be possible to stabilize the world economy but "the chances would be greater if the Vietnamese war ended." Likewise, in a report to investors, Goldman, Sachs economists simply explained that reduced spending in Vietnam "could contribute significantly to the solution of many of the problems currently plaguing the US economy."[54] William McChesney Martin, the chair of the Federal Reserve Board, was likewise alarmed by the continuing costs of military intervention, fearing a repeat of the depression of 1929 and complaining that "I have been trying for the past two years to make the point on 'guns and butter' and the cost of the Vietnam war, economically, without too much success but I think in due course the chickens will come home to roost."[55]

African-Americans, generally supportive of LBJ, also began to turn on him as Martin Luther King and other black leaders increasingly spoke out against a war in which blacks, though only about 12 percent of the population, were accounting for nearly a third of the casualties. Then, on top of Tet, King was killed in April, and the war and urban rebellion converged. In a real sense, the violence of Vietnam had come home as cities burned and the hopes of a generation seemed shattered. At the Ohio State University, a young history professor, David Green, burned his draft card in class the day after King's death to protest the war and America's racial dilemma. Businessmen, moms, and young radicals all protested the war together, posing a mainstream assault on the Johnson administration. Some younger activists gave up on the system and dropped out of society or joined militant groups. Some hoped to reform the political structure from within and worked on the other candidates' campaigns, only to see Bobby Kennedy too assassinated and Eugene McCarthy lose the nomination. By mid-1968, the country was terribly divided over Vietnam and the war was about to come home.

In August, at the Democratic convention, tens of thousands of demonstrators fought street battles with local police forces. Chicago's mayor, Richard Daley, in conjunction with the Federal Bureau of Investigation, had planted *provocateurs* in the crowd to incite the protestors. Then, on 25 August, 150 police, wielding tear gas and night sticks, attacked an encampment in Lincoln Park. The next day, the protestors struck back with rocks and bottles, and in turn 5,000 army troops were sent into Chicago. After that, local cops stripped themselves of their badges and uniforms and went on a rampage with clubs and mace, injuring hundreds. By 29 August, all hell broke loose as several thousand demonstrators marched on the convention headquarters at the Hilton. As officers charged into the crowd, some yelling "Kill, Kill," young people chanted "the whole world is watching." Inside the convention, Connecticut Senator Abraham Ribicoff was attacking the "gestapo tactics" of the police in the streets, while Daley mouthed "sit down you fucking Jew" to him. Surveying the wreckage of Chicago, the radical journalist I. F. Stone could only lament that "the war is destroying our country as we are destroying Vietnam." Johnson himself, writing after he left office, still did not take responsibility for the crisis, but poignantly observed that "the American people recoiled in anguish in 1968, as violence again struck down national leaders and lit flames in the skies above a dozen cities. We confronted the perils of inflation at home and the danger of the dollar's decline abroad. The agony of an odious war, forced upon us so cruelly for so long, cut deep divisions across our national life. These, with all their shock and sorrow, are forever part of the fabric of that turbulent period."[56]

4

The Empire Strikes Back: The Vietnam War from 1968 to 1975

Tet ended American hopes for victory in Vietnam. Militarily, the Offensive had exposed the US inability to stop infiltration or destroy the enemy. Worse, politically it showed that the NLF remained popular throughout Vietnam while large numbers of mainstream Americans – those who got their opinions from Walter Cronkite – seemed ready to throw in the towel. American leaders recognized failure too and so began a strategy of "*Vietnamization*" – shifting the burden for warfare to the ARVN while continuing to support Saigon with huge amounts of material and money, but also withdrawing American soldiers to quiet the anti-war movement – in hopes of winding down the war.

But at the same time, new President Richard M. Nixon, who had won office promising to quickly bring "peace with honor," contradictorily intensified the American air campaign and geographically expanded the conflict into Cambodia and Laos. Nixon's strategy, as Dove Senator George McGovern later described it, amounted to maintaining the war while "changing the color of the corpses" from white to yellow. If Tet and the Gold Crisis had signaled a dramatic transformation of American power, then Nixon's policies sent the message that the American empire was still alive and capable of inflicting great damage on its enemies. If Ho and the NLF were to win, it would be at a tremendous cost.

The Age of Nixon

Two years before the next scheduled presidential election, Democratic Senator Stuart Symington warned LBJ that "Nixon will murder us" in 1968. "He will become the biggest dove of all times," the senator feared. "There has never been a man in American public life that could turn so fast on a dime."[1] In the course of five and one-half years in the White House, Nixon would repeatedly prove the accuracy of Symington's earlier observation. As Commander-in-Chief, Nixon would act as peacemaker and then unleash more bombs, pose as madman and complain about unfair "liberal" media treatment, pledge to uphold American credibility and violate the Constitution. Meanwhile the war in Vietnam continued, while bloodlettings in Cambodia and Laos intensified as well. At home, paranoia over the anti-war movement led to the Watergate scandal. Fittingly, the war in Vietnam and Richard Nixon's political career ended in the same period.

Nixon had campaigned in 1968 with, he said, a "secret plan" to end the war. At the same time, his associates were secretly talking with RVN President Nguyen Van Thieu to make sure that peace talks did not take place before the election and thereby hurt his chances. Thus Nixon won by a slim margin in November 1968 and the new president set out to extricate America from Vietnam. To do so, Nixon pursued several paths, including talks, terrorism, expanding the war, and accelerating B-52 bomber strikes. The centerpiece of American strategy, developed and conducted by the president and his Machiavellian National Security Adviser Henry Kissinger, would be Vietnamization to wind down the war. But at the same time Nixon would not go gentle into the night, urging staffers to consider new options, even nuclear weapons, for Vietnam. As Kissinger put it, "I refuse to believe that a little fourth-rate power like North Vietnam does not have a breaking point."[2]

Such arrogance would typify the Nixon–Kissinger approach to the war and so the United States, while trying to get out of Vietnam, built up the war as well. The United States increased the size of the ARVN to one million soldiers by 1970, and provided it with a million M-16 rifles, 12,000 M-60 machine guns, 40,000 M-79 grenade launchers, and 2,000 heavy mortars and howitzers. Nixon also began "*Operation Phoenix*," which would "neutralize" – arrest or kill – suspected VC supporters in the south. Phoenix, according to one reporter, was a program of "calculated brutality," in which innocent villagers were systematically arrested, tortured, or killed to meet quotas. As one CIA official described it, Phoenix was "thought up by geniuses and implemented by idiots."[3] It did, however, damage the VC infrastructure in the south; by arresting and killing so many villagers, Phoenix operatives were bound to bag a large number of the enemy as well. Though arming the ARVN and "neutralizing" the enemy were important, the keystone of the "Nixon Doctrine" became the unbridled use of American technology, especially air power, against not only the VC, but all of Indochina. Vietnamization, intended to end the war, was expanding it.

Sideshows

The United States had been involved in Laos and Cambodia well before the Nixon years, but they became central battlegrounds after 1969. In Laos, America had fueled a "secret war" against the Pathet Lao rebels from the mid-1950s onward, while using CIA aircraft – the infamous Air America – to transship heroin out of the region. In Cambodia, the United States helped oust the neutral government of Prince Norodom Sihanouk, invaded the country, unleashed a torrent of B-52 bombings, and helped facilitate the emergence of the bloody Khmer Rouge regime.

Between 1964 and 1969, the Johnson administration flew sorties over Laos with B-52s, long-range bombers which carried eighty-four 500-pound, and twenty-four 750-pound bombs, and which could saturate an area of two square miles per sortie. In five years, American B-52 pilots dropped nearly 150,000 *tons* of bombs over the Plain of Jars, a Pathet Lao area in northeastern Laos. As a United Nations representative described it, "the intensity of the bombing was such that no organized life was possible in the villages."[4] Such destruction notwithstanding, Nixon took even more drastic action. Both to show that the ARVN was capable of fighting by itself – per the doctrine of Vietnamization – and to convince the enemy that he might be a "madman" capable of inflicting untold damage on them, Nixon ordered an invasion of Laos in February 1971. The operation, known as Lam Son 719, or Dewey Canyon, was a disaster. The ARVN was supposed to attack the northern section of the VC's supply route, the Ho Chi Minh Trail; strike the PAVN's troop encampments and supply depots; and disrupt the enemy's offensive plans. But RVN President Thieu had given his commanders orders not to sustain too many casualties, and ARVN intelligence was terrible, so about 40,000 PAVN troops ambushed the southern army, inflicting casualty rates of over 50 percent and destroying or damaging 543 of 659 US helicopters flying support missions. Only by dropping 48,000 tons of bombs did the United States prevent an even more horrific rout. The Laos invasion, intended to show the virtues of Vietnamization, instead proved that the southern state and the ARVN could exist only with massive US support. As one American soldier put it in blunt terms, "the enemy was a tough, hard, dedicated fucking guy, and the ARVN didn't want to hear about fighting. It was LaLa Land. Every, every, every, *every* firefight that we got into, the ARVN broke, the ARVN fucking ran."[5] Kissinger himself conceded that "as for the South Vietnamese, Laos exposed many of their lingering deficiencies." ARVN planning was "largely abstract" and Kissinger doubted if it "ever really understood what we were trying to accomplish." Because of the failure of the Laos invasion, it was likely that the United States would face "another major military challenge" in the coming years.[6]

A Pitiful Helpless Giant

Even more than the Laotian intervention, US involvement in Cambodia had an enormous impact on events in Indochina and at home. Nixon had become increasingly frustrated with Prince Sihanouk, who, though technically neutral, was not preventing the VC from receiving supplies via his territory, including the port of Sihanoukville, and seeking refuge there from American troops. Accordingly, in March 1969, the president began Operation Menu – with raids codenamed Breakfast, Lunch, Snack, and Dinner – a series of "secret" bombings of Cambodia (secret to the American people but not to the Cambodians being struck by them) in which tens of thousands of sorties would be flown and hundreds of thousands of tons of bombs dropped on the small country. But Nixon still was not satisfied, so, in March 1970, the United States helped a palindromic Cambodian politician named Lon Nol overthrow Sihanouk. As one of his first acts, Lon Nol "invited" the southern Vietnamese to enter Cambodia to expel VC and PAVN forces from its territory.

Nixon, claiming that the "nerve center" of the enemy operations – the VC's pentagon, as it were – was in Cambodia, thus authorized an invasion, or "incursion" as he termed it, in late April, ironically just a week after announcing the withdrawal of another 150,000 US troops from Indochina. To Nixon, the Cambodian invasion would show the world that he was tough, if not mad, and that American credibility remained strong. As the president explained in a televised address on 30 April, "if when the chips are down, the world's most powerful nation acts like a pitiful, helpless giant, the forces of totalitarianism and anarchy will threaten free nations and free institutions throughout the world."[7] Meanwhile the air war continued, with US pilots flying over 8,000 sorties between July 1970 and February 1971, over 300 a day. All of Cambodia had essentially become a free-fire zone, but, as in Laos, with little effect on the war. In both Cambodia and the United States, however, the events of April 1970 made a huge and long-lasting impact.

In Cambodia, a Communist rebel group, the *Khmer Rouge*, which had been previously marginal, exploited the US-caused terror to gain a much larger following and, after the Lon Nol coup, joined an alliance with Sihanouk, thereby giving it credibility. Building on the revulsion against the United States and Lon Nol, the Khmer Rouge grew and took control of more area throughout the early 1970s, culminating in victory in April 1975. In power, the regime, led by Pol Pot, instituted the infamous "killing fields" in which the Khmer Rouge eliminated perhaps over a million Cambodians, by starvation and also by execution, often for spurious reasons such as speaking French, wearing eyeglasses, or being "enemies" of the people. The Cambodian people, in less than a decade, had to deal with the twin terrors of the US air war and the Khmer Rouge genocide.

The War Comes Home

At the same time, the movement against the war at home became the target of state violence, and Nixon anticipated this. As he prepared his "pitiful helpless giant" soliloquy, he warned his daughter Julie, a graduating senior at Smith, that "it's possible that the campuses are really going to blow up after this speech."[8] And they did. Although public opinion polls showed support for the invasion, colleges and universities nationwide erupted in protest. Students at over 1,300 campuses held demonstrations; 536 campuses were shut down completely with 51 closing for the remainder of the academic semester. In California, the nation's largest public system, Governor Ronald Reagan shut down the entire state university structure, while the Pennsylvania university system ceased operations indefinitely.

At *Kent State University*, a working-class school in northeastern Ohio, the war came home more starkly than ever. Students there began organizing demonstrations right after Nixon's "incursion" speech and on 2 May torched the campus Reserve Officers Training Corps (ROTC) building, a frequent target of anti-war protest on most campuses. Ohio's governor, James Rhodes, comparing the students to Nazis, Communists, and Klansmen, deployed the National Guard to the campus. On 4 May, after students, standing hundreds of yards away, threw rocks and bottles at the Reservists, several soldiers opened fire, killing four and wounding 13 others. Nixon, who days earlier had called young protestors "bums

. . . blowin' up the campuses," offered no sympathy to the Kent victims. Vice-President Spiro Agnew in fact found the killings "predictable" and said that campus demonstrators were part of the "psychotic and criminal elements in our society." J. Edgar Hoover, zealous FBI director and the Dennis Rodman of his day, told White House officials that one of the young women killed "was nothing more than a whore anyway."[9]

The events at Kent State galvanized America's youth. With almost no planning, a rally held on 9 May in Washington drew over 100,000 protestors. Nixon, trying to show his rapport with young people, went to the Lincoln Memorial to meet with demonstrators. Instead of discussing the war, however, he talked about football. "He just kept rambling," one student said, "and he didn't make any sense."[10] Nor did he do much to bring calm to the country. Amid the climate of anger and frustration, protests and violence continued. At Jackson State University, a historically black institution in Mississippi, state police and national guardsmen attacked a dormitory and killed two students. By mid-1970 then, the United States was in a wider war in Cambodia, helping to unleash the Khmer Rouge, and using violence against students at home. "Peace with honor" seemed as far away as ever.

Talking . . .

Despite constant rhetoric about its desire for peace in Vietnam, the Johnson and Nixon administrations made no sincere effort to negotiate an end to the war in the 1960s. American offers to talk with Ho repeatedly included the requirement that the NLF *not* be a participant in any negotiations, a provision that southern nationalists and Hanoi were sure to reject. On the rare occasion when negotiations seemed to hold promise, things quickly fell apart – as when Nixon and Kissinger torpedoed talks just prior to the 1968 elections. But in February 1970, without even informing Secretary of State William Rogers, Kissinger opened secret negotiations in Paris with Le Duc Tho, the DRVN representative. On the major issues, however – a bombing halt, a political role for the NLF, and American support for the RVN – the United States and Vietnam remained far apart, and in June, to protest the Cambodian invasion, Le Duc Tho suspended the secret talks. Negotiations reopened in May 1971, and in July, to gain the diplomatic initiative, Hanoi and the southern-based Provisional Revolutionary Government (PRG), the successor organization to the NLF, announced their own peace proposal, which included a coalition government in the south, the withdrawal of American troops, and the return of prisoners of war (POWs) from all sides. To Hanoi, it was essential to hold reasonably free elections in the south, which it assumed would bring to power a government in the RVN willing to negotiate an end to the war. Kissinger must have expected that as well, for instead of considering the proposal he told the media that the DRVN was demanding the "overthrow" of Thieu and that the United States would never submit to such ultimatums. Free elections in the south, Kissinger warned, were a source of "turmoil and uncertainty."[11]

. . . and Fighting

With such an approach to negotiations, the war was bound to continue – and it did, reaching new intensity in 1972. Nixon had actually increased his options in Vietnam in 1972 by pursuing a policy of détente with the major Communist powers, the Soviet Union and China, even traveling to the PRC in early 1972. Thus, by mid-year, he could escalate the air war without the same fear of Soviet or Chinese retaliation that had influenced LBJ's air campaign. The immediate cause of the new B-52 strikes came with the enemy's so-called Easter Offensive. On 30 March 1972, after months of construction and military preparations in the regions where Vietnam, Cambodia, and Laos meet, three PAVN divisions, supported by artillery and T-54 tanks acquired from the Soviet Union, swept across the seventeenth parallel and into the northern RVN. Hanoi's goal was to again show the failure of Vietnamization and to demonstrate to Nixon that he faced endless war unless he talked with the enemy in good faith. The first goal was proven immediately, as the ARVN fell apart and the PAVN and VC captured various cities in the Demilitarized Zone (DMZ), as well as Quang Tri Province. Creighton Abrams, the American commander, feared that the southern Vietnamese "have lost their will to fight . . . and that the whole thing may well be lost."[12] The ARVN, with desertions nearing 20,000 a month and casualty figures approaching 150,000, was simply bolting as the PAVN-VC offensive roared into Kontum Province in the central highlands and had a clear path to Hué in the northeastern RVN. Even Hanoi was surprised by the speed of the offensives and hesitated before moving in for the kill.

In the meantime, Nixon rallied. He insisted that he would not negotiate under current conditions. "No nonsense. No niceness. No accommodations," he told Kissinger, and he unleashed a new series of air strikes that finally blunted the PAVN advance. Codenamed *Operation Linebacker*, the Air Force began non-stop B-52 attacks north of the seventeenth parallel in early April. Boasting that "the bastards have never been bombed like they're going to be bombed this time,"[13] Nixon had US pilots conduct over 700 B-52 sorties in the DRVN, over 300 in or near Kontum over a three-week period, and daily hit Quang Tri Province with 40 B-52 sorties, each carrying over 30 tons of bombs. Nixon even began bombing Hanoi and the port at Haiphong – where non-combatant countries, including the Soviet Union, delivered supplies to the DRVN – and on 8 May mined the harbor at Haiphong. By that time, the Easter Offensive had run its course. The B-52s had prevented a collapse in the RVN, but the damage already done was severe. In addition to the ARVN's losses and desertions, the attacks created about a million more refugees, the NLF remained in control of northern Quang Tri, and guerrilla forces had exploited the mayhem in the north by establishing positions all over the delta and central coast. Nonetheless, Linebacker continued for seven months, in which time the United States flew about 42,000 sorties and dropped over 155,000 tons of bombs on DRVN storage facilities, air bases, power plants, bridges, tunnels, hospitals, and homes. Despite the relentless barrage, American prospects in Vietnam were not markedly better than before, while at home the American people continued to oppose the war.

Vocal Opposition and the "Silent Majority"

Because of Nixon's escalation, millions of Americans joined protests against the war. The nature of the Peace Movement and of demonstrations against continued American involvement in Vietnam changed significantly, however. In October 1969, radical activists in SDS and a splinter group, the Weathermen, returned to Chicago, site of the 1968 police riots, to conduct their "Days of Rage," blowing up a statue dedicated to Chicago police and engaging in pitched battles with law enforcement officials. And barely six months later, following the Cambodian invasion, numerous campuses erupted, while in the summer of 1970 violence against draft boards and military installations was not uncommon. But the typical protest was not like Chicago or Kent State, though Nixon would try to depict it as such. Rather, leaders of the movement against the war tried to broaden demonstrations to include "mainstream" Americans – clergy, businessmen, housewives, high school students, and others – and to present a more moderate, though still firm and aggressive, opposition to the war.

Along those lines, in 1969, the National Moratorium Day, on 15 October, and the New Mobilization to End the War, or "Mobe," a month later, constituted probably the biggest actions against the war in the Vietnam era. Over a million Americans participated in the Moratorium: over 100,000 protestors met in Boston Common; in Manhattan, political leaders and Woody Allen, Shirley Maclaine, and Stacy Keach spoke against the war; in Washington, after speeches by Dr Benjamin Spock and others, Coretta Scott King, Martin Luther King's widow, led a candlelight march on the White House. Among supporters of the Moratorium were John Laird, son of Defense Secretary Melvin Laird; Antonia Lake, wife of Kissinger aide Tony Lake; Susan and Peter Haldeman, children of Nixon's Chief of Staff H. R. Haldeman; and the children of both Treasury Secretary George Shultz and Office of Management and Budget Director Caspar Weinberger; even Vice-President Spiro Agnew's 14-year-old daughter wanted to participate – more examples of the war literally coming home to the administration.

The Moratorium infuriated the White House. Pat Buchanan, a Nixon aide, wrote the president that the war "will now be won or lost on the American front." The public was "confused and uncertain and beginning to believe that they may be wrong and beginning to feel themselves the moral inferiors of the candle carrying pessimists who want to get out now." Nixon claimed that the protests were actually prolonging the war by sending the message to Hanoi that it would not have to compromise so long as the American people were demanding an end to the conflict. To rally support for the war, the president, while addressing the nation two weeks after the Moratorium, claimed that a "silent majority" of Americans in fact supported the war, but were not staging huge rallies to state their opinion, as the anti-war forces were.[14]

A month later, however, even more Americans vocally participated in the "Mobe," thereby laying bare Nixon's attempt to discredit them. On 13 November, the protestors began a "March Against Death," hanging cards around their necks with the names of dead American soldiers and pausing in front of the White House to announce the names of Americans killed in Vietnam. "For almost forty hours, through rain, hail, and bright sunlight, the death parade continued unabated. Forty-five thousand marched in all."[15] On the 15th, over a quarter-million people met on the Mall to demonstrate against the war, while in San Francisco, amid steady rains, another 150,000 turned out for the Mobe. Again the Nixon administration was reeling. To Attorney General John Mitchell, the Mobe evoked images of the Russian Revolution as the DC police unleashed tear gas against the protestors; he then, hopefully not seriously, turned to John Dean, buttoned-down White

House counsel, and said "Dean, you're a revolutionary like those kids – what do they want?" Kissinger felt similarly, describing the actions as "fascism of the streets" in Washington.

The views of Mitchell and Kissinger were out of touch with most Americans, "silent" or otherwise. After Kent State, mainstream opposition to the war grew as even the establishment – senators and representatives, the media, the business community, and others – began to bail out on Vietnam. In mid-1970, Senators John Sherman Cooper (R, Kentucky), a conservative, and Frank Church (D, Idaho), a liberal, successfully sponsored a bill to cut off funding for the war in Cambodia unless Congress specifically approved the expense, and also repealed the Tonkin Gulf Resolution, the legislation that gave LBJ the go-ahead on the war in August 1964. In 1971 Senators George McGovern (D, S Dakota) and Mark Hatfield (R, Oregon) tried to go even further, offering an amendment to cut off all funding for the war by the end of the year. Their effort failed, but in the meantime even more members of the clergy, military, press, and corporate community were speaking out against the war, especially after the July 1971 publication of the *Pentagon Papers* – a "secret" history of the war – leaked to the *New York Times* by Pentagon official Daniel Ellsberg and highly revealing of the motives behind the war and the behavior of ranking officials.

Ironically, however, Nixon's continued withdrawal of American troops – he would pull out 70,000 by 1 May 1972, leaving just 69,000 in Vietnam – took the steam out of the anti-war movement. Although spontaneous protests broke out in numerous areas during the April Linebacker campaign and at the Republican convention in Miami in August, there were no more massive and dramatic demonstrations as there had been in the previous years. But Nixon was unable to understand his success and, in July 1972, burglars authorized by the White House, in an effort to discredit the Democrats' peace candidate, Senator McGovern, and the anti-war movement, broke into Democratic National Committee headquarters at the Watergate complex in Washington – thereby setting into motion a chain of events that would lead to Nixon's resignation in disgrace in August 1974. In the end, the Peace Movement helped drive Nixon out of office, perhaps unwittingly, but, despite its fervent efforts, could not end the war at an earlier date.

Soldiers in Revolt

There is still today great debate over the impact of the anti-war movement, with many of those who protested the war claiming that they forced American policymakers to de-escalate the war in Vietnam, while many supporters of the war charge that the demonstrators were essentially traitors who gave aid and comfort to the enemy. Both views are problematical, and for the same reason: they place the focus of the war on the United States, whereas in reality the outcome was decided in Vietnam. The NLF was able to consistently appeal, politically and culturally, to the people of southern Vietnam, while the RVN government never overcame the label of a US "puppet" regime. Militarily, the VC enjoyed the respect and/or fear of the southern populace, while the ARVN was riddled with desertions and corruption. And in the north, the people of the DRVN withstood the stunning barrage of B-52 attacks with their will unbroken, and the PAVN, as shown during the Lam Son 719 and Easter campaigns, was an organized and efficient military machine.

Worse for the Americans, their own military establishment in Vietnam was deeply troubled and deteriorating as the war was winding down. Problems of morale, discipline, drugs, racial conflict, and anti-war activity – already serious during the Johnson years – mushroomed in the early 1970s, leading to one of the more serious crises for the US military in its history. American soldiers often lacked any incentive to fight in Vietnam, violating rules or ignoring their officers because, as they often said, "what are they going to do about it, send me to 'Nam?" With such attitudes, American troops in Vietnam engaged in behavior that was often shocking.

The drug problem that was already in evidence became a

crisis in the final years of the war. There was always a steady supply of cheap and potent drugs, especially marijuana and heroin, available to American soldiers in Vietnam, and they took advantage of the consumer's market in mind-altering substances. Marijuana in Vietnam had a particular kick to it, with THC levels of 5 percent, compared to 1 percent in the grass usually available in the United States; in addition, most dope in Vietnam was treated with opium, intensifying the high. Heroin was also widely available by 1969. It was 95 percent pure but incredibly cheap – where a vial in the United States might cost $200, in Vietnam it would be a dollar or two. By 1973, the Pentagon admitted that about one-third of American troops were using heroin and about 20 percent were addicted at one time. According to a 1971 congressional survey, drugs in Vietnam were more plentiful than cigarettes or chewing gum. Indeed, the drug problem became so severe that on some bases, commanders would allow prostitutes into the barracks so that the soldiers could avoid the downtown brothels, where illicit substances were sold and bought so easily. For the soldiers, drugs were a way of coping with, or forgetting about, the war.

By itself, the serious substance abuse problem in the armed forces was a huge barrier to effective military action. But the military also had many other serious problems in the Vietnam era. Given the nature of the war, one of the few ways for the United States to claim progress was to cite the impressive "body counts," the number of enemy soldiers killed in combat, artillery attacks, or air strikes. In pursuit of high numbers, US officers, to impress their superiors and get promotions, often wildly inflated the figures, coerced their men into battle, or had their troops engage in brutalities. There was thus a marked difference in the Vietnam experience of officers and the so-called grunts. Between 1965 and 1972, of the more than 27,000 Army personnel killed in Vietnam, only 3,200 were officers, and of the 43,000 Americans with the rank of major or higher, only 201 died in Vietnam (mostly majors). Among frontline officers, most were ROTC products, but enrollment in that program at American schools dropped from 231,000 in 1965 to 73,000 seven years later.

Among soldiers in Vietnam, there was also a clear correlation between status and education and their chances of survival. Draftees were far likelier to get killed or wounded than enlisted men. Soldiers who had not graduated from High School had casualty rates three times higher than those who had a diploma, while young men whose families had incomes in the $4,000–7,000 range were three times more likely to die or be hurt than those with incomes over $17,000. African-American casualty rates were higher as well – 25 percent of the US total between 1965 and 1968 and 13 percent for the entire war, and the average combat rifle company was over 50 percent black and Hispanic. In addition, white soldiers from southern states, the poorest in the country, had much higher casualty rates than the norm. Not surprisingly, then, many soldiers resented their officers and rebelled accordingly. As Naval Lieutenant John Kerry, an anti-war activist, put it, "how do you ask a man to be the last man to die for a mistake?"[16] Thus "search and evade" tactics were more common; fraggings grew dramatically, with some estimates that over 2,000 fraggings were committed and about 100 US officers killed; hundreds of thousands of soldiers received less-than-honorable discharges; and most importantly, organized dissent within the armed forces badly shook the military establishment.

Soldiers' opposition to the war could be subtle, such as listening to anti-war music at a GI Coffee House, or wearing a peace sign or the letters "F.T.A." ("Fuck the Army") on one's helmet. Or resistance could be more overt, such as sailors aboard the *USS. Kitty Hawk* refusing to sail for Vietnam and circulating an anti-war newspaper, *Kitty Litter*. On other Navy ships, sailors sabotaged the radar center and gears to avoid deployment to Indochina. In November 1972, one of the greatest mass mutinies in US naval history occurred, as 144 sailors refused to reboard the *USS Constellation* in Southern California and then laughed at the officers trying to round them up. Given such internal problems, it was no surprise that the respected military writer Colonel Robert Heinl, quoting the comic strip character *Pogo*, could only lament about the US armed forces in Vietnam, "we have met the enemy, and he is us."

Not surprisingly, organized anti-war groups within the military had a great impact, and among them the Vietnam Veterans Against the War was the most significant, especially in 1971. Up to that point, VVAW had organized and participated in anti-war actions – most notably a New Year's Eve takeover of the Statue of Liberty – but considerably increased its activities during the trial of William Laws Calley. Lieutenant Calley had been a young platoon leader in Charlie Company, attached to the Americal Division, operating in the village of *My Lai* in central Vietnam near the coast in March 1968, when he and his troops, under orders to destroy everything and everyone they encountered, massacred over 400 Vietnamese, including old men, women and babies but no VC, until an American helicopter pilot, Chief Warrant Officer Hugh Thompson, threatened to open fire on Calley's men unless they ended the slaughter. For eighteen months, until another veteran, Ron Ridenhour, came forth to relate the story of "something rather dark and bloody," the story of My Lai remained unknown. Once revealed, the Army held Calley principally responsible and court-martialed him. VVAW, appalled at government claims that My Lai and Calley were unique, thus began its own "Winter Soldier Investigation" in January 1971, during which over 200 Americans who had served in Vietnam testified about atrocities that they had been involved in or seen. To the Winter Soldiers – whose name derived from Thomas Paine's pamphleteering about the "summer soldiers and the sunshine patriots" during the War for Independence – incidents like My Lai were part of official American policy, engendered by obsessive anti-Communism, free-fire zones, and body counts. As a result, Marine Sargeant Scott Camil could offer "testimony involv[ing] burning of villages with civilians in them, the cutting off of ears, cutting off of heads, torturing of prisoners, calling in of artillery on villages for games, corpsmen killing wounded prisoners, napalm dropped on villages, women being raped, women and children being massacred . . . bodies shoved out of helicopters."[17]

The Winter Soldiers and VVAW attracted significant attention. One congressional committee considered them the third
most dangerous subversive group in the country, behind the
Weather Underground and the Black Panthers. On the other
end of the spectrum, Senator Hatfield had the entire testimony placed in the *Congressional Record* to make Americans
recognize the brutal nature of the war in Vietnam. For VVAW,
it set the stage for *Dewey Canyon III*, its "limited incursion
into the country of congress" in April 1971. Dewey Canyon
III was one of the more powerful and memorable demonstrations of the Vietnam era for it involved thousands of veterans,
many of whom had been decorated for their service in the
war, coming to Washington to renounce their behavior and
demand an end to the fighting. Many veterans threw away
their awards, including a Medal of Honor winner; veterans
and Gold Star Mothers (women who had lost sons in the war)
marched on Arlington Cemetery, where they were denied entry by military police; others staged guerrilla theater – wearing fatigues, carrying toy weapons and staging mock raids on
"civilians." Politicians and celebrities visited the vets on the
Mall, and in the Senate McGovern and Philip Hart (D, Michigan) conducted hearings on war atrocities. Most powerfully,
John Kerry, who had won the Silver Star, Bronze Star, and
three Purple Hearts in Vietnam and in 1984 became a Massachusetts senator himself, testified before the Senate Foreign
Relations Committee, emotionally ending

> We wish that a merciful God could wipe away our own memories of
> that service [in Vietnam] as easily as this Administration has wiped
> away their memories of us. But all that they have done and all that
> they can do by this denial is to make more clear than ever our own
> determination to undertake one last mission – to search out and
> destroy the last vestige of this barbaric war, to pacify our own hearts,
> to conquer the hate and fear that have driven this country these last
> ten years and more, so when thirty years from now our brothers go
> down the street without a leg, without an arm, or a face, and small
> boys ask why, we will be able to say "Vietnam" and not mean a
> desert, not a filthy obscene memory, but mean instead the place where
> America finally turned and where soldiers like us helped it in the
> turning.[18]

Kerry's words, though powerful, were ultimately empty, for in Paris Kissinger was playing politics and in Vietnam Nixon was making war. As for Lieutenant Calley, he had become something of a folk hero to the political right, with Charlton Heston and other celebrities sponsoring a defense fund for him. After his conviction, Calley spent three days in military prison until Nixon released him into House Arrest; three years later he was paroled and now runs a pawn shop in Columbus, Georgia. In the village of My Lai, there are a number of memorials to the victims of the slaughter there.

Peace Is at Hand

Amid the Linebacker bombings, both the DRVN and the United States felt pressured to return to negotiations. In Hanoi, the leadership could no longer count on the same levels of support from the Soviet Union and China as in the past. Nixon's détente was working, as Moscow and Beijing both were urging Pham Van Dong, Ho's successor, to moderate the DRVN's demands. In America, continued congressional criticism and attempts to cut off funding for Vietnam made it clear to the White House that the war could not continue indefinitely. Though only 47,000 ground troops remained in Vietnam in mid-1972, the US role was not diminishing, as air strikes, targeted against all of Indochina, were originating from the RVN, Thailand, Guam, and carriers in the South China Sea.

In July 1972, then, Kissinger and Le Duc Tho resumed their private talks in Paris. The United States was willing to back off its insistence that northern troops be withdrawn from the south – after all, if the US military could not dislodge them, then they were not going to leave on their own. For its part, the DRVN backed down from its demand that the United States end support for the Thieu regime and replace it with a coalition that would include the Provisional Revolutionary Government. On 8 October, Le Duc Tho offered Kissinger a nine-point proposal to end the war. In it, he rescinded calls for Thieu's removal and the establishment of a coalition government; was willing to accept a cease-fire prior to a political settlement; called for the removal of all "foreign" troops; and wanted to limit all military aid to the replacement of used supplies. Politically, Tho was willing to recognize two "administrative entities" in the south – the Thieu government and the PRG. Kissinger, eager for an agreement before the 7 November presidential elections, assented to the proposal, declaring to the world that "peace is at hand." If only Nixon and Thieu had agreed!

The southern Vietnamese had been left out of the negotiations between Kissinger and Le Duc Tho, so Thieu immediately began to monkeywrench the process. In late October, the RVN leader listed 69 objections to the nine-point program. Thieu was enraged that northern troops would remain in the south and that the PRG was recognized as an institutional entity. He also issued "Four Nos" regarding any agreement: no recognition of the enemy; no neutralization in the south; no coalition government; and no surrender of territory. Kissinger was furious at Thieu and wanted Nixon to threaten to cut off all aid to the RVN unless its president fell in line with the deal. By that time, however, Nixon was quite sure that he would easily be re-elected, with or without a settlement in Vietnam, so he simply dismissed the agreement between Kissinger and Hanoi. In turn, Kissinger issued a new round of threats to the DRVN, promising more air strikes and breaking off talks, while also demanding to reopen the question of northern troops remaining in the south. In short order, Kissinger had double-crossed Thieu; Thieu had done the same to Nixon; Nixon then did it to Kissinger; and Kissinger to Le Duc Tho. Years earlier Bob Dylan had written that "to live outside the law you must be honest." Apparently, Nixon and Kissinger had not been listening to *Blonde on Blonde*.

In both Saigon and Washington, there were immediate and catastrophic repercussions to the breakdown. In the RVN, Thieu began a series of large-scale arrests of so-called dissidents, detaining many without trial, and he began reclassifying political prisoners as "criminals" in order to exclude them from any prisoner of war exchange or amnesty. In the United States, Nixon won a landslide re-election victory against George McGovern, though he still had not unveiled his "secret plan" to end the war from 1968. Kissinger, citing "nuances" and "technicalities," was still blaming the DRVN for the failure of the October talks, and he described Hanoi's representatives as "just a bunch of shits. Tawdry, filthy shits."[19] And the US media just went along for the ride, creating the impression that the Vietnamese had disrupted the peace process. Nixon, thus politically protected and emboldened, played "madman" once again and commenced Linebacker II, better known as the "Christmas Bombings." Beginning on 18 December and lasting eleven days, the saturation bombing campaign "was a final and devastating evidence of Nixon's willingness to unleash US power."[20] Fighter jets such as F-105s, F-4s, and F-111s and over 200 B-52 bombers flew round-the-clock missions for a week and a half against the DRVN in what Kissinger's aide Roger Morris called "calculated barbarism."[21] Air Force tactical aircraft flew over 1,000 sorties and B-52s another 750, and they dropped a combined total of over 40,000 tons of bombs, hitting not only military and communications facilities but also docks, shipyards, workplaces, residential areas, and the DRVN's biggest hospital. In some places, the B-52s left craters with diameters of 50 feet. The northern Vietnamese had prepared for the raids in underground shelters and tunnels, and still lost 1,600 civilians, which was not a significant number compared to other civilian deaths during the US air war.

Linebacker II caused serious destruction in the DRVN, but at a great cost. North Vietnam, utilizing its own considerable anti-aircraft capabilities – with over 1,000 surface-to-air missiles – downed well over 20 tactical aircraft and 15 B-52s (though Hanoi claimed to have downed 34 and the US Pentagon privately admitted to higher numbers), and also shot down 44 American pilots. Politically, Nixon's air attacks were condemned across the globe, with the Vatican and European leaders speaking out against the bombings – Swedish Prime

Minister Olaf Palme compared them to Nazi atrocities – and both the Soviet Union and China threatening to reconsider détente. Soviet leader Leonid Brezhnev publicly blasted the "longest and dirtiest" war in US history while Zhou Enlai and Mao's wife attended a mass rally in Beijing in support of the PRG and its foreign minister, Madame Nguyen Thi Binh.[22] At home, about two-thirds of US senators polled opposed the Linebacker bombings and were threatening to pull funding for the war, while the president's approval rating, barely a month after his overwhelming re-election victory, fell to just 39 percent. Nixon would claim, in 1973 and repeatedly thereafter, that the Christmas bombings had forced Hanoi to accept the treaty that ended the war; in truth, the United States bombed itself into a final settlement. Linebacker II amounted to a terror bombing campaign, had little, if any, military purpose, and backfired politically. By January 1973, even Richard M. Nixon could see that the war in Vietnam had to end.

War Is Over (If You Want It)

On 20 January 1973, Nixon was again inaugurated as president in Washington, DC; two days later his predecessor, LBJ, died on his ranch in Texas; the next day, the 23rd, Nixon announced that an agreement to end the US war on Vietnam had been reached in Paris and that a cease-fire would take effect on the 27th. These events, converging as they did, provided a fitting denouement to the Vietnam experience. "Lyndon Johnson's war" was now ending, though he had not known it, while Richard Nixon, like a tragic Greek figure, was heading inexorably to his downfall. In Vietnam, despite the peace agreement, the bleeding continued.

The final peace treaty was virtually identical to the October agreement and indeed followed many of the general lines of North Vietnamese proposals from 1969 onward. The accord established a "National Council of Reconciliation and Concord," with representation for the PRG; created a temporary demilitarized zone; allowed northern personnel to remain in the south while US troops would depart in full; and provided that all POWs be returned to their homelands. Nixon would claim that he had achieved "peace with honor," and Kissinger, along with Le Duc Tho, would receive the Nobel Peace Prize (which Tho refused), but the pact mainly reflected the fact that the United States could not end the revolution in southern Vietnam nor break the will of the north. To Nguyen Van Thieu, the recognition of the PRG and presence of northern troops put his government in a precarious position, so Nixon had to demand that he sign the treaty and then confidentially promised him that America would continue to support the RVN. Hanoi, though compromising on its demand for Thieu's removal, continued to seek, as in 1954, national reunification. Nixon, to seal the deal, also secretly agreed to pay the DRVN $3.5 billion in reparations, with no strings attached. Despite the agreement and secret codicils, the treaty accomplished nothing besides US withdrawal. Critics such as ex-CIA officer Frank Snepp would later claim that American disengagement was Nixon's only goal anyway, that he wanted to remove US forces to allow a "decent interval" before the RVN inevitably fell. Indeed, since Tet in 1968, Americans had little realistic hope of "winning" in Vietnam – whatever that meant – but still unleashed a vicious and destructive war against the people of Vietnam on both sides of the seventeenth parallel. During the first Nixon administration, 1969–73, over 15,000 Americans died in Vietnam, while over 100,000 southern Vietnamese and over 400,000 northern Vietnamese perished as well. Not content with that, the United States continued to wage war in Indochina even after the 1973 "peace" treaty.

Et Thieu?

The ink was barely dry on the peace accords when the violations began. After initialing the treaty, Thieu, confident of Nixon's continued support, told his troops that if "Communists come into your village, you should immediately shoot them in the head," while those who "begin talking in a Communist tone . . . should be immediately killed."[23] In March, Thieu established the Dan Chu, or "Democracy," Party and then, shades of Diem, forced all civil servants to join it, rigged national elections, banned rival parties, shut down the media, and established martial law. Contrary to the Paris agreement, the RVN president continued to reject any PRG role in southern politics. Militarily, the ARVN, because of American funding, could count on over 1,000,000 troops, much more than the north had, and a sizeable Air Force as well, both of which were used against PRG zones and even against neutral members of the Joint Military Commission who were trying to map each side's zones of control in the southern countryside.

Because northern troops remained in the south against his wishes, and other forces moved below the seventeenth parallel, Thieu felt no responsibility to maintain the peace pact and he still relied on Nixon to keep him in power in the RVN. And, for a time, US money did continue to flow into Thieu's purse. Throughout 1973, however, Nixon's options were narrowing, as the Senate began to reduce funding for Vietnam and passed the War Powers Act to limit the president's ability to make war. More importantly, the Watergate crisis was engulfing the White House, pushing events in Indochina onto the back burner. In the RVN, meanwhile, the economy was in disarray – with inflation rates of 90 percent; Buddhist opposition to the government resurfaced; and the ARVN was still plagued by corruption and suffering heavy desertion rates. Because of refugees, the population of Saigon soared from 1,000,000 to 4,000,000, with serious housing shortages, a thriving black market, brothels everywhere, drugs, enemy infiltration, and con men making the situation even worse. Even with over $3 billion in American aid in 1973–4, the Thieu regime was losing its ability to control the RVN.

The Beat Goes On: Laos and Cambodia

The 1973 peace accords did not include the other states of Indochina so, along with continued fighting in Vietnam, Laos and Cambodia remained in bloody conflict too. In Laos, where the United States had dropped a million or so tons of bombs prior to 1973, the American State Department had vowed to defend the Royalist government against Pathet Lao rebels, and a US skeleton crew remained there into 1974. In April of that year, however, the various factions in Laotian politics formed a coalition government and, despite American efforts to supply the Royalists with weapons to use against the Pathet Lao, by early 1975 the Communist rebels clearly had the upper hand in the government and they assumed power in Laos later that year.

With regard to Cambodia, Kissinger announced in January 1973 that both Lon Nol and the United States would suspend attacks and bombings against the Khmer Rouge, but would take "necessary counter measures" if the rebels did not obey the cease-fire. The Khmer Rouge, however, did not trust Kissinger's word, feared that their "allies" in North Vietnam would conquer Cambodia if they quit fighting, and were tempted by Lon Nol's weaknesses to oust him sooner rather than later, so they continued their struggle against the American puppet government. Thus, on 9 February, Nixon and Kissinger reopened the American air war "with greater intensity than ever before," as William Shawcross explained it. "Within a few months an enormous new aerial campaign had destroyed the old Cambodia forever." Up to January 1973, the White House had justified its air war in Cambodia as a way to disrupt sanctuaries and infiltration by the northern Vietnamese. But now, after the peace treaty, those reasons were no longer valid, so Nixon publicly claimed that the new air strikes would protect the Lon Nol government from Communist attacks. In fact, the continued bombing was directly linked to US promises of support to Thieu. With the Americans forbidden from attacking Vietnam by the peace pact, the Cambodian campaign was a way to keep US power in Indochina to protect the RVN if need be – to serve as a "firehose" for Thieu. As the Director of Central Intelligence, William Colby, admitted, "Cambodia was then the only game in town."[24]

The impact of the air war after January 1973 was catastrophic. Cambodia was turned into a desolate "parking lot." Whereas American B-52 pilots had dropped 37,000 tons of bombs on Cambodia in all of 1972, they dropped 24,000 tons in March 1973 alone, 35,000 tons in April, and another 36,000 tons in May, while fighter bombers were unleashing between 15,000 and 20,000 tons per month as well. At home, the US Congress finally put its foot down and voted to end American air operations in Cambodia as of 15 August 1973, and it later included the "secret war" as an article of impeachment against Nixon. That charge was later dropped, prompting an exasperated Representative William Hungate (D, Missouri) to admit that "it's kind of hard to live with yourself when you impeach a guy for tapping telephones and not for making war without authorization."[25] Inside Cambodia, Khmer Rouge strength grew as the American attacks increased, and by 1974 they controlled 80 percent of the country while the Lon Nol regime was moribund. In April 1975, the Khmer Rouge victoriously entered the capital of Phnom Penh and declared the establishment of Democratic Kampuchea.

In large measure, they emerged and triumphed *because of*, not *despite*, the massive US air assault. As David Chandler, an eminent scholar of Cambodia, explained it, "the bombing destroyed a good deal of the fabric of pre-war Cambodian society and provided the [Khmer Rouge] with the psychological ingredients of a violent, vengeful and unrelenting social revolution. This was to be waged, in their words, by people with 'empty hands.' The party encouraged class warfare between the 'base people,' who had been bombed, and the 'new people,' who had taken refuge from the bombing, and thus had taken sides, in Khmer Rouge thinking, with the United States."[26] Once in power, the Khmer Rouge were led by Pol Pot, who was impressed with the Chinese Cultural Revolution of the 1960s and too wanted to eradicate all western influences in his country, while at the same time guarding against any possible intervention by his longtime enemies, the Vietnamese. Thus, he emptied out urban areas in the hopes of establishing a pure form of peasant Communism. Calling his experiment "Year Zero," to imply that Cambodia was beginning its history over again, the Khmer Rouge engaged in mass executions of hundreds of thousands of their own people, especially ethnic Chinese and Vietnamese, Muslims, and Buddhists. Even more died of starvation due to Pol Pot's failed agrarian policies. Cambodia, a small country suffering from dire poverty to begin with, thus experienced, in barely a decade, two indescribable horrors: the American air war and the Khmer Rouge genocide, both linked together politically and historically.

The Enemy and the Burden of Protracted War

For the NLF, VC, and North Vietnamese, the period from Tet to ultimate victory was filled with trial, loss, and redemption. While most scholars, conservative and liberal alike, have argued that the NLF and VC were devastated by the early 1968 Tet Offensive, the enemy in fact was not irrecoverably hurt and recuperated rather quickly. But, as the respected scholar Ngo Vinh Long has shown, the VC came back for two "mini-Tets" later in 1968 instead of regrouping in their bases in the countryside to rebuild, and in those engagements they suffered much heavier losses. Along with the damage being done by the Phoenix program, the enemy, by 1969, was licking its wounds. Psychologically, Vietnam was rocked as well when, on 2 September 1969, Ho died of congestive heart failure. Millions of Vietnamese mourned their late leader, and his successors – Pham Van Dong, Le Duan, and Vo Nguyen Giap – wept openly at his funeral. Though he had insisted on a simple ceremony and asked to be cremated, with his ashes spread in the countryside in the three regions of Vietnam, the new leaders instead buried him, Lenin-like, in a large mausoleum in Hanoi. Even in death, the revolution's leaders continued to rely on Ho as a symbol of nationalism, resistance, and liberation, and as a "guardian angel." As Vietnamese heroes in the past could invoke the memories of past national liberators, "so now could his followers call on the unsullied and larger-than-life memory of Ho Chi Minh, a mighty reservoir of solace and inspiration."[27]

While 1969 and 1970 were difficult years for the Vietnamese revolution – exacerbated by Phoenix and the fallout from Ho's death, as well as the American air wars – the NLF was able to regroup, hold onto its high levels of popular support, successfully recruit and infiltrate in the south, and by 1971 was stronger than ever. As Ngo Vinh Long concludes, "popular support in the South allowed the NLF to rise from the ashes of defeat like a Phoenix in spite of the American efforts to destroy it."[28] At the same time, however, America's extensive use of airpower was killing masses of Vietnamese in the north, especially civilians, and destroying much of the countryside, while the continued use of airpower and herbicides was doing the same to the south. Accordingly, General Giap in 1972 decided that only a general military offensive could end the destruction and convince Nixon of the futility of continued war – hence the Easter Offensive. Indeed, by 1972–3, the PAVN took on more responsibility as the war assumed a more conventional character than it had before. By mid-1973, Le Duan and others were urging a final offensive to reunify Vietnam. As they saw it, the peace accords, Watergate, the Arab oil embargo, and economic recession in the United States would make it impossible for American forces to return to bail out the RVN. In addition, the PRG had about 100,000 of its own forces killed in the two years *after* the cease-fire, so ending the bloodshed by winning the war was an incentive as well.

Let Saigons Be Bygones: the Final Offensive

By 1974, Hanoi had given up hope that the peace treaty would end the conflict and achieve reunification. It was, to the PRG and North Vietnamese, a bleak reminder of the 1954 Geneva settlement. Thus they began to build a vast highway running from the seventeenth parallel to the Saigon area, about 1,000 kilometers, with vast connecting routes for supply and communication. By early 1975, the road network, Corridor 613, could handle 10,000 trucks in traffic and refuel them via a 5,000-kilometer pipeline. Ironically, however, Corridor 613 was barely used, for when the final offensive began, PAVN and PRG forces so totally overwhelmed the ARVN that they simply used the existing highways in the RVN.

In December 1974, Hanoi decided on a strategy to attack Vietnam below the seventeenth parallel in two stages lasting two years, hoping to wear down the ARVN and gain victory in 1976 or 1977. Initially, Hanoi planned to liberate the central highlands, in constant fighting throughout 1975, but southern-based military commanders, more aware of how weak the ARVN really was, lobbied for attacking further southward. So on 26 December 1974, General Van Tien Dung, with 22 infantry divisions, hundreds of tanks, and thousands of artillery pieces, began bombarding Phuoc Long province near the Cambodian border and only about 50 miles from Saigon. By 7 January 1975 the entire province came under PRG control as the ARVN barely resisted and American B-52s did not reappear, as South Vietnam had hoped and the enemy had feared. Hanoi was thrilled, as the offensive had exceeded its most optimistic hopes. As Le Duan exclaimed, "never have we had military and political conditions so perfect or a strategic advantage so great as we have now."[29]

Next, General Dung planned to cut the RVN in half, driving from the central highlands near Cambodia across Vietnam to the South China Sea. On 9 March, three PAVN divisions attacked Ban Me Thuot, the largest urban center in the central highlands, about 150 miles northwest of Saigon. The ARVN, thinking the attack was a diversion, did not fight back and the city fell three days later. The PRG, hardly able to keep pace with the southern army's collapse, decided to shift its focus to the capital. Thieu had abandoned the central highlands and called for an ARVN retreat toward Saigon and the delta. General Dung, while preparing for the final assault in the south, also had his forces attack Hué, Da Nang, and Kontum, all of which fell in just weeks. Thieu's days were obviously numbered, but he refused PRG offers to negotiate a solution based on his resignation. On 20 April, however, after the US Congress refused President Gerald Ford's request to send $700 million to the RVN, Thieu finally quit, though the

United States did "loan" him aircraft to conduct terror raids on his way out. On 26 April, General Dung began the "Ho Chi Minh Campaign" and the ARVN fully collapsed. American helicopters scrambled to get over 7,000 American and RVN personnel out of the capital while US ships in the South China Sea evacuated another 70,000 Vietnamese out of the country. On 30 April 1975, tanks rolled toward the presidential palace, crashed through the gates, liberated, or conquered, Saigon, and flew the PRG flag from the palace balcony. "Saigon" ceased to exist and the capital was renamed "Ho Chi Minh City," while in Hanoi crowds began chanting "Long Live Ho Chi Minh." General Tran Van Tra, who led the final assault, was overtaken with emotion and "suddenly felt as if my soul was translucent and light, as if everything had sunk to the bottom."[30] The Vietnam War had ended . . .

Vietnam After 1975: The Perils of Peace

In his final testament, written just a few months before he died, Ho poetically envisioned that "our rivers, our mountains, our people will always be; The American aggressors defeated, we will build a country ten times more beautiful." Had the wars in Indochina ended years earlier, before the destruction became incomprehensible and the bitterness so deep, Ho's dream might have been fulfilled. But by 1975, after thirty years of open warfare against the French and Americans, and against each other, the most obvious characteristic of Vietnamese society was the devastation, north and south. During the "Second Indochina War," the United States conducted warfare on a scale that would have been unimaginable to an earlier generation. Millions of tons of bombs, artillery, herbicides and the like tore Vietnam apart on both sides of the seventeenth parallel (though, ironically, the United States dropped six times more bombs on its ally, the RVN, than on the enemy, the DRVN) and caused human tragedy on a mass scale. Disease epidemics, starvation, and poverty occurred at frightening rates as well. The US presence in Vietnam also fundamentally altered the structure of traditional society there. Americans flooded what had been an agrarian country with technology, money, and consumer culture, thereby reversing many of the cultural values that the Vietnamese had held. The drug trade, black market, prostitution, and other underworld activities flourished. Not surprisingly the natives resented this. Just as many Americans held the government and army of the RVN in contempt, a good number of Vietnamese believed that the Americans had encouraged them to fight a war, had not treated them as equals, introduced western vices to their society, had a drug-addicted army, often supported the enemy, and betrayed them after 1973. Both physically and morally, Vietnam was a dramatically different place because of the Americans. Though militarily and politically foiled and its hegemony challenged, the US empire had struck back, repeatedly, against Vietnam. So amid the victory celebrations, a new batch of problems was emerging. As Pham Van Dong recognized, "waging a war is simple, but running a country is very difficult."[31]

Hanoi had been counting on Nixon's promise of reconstruction aid to start the long and difficult task of rebuilding the newly renamed *Socialist Republic of Vietnam*, or SRV. The Ford and Carter administrations, however, refused to follow through on their predecessor's agreement, with Carter, the "human rights president," incredibly claiming that "the destruction was mutual" between the United States and Vietnam.[32] Congress, once more aggressive after the "dovish" Vietnam years, in fact passed laws forbidding American aid to the SRV, and then cutting Vietnam off from international lending agencies to which it contributed, such as the International Monetary Fund and World Bank. Reconstruction, hard enough already, would become virtually impossible without access to outside capital. In large measure, the United States justified its hard line on aid to the SRV because of alleged failures by Hanoi to fully account for Americans who had been held as POWs or were listed as "Missing in Action" (MIA) during the war. But the charges were a sham. No credible evidence had ever existed that any Americans were held against their will by the Communists in Indochina, but the allegations, cleverly contrived by Nixon and Ross Perot and parroted by other politicians, the media, and Hollywood, struck a nerve in the United States. Americans, perhaps humiliated by the failure in Vietnam, were not about to send funding to Vietnamese Communists while "our boys" were imprisoned there.[33]

Inside the SRV, as the poverty and bitterness increased, Hanoi had its own missteps. Though no "bloodbath," as predicted by American conservatives and RVN leaders, ever took place, perhaps over a hundred thousand supporters of the Saigon regime were sent to "re-education camps," prisons, as reprisal and for indoctrination, while many others were kept under surveillance by the government and not allowed to leave the country. Vietnam also had to deal with a series of foreign policy crises. In late 1978 – as the Khmer Rouge genocide continued and China was promising to teach "a lesson" to the "ungrateful and arrogant" Vietnamese, whom President Deng Xiaoping called "dogs" – Pham Van Dong decided to take pre-emptive measures, invading Cambodia, which had Chinese support, on Christmas Day and pouring into Phnom Penh on 7 January 1979, thereby mercifully closing the "killing fields," placing a new government in power, and leaving 120,000 troops to occupy the country. For many years thereafter, the United States would vote to seat the Khmer Rouge as the official government of Cambodia at the United Nations. Though they were Communists and killed huge numbers of their own, they too hated the Vietnamese, and that was what mattered. Just six weeks after the Vietnamese incursion into Cambodia, China, with American approval, invaded Vietnam once more, crossing into Tonkin and clashing with over 100,000 regional and local military groups. Though outnumbered two to one, the Vietnamese, despite heavy losses, held off the PRC forces, causing about 20,000 casualties and forcing them to retreat. For Hanoi, the wars just would not end.

Through the 1980s and 1990s, the SRV diverged markedly from the revolutionary path that brought it national liberation, and began to take on many of the characteristics of the western invaders it ousted. Politically, Hanoi cracked down on movements for democracy and equality, suppressing both labor and veterans of the war in the process. Economically, it began a policy of *doi moi*, similar to Mikhail Gorbachev's *perestroika* in the Soviet Union, which was an integration of capitalist ideas into its nominally socialist economy. The SRV offered enticing terms to lure in foreign investment, while Vietnamese workers and peasants were often without work and land, and hundreds of thousands of young women worked as prostitutes in urban areas. Within the government and army, corruption was becoming a major problem as well. As Hanoi official Nguyen Van Linh complained in 1993, "bureaucratism, corruption, and bribery . . . have reached a serious level without any sign of abating . . . [They] have reached such a widespread and alarming proportion that many people regard them as a national disaster."[34]

Such conditions have continued as the market economy has expanded in Vietnam. Asian investors, particularly Japanese, have developed an infrastructure and tourist industry, and, as of 1996, American corporations have been moving into the SRV after President Bill Clinton normalized relations with Vietnam. For the Vietnamese, however, *doi moi* is at best a mixed blessing; the US shoe company Nike, for instance, has invested millions in the Vietnamese economy, but pays its workers about $30.00 a month, not really a living wage, and forbids any attempt to organize or act collectively. As foreign firms set up shop in Vietnam then, many contradictions between Ho's vision and the realities of bureaucracy and the market are obvious for all to see: vast inequality, unemployment, class antagonisms, corruption, and authoritarian politics. In 1995, during the twentieth anniversary celebration of the end of the war, an official sponsor of the festivities was Pepsi-Cola, making one wonder who won the Vietnam War after all.

The United States After 1975: Kicking the "Vietnam Syndrome"

The American defeat in Vietnam was a natural outcome of the way the war was developed and fought. The enemy – the

NLF, VC, PAVN, and PRG – was popular, dedicated, and effective – while the ally, the government and army of the RVN, was corrupt, repressive, and not terribly competent, and American soldiers were often as interested in getting high or fighting among themselves as with engaging the enemy. America's military leaders were never enthused about intervening in Vietnam and, once there, were internally divided over the nature of the war and US strategy; they never achieved the unity of purpose so essential to warmaking. Significant segments of the public at home resisted the war as well, adding to the sense of crisis that Vietnam was causing. The war also caused international distress, as America's European allies wanted the United States to de-escalate and disengage, both because the war was hurting the world economy and because its primary interests were not in Indochina but in the developed western world. Henry Kissinger recognized this and declared 1973 the "Year of Europe," but also delivered a stern lecture to the allies about the responsibilities of American world leadership, which did not go over well. In retrospect, all these factors put the United States at a great political and military disadvantage in Vietnam. The Americans were simply on the wrong side of history, fighting an implacable enemy which had a national tradition of ousting foreign interlopers. While the United States was not even 200 years old when the Vietnam War occurred, the Vietnamese had 2,000 years of experience fighting for independence under their belts.

America's defeat, even if it was unavoidable, caused anguish at home. The air of invincibility that had developed throughout the Cold War was punctured and Americans, for the first time in many of their lives, had to think about the limits of US power. For a few years after Vietnam, this debate continued, but by the 1980s, influential Americans were trying to rewrite the memory of the war. In the immediate aftermath of Vietnam, the United States conducted itself in a somewhat more circumspect manner internationally, but remained clearly engaged in world affairs. Because of the economic effects of the war, Nixon had significantly reduced defense spending after 1970, and, perhaps because of the bad taste left by Vietnam, did not intervene in a civil war in Angola ultimately won by a Socialist group. At the same time, Nixon escalated the amount of American weapons sold abroad, had the CIA sabotage the Cuban economy by introducing a swine flu virus, supported the apartheid regime in South Africa, and helped facilitate the overthrow of President Salvador Allende in Chile in 1973. Despite the impression that Vietnam was causing America to retreat from its global "responsibilities," it was, in many fundamental ways, "business-as-usual" in the Nixon years. Indeed, any funk or malaise associated with the Vietnam War did not last terribly long.

In 1980, Republican presidential candidate Ronald Reagan called the Vietnam War a "noble cause" and many national leaders, military officials, and scholars began to re-evaluate the war in a more positive light, often claiming that the United States had gone to war for all the right reasons – anti-Communism, democracy, national security – in Vietnam, had conducted itself with skill and admiration during the war, but had been "stabbed in the back" by the media and anti-war movement at home. Hollywood added to this revival with pro-war or pro-military movies such as *Uncommon Valor, Red Dawn,* and especially Sylvester Stallone's *First Blood* and *Rambo II,* while the militarist novels of Tom Clancy helped lift Americans out of their post-Vietnam self-doubt as well. To some degree, then, this rehabilitation of the war emboldened the Reagan administration to conduct large-scale and initially "secret" wars against insurgent groups in Latin America and the leftist Sandinista government in Nicaragua, using much the same rationale in that part of the world in the 1980s as its predecessors had in Indochina in the 1960s. In fact, Secretary of Defense Caspar Weinberger invoked the revisionist interpretation of Vietnam explicitly when he claimed that, unlike in Vietnam, "we must never send Americans into battle unless we plan to win." In 1991, that school of thought reached its apex as George Bush linked the US war against Saddam Hussein with Vietnam, and at its conclusion boasted that "by God, we've kicked the Vietnam Syndrome once and for all."[35]

Bush's glee was somewhat premature and not totally justified, however. As he and his successor, Bill Clinton, would discover, the issue of Vietnam would just not go away. During the 1992 draft, Clinton ran into trouble after the media reported that he had tried to pull strings to avoid service in Vietnam. Moreover, comparisons to Vietnam would pop up whenever the United States was debating involvement in foreign lands. During the 1980s, following the example of the Vietnam anti-war movement, a strong anti-intervention movement emerged to protest Reagan's aggression in Central America, and a popular slogan was "El Salvador is Spanish for Vietnam." Likewise, references to the war in Indochina were omnipresent whenever US policy toward Haiti, Somalia, Bosnia, and other lands was discussed. It seems as if virtually every interview concerning US foreign policy today ultimately comes to the question of whether this could turn into "another Vietnam." And the American people continue to believe that the war was "fundamentally wrong and immoral" – 70 percent in a 1991 poll.

On a more personal level, the war hurt millions of Americans too. In addition to the over 58,000 soldiers killed in the war, untold numbers of veterans have had a difficult adjustment back to "normal" lives after Vietnam. Although Hollywood often has unfairly stereotyped veterans as being deranged and troubled, in fact hundreds of thousands suffer from "Post-Traumatic Stress Disorder," a psychological and emotional condition involving a wide array of problems such as recurring nightmares, jumpiness, flashbacks, paranoia, and others. Many other veterans are addicted to drugs and alcohol, and have violent or abusive personalities, while, amazingly, almost twice as many veterans have committed suicide since the war ended than died in Vietnam. Thousands of other Vietnam-era soldiers have also suffered health problems such as cancer and immune system disorders, as well as high rates of birth defects in their children, due to their exposure to Agent Orange and other herbicides.

In 1982, one of the more powerful moments in the Vietnam era occurred when "The Wall," the Vietnam Memorial, was dedicated on the Mall in Washington, DC. Two long narrow blocks of black concrete which contain the names of every American killed in Vietnam, the monument emotionally details the human costs of the war to the United States. But the country of Vietnam would need perhaps 40 or 50 such "walls" to commemorate their own losses during the American War. Instead, still-destroyed buildings, burned-out villages, land mines, disabled young men, and bitterness and recrimination mark their war. It will certainly be some time, if ever, before the Vietnamese, as Ho Chi Minh wished, will build a country "ten times more beautiful."

Part II

The Movements of the 1960s

5

"Many Deeds of War": Hope and Anguish in the 1960s

John F. Kennedy had "vigor," as his friends and supporters would say. The youngest man elected to the White House, JFK became president in January 1961 proclaiming that the "torch had been passed" to a new generation of leaders, vowing to get the country moving again, and memorably exhorting Americans to "ask not what your country can do for you – ask what you can do for your country." The aging poet Robert Frost added to that theme, reading "The Gift Outright," essentially a tribute to America's manifest destiny: "The land was ours before we were the land's," he began. "She was our land more than a hundred years before we were her people . . . Such as we were we gave ourselves outright. The deed of gift was many deeds of war."[1]

Kennedy, with his famous background, Harvard degree, heroism in World War II, and beautiful family, symbolized both the limitless opportunities that the new decade could bring and the aggression and violence that Frost's poem invoked. Moved by his inaugural address, young people joined the military, Peace Corps, and other service organizations. As he reached out to Martin Luther King during the 1960 campaign, Americans raised their hopes for racial harmony. The country's best days, most believed, lay ahead. While it would be a stretch to cast JFK as an American version of Ho Chi Minh or other Vietnamese nationalists, he embodied many of the same characteristics – the martial spirit, eloquence and empathy, national pride, virility. Ironically, or maybe inevitably, those traits led the United States into the Vietnam War and spilled over into all other aspects of American life, transforming the nation in the process. During the 1960s, the war in Indochina time and again intersected with the major political and social movements of the day – Civil Rights, the New Left, the war on poverty, Women's Liberation, and many others, and helped shape them accordingly. This was, in every sense, the Vietnam generation.

The Promise of Liberalism . . .

Just as the vision of creating global liberalism drove American leaders after World War II to intervene abroad, as in Vietnam, their hope for a liberal domestic order characterized 1960s America. There existed a liberal consensus on "the rhetoric of egalitarianism; a positive role for government, particularly against business excesses; [and] the achievement of civil rights through federal action," as well as activism in foreign affairs.[2] With this vision in mind, US leaders, at first haltingly and then more forcefully, would put the weight of government behind the African-American civil rights movement, recognize the need to address gender, racial, and ethnic inequality, and conduct a "war on poverty" to confront the economic gap between haves and have nots. Pressure for such actions, however, usually came from below. The "modern" civil rights movement emerged in the mid-1950s in various areas throughout the south. Movements for women's liberation, Chicano rights, and gay rights began at the grassroots level, in the streets and fields. And even the war on poverty, though centrally directed, was in good measure a response to community concerns voiced by labor representatives, liberal intellectuals, and the poor themselves.

By the early 1960s, then, activists on several fronts were calling for change, for national action to address discrimination, inequality, and poverty. As liberalism demanded, the government responded, both symbolically and in practice. Because the US economy was strong and still growing, American leaders had a unique opportunity to pursue reform without asking for undue sacrifice from particular groups, particularly working-class whites. So, within a few years, the president and Congress were cutting taxes, trying to resolve major civil rights issues, admitting to the scope of American poverty, opening a discussion on gender discrimination, and trying to create a "great society." But at the same time, events far away were threatening reform at home.

. . . The Peril of Vietnam

By mid-1965, Lyndon Johnson had already recognized that "two great streams in our national life converged – the dream of a Great Society at home and the inescapable demands of our obligations halfway around the world." Domestic reform and Vietnam would hence "run in confluence until the end of my administration."[3] Indeed, as the president noticed, the spectre of Vietnam would haunt America from the mid-1960s forward, and transform the nation's political and social fabric along the way. The war, by becoming the dominant national concern, took up resources and energies that might have been devoted to domestic programs. At the same time, millions of Americans of differing backgrounds joined the movement against the war, likewise shifting their attention onto Vietnam instead of civil rights or the Great Society, and in the process creating new movements and organizations. Because of the war, then, the United States, both internationally and at home, would become a dramatically different place than it had been in 1960.

The centrality and impact of one major event or movement, in this case the Vietnam War and the resistance against it, on other organizations or issues is common in US history. Sometimes a traumatic national event, such as a war, transforms existing movements, possibly giving them life, co-opting them, creating more militancy, or crushing them. Progressive Era reform, for instance, stalled and died during World War I as American leaders portrayed criticism of American social policies as unpatriotic. In World War II, however, African-Americans were able to gain some political rights by comparing their own struggle to the fight for freedom against Nazi Germany or, after the war, the Soviet Union. At Yalta, so the story goes, Joseph Stalin had responded to a lecture from Franklin Roosevelt about human rights in Poland with a long draw on his pipe and the rhetorical question "What about Mississippi?" Though the dialogue may be apocryphal, Americans did recognize that it would be easier to criticize Communism if its own house, including Ole' Miss, was in order. Again, during the Korean conflict, war and domestic politics intersected as the struggle against nationalism and Communism in North Korea was linked to Senator Joseph McCarthy's crusade against alleged subversion and Communism at home.

Major crises can also bring other movements to life. Reform issues such as temperance, penal reform, and, most importantly, abolitionism emerged in good measure from the Great Awakenings of the eighteenth and nineteenth centuries. The first significant women's movement in the 1840s in turn grew from the abolitionist movement. Many labor activists in the latter nineteenth century then cut their teeth on the abolitionist movement – seeing themselves as "wage slaves" – or drew ideas from fundamentalist religion – calling for a "Christian commonwealth." Out of the Populist and Progressive eras of the late nineteenth and early twentieth centuries came mobilizations and organizations dedicated to political reform and accountability, women's suffrage, birth control, minimum wage and child labor laws, and cultural toleration, among others. National movements, such as abolitionism or unionism, often created open spaces and communities of support in which other issues could develop. Anti-slavery action, for instance, had flowed logically from existing reform movements. Sometimes, the limits of reform groups forced others to splinter off; Lucretia Mott and Elizabeth Cady Stanton, for example, began to focus on women's rights after being denied seats at an anti-slavery conference. Males in the abolitionist movement, they discovered, could be as paternal and discriminatory as pro-slavery men.

Events and movements already in existence, then, had great consequence on what was to follow. National issues such as slavery or war engendered national discussions and movements, for and against. In turn, those movements created analyses, language, and tactics that other groups would adopt and adapt to other issues. This most assuredly happened in the Vietnam era, as blacks, women, the poor, and so many others developed a new critique of liberalism and the government because of the war, and various reform groups grew out of or in opposition to other movements. Vietnam created a climate in which the inherent limits of liberal reform became visible, making some existing groups more militant and giving rise to new movements. In the end, few could fail to notice and respond to the increasing and traumatic American role in the war in Indochina.

The Upheavals of the 1960s: Origins and Transformation

The Vietnam War by no means created the political and social movements of the 1960s. Civil rights for African-Americans had been a mainstream political issue since the *Brown v. Board* decision and Montgomery bus boycott of the mid-1950s (to which we will return). Critics of American inequality and aggression abroad had been emerging before the major commitment to Indochina of 1965. The roots of Women's Liberation – the establishment of a President's Commission on the Status of Women, the publication of Betty Friedan's *The Feminine Mystique*, the passage of Title VII of the Civil Rights Act – likewise preceded the major buildup in Vietnam. And culturally the "Beats," birth control, and rock and roll, for instance, were well known by the early 1960s. All these movements, however, would begin to change markedly in mid-decade, in principal measure because of intervention in and escalation of the war in Vietnam. As Todd Gitlin, a leading activist of the decade, bluntly observed, "the war was driving us nuts."[4]

Millions of others no doubt felt the same. By the latter 1960s, the hope and promise of a new era had for the most part disappeared. Political, media, and community leaders were now using words like "turmoil," "ordeal," "tragedy," "anguish," and "rage" to describe American society. Liberalism was on the run as Richard Nixon was elected president in 1968. The optimism of the Civil Rights movement was waning even before Martin Luther King's assassination. The Women's Liberation movement was emerging from the anti-war movement and criticizing America's gender policies and the political structure which was creating them. Mexican-Americans, Indians, environmentalists, gays, and others were expanding their struggles for civil and political rights as the war grew as well. Even Lyndon Johnson "totally agreed" that "the war poisons everything else."[5]

The Vietnam War thus affected American life in innumerable ways, creating new forms of politics and culture. Sometimes, as with King's April 1967 speech, the links between the war and various other movements were direct and clear; sometimes, they were more subtle. While there are countless, and often complicated, examples of the ways in which the war transformed American society, to make these concepts more manageable, we will establish three major and interrelated characteristics of the intersection between Vietnam and the social and political movements of the 1960s.

Priorities, and the Limits of Liberalism

Before the major decisions for war in 1965 and thereafter, the government's top goal seemed to be the dismantling of apartheid in the US south and the creation of a Great Society, with equal opportunity and access for all. Toward that end, the Kennedy and Johnson administrations had established programs to attack poverty and to ensure voting rights and equal accommodations for African-Americans, and had begun to examine issues of gender and class inequity. But after 1965 the emphasis on domestic reform faded as Vietnam grew in importance. As LBJ, in his blunt Texas style, would later complain, the "whore" of a war in Vietnam had taken him away from "the lady I love," the Great Society. At the same time, the commitment to Indochina would expose the limits of and ultimately delegitimize Cold War liberalism and upend the political coalition that had put and kept liberal Democrats in power since the New Deal, while provoking a right-wing backlash against the state that was still dominating political discourse in the 1990s. The Civil and Voting Rights Acts of 1964 and 1965 had highlighted the possibilities of liberal reform. The nation could integrate blacks into the political and social structure without impinging on other groups' rights. The government, with popular backing, would continue to broaden political rights and economic opportunities at home, while spreading democracy abroad, or at least liberals hoped it would. But Vietnam changed that too. Because of the war, many liberals began to lose faith in the system and in the ability of the Johnson administration to ensure stability, equality, and justice, and they began to analyze the structural causes of the war and how they affected domestic needs. Blacks, working people, community activists, and intellectuals – the backbone of the liberal consensus – began to question both the government's ability to ensure social harmony or its commitment to equality and justice, and the ability of the system to address such issues. Hope had given way to disillusion and, often, violence and rage. The soaring rhetoric of Kennedy's inaugural address or Lyndon Johnson's overtures to Martin Luther King would fade into memory as the angry rhetoric of young radicals or street scenes from Chicago entered the national psyche.

Radicalization and Rebirth

As a good many liberals, especially the young and racial and ethnic minorities, lost faith in their access to mainstream political solutions to problems of poverty, racial discrimination, or gender equality, they became increasingly militant. Movements which had been established and even gained success by working "within the system" became increasingly frustrated and began to attack the very political structures in which they had come to life. By the mid-1960s, for instance, King's "dream" of integration was hard to find in the smoke of urban riots and the increasing awareness by black leaders that civil rights had taken a back seat to Vietnam. Consequently, more militant African-American leaders emerged, linking their own situation to that of the Vietnamese. As Huey Newton, a founder of the Black Panther Party, explained, "as Vietnam should be able to determine its own destiny . . . we in the black colony in America want . . . power over our destiny."[6] Likewise student radicals, who had originally become politicized because of issues such as Free Speech or participatory democracy, were increasingly enraged by the war and helped form the largest mass anti-war movement in history. They too had lost faith in liberalism's ability to address their agenda and grew increasingly alienated from the system of government and society itself. Groups like the Students for a Democratic Society (SDS), at first a movement of middle-class students for political renewal, became the leaders of the anti-war movement, and were driven into street battles in Chicago in 1968, while working-class students at Kent State faced National Guard bullets in 1970.

At the same time, the radicalization of various groups led to the establishment of new movements. Though issues such as women's rights, Chicano rights, gay liberation, ecology, and a counterculture surely existed prior to 1965, they gained momentum from the rising movement against the war and the distrust and anger that it had produced. By the later 1960s, then, these other movements were gaining strength and attention because they could link their own causes to Vietnam. A nation that was capable of waging war against the Vietnamese, they reasoned, was just as willing to contain or oppress, often violently, democratic forces at home. The war in Vietnam thus served as something of a "conveyor belt," helping create new movements and placing them within the political system.

"Holistic" Criticism and a National Experience

Prior to the 1960s, most criticism of America's political or social system was conducted within the safe and self-limited parameters of liberal dissent. Thus George Kennan or Walter Lippman could worry about the nature of the Cold War, or Margaret Chase Smith and others could attack McCarthyism, because America's problems were seen as aberrant or the fault of "bad people." The early civil rights movement had its villains such as "Bull" Connor (sheriff of Montgomery, Alabama) or George Wallace (governer of Alabama) as well, but the nation genuinely felt that desegregation could be achieved once bad men were removed from power. But, again, Vietnam exposed that as myth. Americans were beginning to develop a comprehensive, or holistic, analysis of American political culture and linking events abroad and at home. Vietnam was not an aberration, many believed, but rather a natural outcome of the Cold War. Likewise, Bull Connor was more than a redneck, racist southern sheriff; he in many ways represented fairly common thought about blacks in America. Indeed, many activists began to see Vietnam, civil rights, women's liberation, poverty, and other problems as part of a larger structure and process. While that transformation might have occurred even without Vietnam as the systemic and structural limits of liberalism became more clear, there is no doubt that the war crystallized and hastened the nation's awareness of the interrelated nature of Vietnam and domestic needs.

And it did so on a national level, creating an "American" experience that crossed class, race, gender, or ethnic lines. While the initial push for civil rights focused on the southern states, the Great Society aimed to help the poor, and women, Chicanos, gays, and others had their own agendas, Vietnam affected virtually everyone. By decade's end, all Americans had some knowledge of and opinions about the war. Millions of young men had been in the military and countless others had dodged service. Many more – a diverse group which included campus radicals, hippies, housewives, business people, the clergy, and others – had joined the movement against the war. Albeit for unfortunate, and often tragic, reasons, Vietnam was a unifying force, for Americans of all stripes, unlike any other social movement of the period could be. And as a result, the American people would be more cynical and angry; "Camelot" – the fantastic kingdom featured in the Kennedys' favorite musical – would remain a myth.

Two, Three, Many Vietnams

Though the war in Vietnam dominated American life after 1965, the decade was just as importantly marked by intense conflict at home. The intervention in Indochina occurred in the midst of one of the more intense and divisive, yet successful, reform periods in US history. In just a half-decade, however, much of the hope and optimism of the early 1960s lay shattered. American priorities had changed from addressing needs at home to containing the NLF in Vietnam. In turn, millions of Americans were variously disillusioned, alienated, and radicalized, and developed a comprehensive critique of national politics and society in the process. In turn, they developed a huge movement to resist the war. Building upon that, other movements emerged or became more militant in pursuit of other goals, including political and social rights for peoples of different races, genders, ethnicities, sexual orientation, and cultures, challenged the structure of the state and society along the way, and also prompted government efforts to contain such forces of democracy at home, as in Vietnam.

Ché Guevara, the revolutionary icon of the 1960s, had called on the peoples of the Third World to fight against American imperialism on every front, to create "two, three, many Vietnams." Ironically enough, Americans put Ché's words into practice at home. Politically, Vietnam led to a crisis in and ultimate delegitimation of liberalism. The war exposed liberalism, upended the civil rights movement, and helped give strength to an emerging Women's Liberation movement. Culturally, Vietnam led millions to question authority and reject "traditional" values and practices. The war, on so many levels, transformed national life, causing mass tragedy and unleashing forces for change, and giving birth to a new America. A generation later, however, Vietnam and the 1960s have entered the media as a tragic war in a distant place or as hippies obsessed with "sex, drugs, and rock and roll" trying to create a new culture. But the activists of that era were not the caricatures they are often portrayed as today. Many were trying to create something new, a society in which blacks had civil rights, where political institutions were democratically organized, where poverty and inequality would be addressed, in which a bloody and terrible war would end. As the legacy of Vietnam continues with an accused draft-dodger as president, a national attack on "reverse discrimination" against white men, and a movement for "family values," knowledge about the 1960s is essential to understanding how we have arrived at this point in our national history.

6

Love Me, I'm a Liberal: The Politics of the 1960s and Vietnam

By 1960, the United States had become the world's greatest military and economic power, extending its influence abroad and enjoying steady progress at home, in large measure due to the ideology and political economy of *liberalism*. Though it had been a political and economic organizing principle throughout the twentieth century, liberalism became the crucial element in the establishment of world power after World War II. Though it can take many forms and have different meanings according to time and place, in general liberalism in the Cold War era involved a commitment to economic growth with government involvement, vast international trade and investment, anti-Communism, and the containment of "radical" reform via the incorporation or co-optation of such movements into existing, "mainstream," political structures.

Liberalism's aim, as one of its leading advocates, the historian Arthur Schlesinger, put it, was to create a "vital center" to establish stability and peace while shutting out "extremism" from the left and right. Thus, in the years after World War II, the government intervened in the economy – particularly through military spending programs – to foster higher employment, wages, and profits. By expanding the economic pie, most Americans would get a bigger piece and there would be no need to redistribute wealth and create economic equality. Politically, fundamental differences between Democrats and Republicans lessened as all sides agreed on the overriding need for economic growth and to fight Communism, at home and overseas, and accepted the general outlines of McCarthyism, if not its extremes or the repulsive outlook of its founding father.

Just as a generation of American leaders after 1945 created a liberal world order based on transnational investment, private markets and containment, the Kennedy and Johnson administrations did the same in the 1960s. Organizing the country's business according to liberal Keynesian principles and offering policies to extend corporate power and profits helped the economy grow at a consistent, strong pace. Politically, to protect that vital center, the government practiced containment against reformers and so-called radicals at home as it had against Communists in Eastern Europe, Asia, and elsewhere. An activist foreign policy, economic expansion, and moderate reform at home were interrelated and necessary parts of the US liberal system. In the years following World War II, however, blacks, women, minority groups, cultural critics, and others developed a striking critique of American society, calling for action to promote equality and opportunity for those left behind. While such changes were indeed needed to create consumers, maintain international credibility, prevent upheavals, and for other reasons, US leaders wanted to make sure they were channeled into "safe" directions. Any reform would thus be conducted from the top down; legal obstacles to opportunity might be removed but grassroots empowerment would not be encouraged. African-Americans would thus have significantly more success in demanding the right to ride on buses, eat in restaurants, or vote, than in agitating for jobs and decent housing. Women, many of whom had gained economic independence and personal fulfillment while working in factories during the war years, were encouraged to return home, have babies, and accept the patriarchal order. Young people were expected to get a college degree and a good job, and wear a grey flannel suit to the office every day. When significant segments of these groups questioned such plans and clamored for civil rights, gender equality, or participation in the political process, the liberals balked.

In the JFK and LBJ years, then, this integrated system of

"growth liberalism, " political anti-Communism, and containment – foreign and domestic – was well ingrained in American life and the government, it seemed, could effectively address problems of poverty, inequality, and discrimination to create a truly "Great Society." By mid-decade, however, liberalism began to unravel – both because of its inherent structural limits and, more importantly, due to the growing commitment to Vietnam. In just a few years, the postwar order was in shambles and American politics was on a rightward journey that continues to this day.

The Affluent Society

Between 1960 and 1965, the US gross national product grew by nearly one-third – and by 5 percent annually for the next five years – while corporate profits soared by 88 percent. Unemployment in the 1960s never rose above 4 percent, and median family income went up nearly 25 percent. Though union wages increased by a slower rate than labor leaders wanted – about 3 percent a year in the early 1960s – those raises still exceeded inflation, which ran at about 1 percent. Even after inflation began to quickly rise due to Vietnam, it topped out at 6 percent, still much lower than it would become in the 1970s. America's global economic position was equally strong. The United States controlled over 25 percent of the world's trade; family income was almost $11,000, two to three times larger than that of most industrialized allies; and the world's currencies were pegged at fixed rates to the American dollar. Economically, this was an era of *Pax Americana*.

This economic strength would be critical to the events of the 1960s, offering new opportunities to working-class Americans, facilitating the emergence of the Civil Rights Movement, and, in general, giving the false impression that American growth had virtually no limits. In large measure, the US government had fostered these conditions. First JFK, and then LBJ, were wholly supportive of the American corporate community. JFK essentially suspended anti-trust actions in the Department of Justice, proposed an investment tax credit for businesses, and established new depreciation guidelines for corporate write-offs. In 1962 alone, such measures saved American businesses $2.5 billion in taxes, or 10 percent of their previous year's bill. Kennedy, an economic novice when he took office, was becoming a Keynesian – using government policy to jump start and maintain economic growth. In 1962, the president thus proposed a massive $10 billion tax cut. Current tax rates, JFK contended, had become a drag on the economy, discouraging investment, reducing consumption, and preventing full employment. Even though the government would take in much less revenue, the president argued that the tax cut would "prevent the even greater budget deficit that a lagging economy would otherwise surely produce."[1]

Kennedy's economic strategy would be an integral, if not the principal, part of 1960s liberalism. By using the government, via spending and reduced taxation, to foster economic expansion, Kennedy and his successor would enlarge the middle class, enable more young people to attend college, make jobs, and, maybe most importantly, create hopes and aspirations in groups that had been left out of the postwar economic boom. 1960s liberalism was thus a combination of economic growth and a movement for political reform by marginalized or disenfranchised groups. And for a time in the early 1960s, the government was able to make progress on both counts – expanding the economy and offering some hope to the underclass and minorities. Vietnam, however, dashed that progress, and liberalism's shortcomings were exposed in the process.

Building a "Great Society"?

In the early 1960s Michael Harrington, a socialist scholar, conducted research on poverty in America and found many disturbing conditions. Perhaps one-quarter of the country – 40 million or so people – lacked adequate housing, food, and health care. Harrington's findings, published in 1962 as *The Other America*, shocked Americans, especially liberals such as John F. Kennedy, who had read Harrington's book. The depth of poverty and need within a wealthy and powerful nation represented a major failure of social policy that would have to be addressed in the coming years. Harrington's work alone, however, did not cause national reform. African-Americans, other ethnic groups, women, and working people were also agitating for change from below, calling for jobs, housing, safety standards, and health care. In the early 1960s, then, this awareness of poverty, and the call for action at the grassroots level, would lead to a national commitment to create a "Great Society."

John Kennedy and Lyndon Johnson held power at a unique moment in modern American history. Riding the crest of postwar growth and progress, they naturally assumed that with enough money and commitment America's social problems could be overcome. Kennedy thus proposed a minimum wage increase, more federal support for education, an expansion of Social Security benefits, and a federal commitment to provide housing to the poor. Congress, however, did not really share such a vision and so eliminated the most needy from minimum wage reform, refused to fund a public works program, and rejected aid for migrant workers and youth and for public transportation. At the time of Kennedy's assassination, then, his record was ambivalent at best.

Lyndon Johnson was driven to do more. Having grown up in rural Texas often feeling unloved and ridiculed, he graduated from a teachers' college and worked with poor minority children. Because of this background he claimed an affinity for the less-privileged and he wanted to establish a domestic reform program to rival the "New Deal" of the 1930s. Declaring "an unconditional war on poverty" in his first State of the Union address in 1964, the new president would act quickly to follow up and improve on the Kennedy vision while securing his own place alongside his hero Franklin Roosevelt as the greatest reform presidents of the century. For a time, in 1964 and 1965, LBJ's efforts seemed to be working, as Congress passed a series of measures dealing with health care, housing, education, safety, transportation, and poverty. To a large degree, such reform was made possible by another tax cut, in 1964, which invigorated the economy, boosted the gross national product, increased wages, and lowered unemployment. With a strong economy, reform was possible because Americans could support programs to help the poor without feeling they were making undue sacrifices. At no time did LBJ ever contemplate redistributing wealth or creating material equality between social classes. Rather, he hoped to create a Great Society – which would include civil rights progress as well (to be covered in the next chapter) – in which the poor and minorities would be uplifted, if not equal. To liberals, class harmony, not conflict, would be the norm.

The first major step in Johnson's anti-poverty crusade came with the 1964 passage of the *Economic Opportunity Act*, which created the *Office of Economic Opportunity*, or OEO, headed by JFK's brother-in-law Sargent Shriver. As LBJ envisioned it, the act was not a welfare program but would help prepare the untrained, unskilled, and undereducated for careers of their own. Thus, the OEO would administer the Job Corps, a program in which poor youth could be trained and educated for future employment; VISTA, a "domestic Peace Corps" program for volunteers to travel to underdeveloped areas and assist in training and teaching; and also provide legal aid, mental health services, small business development aid, safety programs, and rural loans. These programs, based on early examination, seemed to be paying dividends. Poor youth, it seemed, were gaining skills and jobs, poor children were better prepared for school, and many underprivileged Americans were gaining self-esteem and dignity. Such results, LBJ hoped, would only increase with future programs.

For the rest of the Johnson presidency, Congress continued to pass such reform programs, though at a decreasing pace and with diminishing results. In 1965, two major pieces of legislation – concerning education and health care – comprised the backbone of the Great Society. The president believed that the American education system was in a state of crisis. Due to the baby boom, school enrollments had grown by 43 percent in just a decade, so classrooms were overcrowded and under-funded. In America's largest cities, about 60 percent of High School students were dropping out. Federal aid was impera-tive, as LBJ saw it; "the kids is where the money ain't," he colloquially described the situation. He thus had made fed-eral support of education a major issue in his 1964 campaign and, upon re-election, began to press for congressional ac-tion. After negotiations with teachers' unions and the Catho-lic Church – which wanted aid to parochial schools included in the federal program – Johnson was able to secure passage of the *Elementary and Secondary Education Act*. As he saw it, the new law would provide the foundation for future progress. Upon signing the bill, the president related that "as a son of a tenant farmer, I know that education is the only valid passport from poverty."[2]

Under the new education act, federal monies would be sent principally to those school districts in which most family in-comes were less than $2,000 a year. To appease the Catholics, LBJ made aid available to parochial school *students*, but not to the schools themselves. The president hailed the new pro-gram as a great success, claiming that millions of poor boys and girls now had access to language and reading training, audio-visual equipment, specialized education for preschoolers, nurses, counselors, bilingual teachers, and, for adults, special classes for High School dropouts. The law, as liberals saw it, was attending to America's education emergency.

On the other end of the life cycle, LBJ also recognized that the nation's elderly lacked adequate health care, and he attacked that problem with vigor as well. Old people had incomes only about half as large as younger Americans but had three times more hospital visits and did not have sufficient health insur-ance. The president thus proposed a national "*Medicare*" pro-gram in which the government, via contributions to the Social Security fund, would provide hospital insurance for Americans over the age of 65. The bill was immediately popular among the aged. "Please try to pass the Medicare for us old folks," one woman wrote to LBJ, "I just don't want to be a burden to anyone."[3] The 89th Congress, dominated by liberals, apparently liked the idea even more and ultimately created a program even more generous than LBJ had envisioned.

The administration designed its original bill to cover just hospital visits for the elderly, but Wilbur Mills, the chair of the House Ways and Means Committee and one of Washington's more powerful legislators, began to expand the program as he sensed the political attractiveness of the concept of providing health care for the elderly, and despite repeated charges by the powerful medical lobby that it would usher in "Socialized medicine." Soon, Medicare included a voluntary insurance program to cover doctors' and surgical fees, with the government and senior citizens splitting the premium payments. Mills then expanded the program more dramatically yet, extending coverage to the poor, regardless of age, in the "*Medicaid*" program. Under Medicaid, participating states would receive matching federal funds to pay the bills of welfare recipients or the medically indigent – the blind, disabled, and so forth – who did not receive welfare but neither could afford to pay for health care.

Johnson proclaimed the new Medicare system a huge victory. "No longer will older Americans be denied the healing miracle of modern medicine," he declared at the signing ceremony, "no longer will illness crush and destroy the savings they have so carefully put away."[4] And the government immediately began to put its money behind the new program, with costs rising from $3.4 billion to $18 billion in the first decade after passage. As a result, almost all aged Americans qualified for hospitalization benefits, and well over 90 percent also purchased supplementary doctor's insurance. About 95 percent of doctors, most of whom originally opposed the bill, eventually participated in the Medicare system. Millions of men and women with health problems who previously could not afford medical care now could be treated. Likewise, the Medicaid program reached large segments of the population, with the number of beneficiaries soaring from 4 to 24 million in a decade and funding growing to $14 billion. Additional measures covering medical research passed Congress as well,

leading to expanded funding in the fights against heart disease, cancer, strokes, and mental retardation. Death rates from
tuberculosis and measles declined, more young people than
ever were immunized from childhood diseases, and thousands
of new doctors and nurses were trained with government assistance. In larger numbers than ever before, the elderly and
poor now had access to basic medical attention and were enjoying a markedly better quality of life.

Though the educational and medical reforms of 1965
marked the peak of the Great Society, other measures continued to pass Congress in subsequent years. LBJ expanded the
food stamp program dramatically, increasing the number of
Americans eligible for such assistance by over 2,500 percent
between 1965 and 1975. Aid to Families with Dependent
Children (AFDC) grew significantly in the Johnson years as
well, with the number of recipients eventually quintupling.
To address America's urban problems, Congress in 1965 created the Department of Housing and Urban Development,
and a year later began to fund model city projects nationally.
In the Motor Vehicle Safety Act, lawmakers for the first time
established safety standards for the auto industry and also
created a Department of Transportation to coordinate new
programs. One of the most useful anti-poverty programs was
Head Start, begun in 1965 as part of the OEO to help pre-
school children from poor families by providing basic education skills as well as meals and medical examinations. In that
summer alone, over 500,000 children – rural and urban, northern and southern – enrolled in pilot Head Start programs. To
LBJ, it was such an impressive start that he expanded the
project and gave it permanent status.

Lyndon Johnson and his supporters believed that the War
on Poverty had gotten off to a generally successful start. Because of LBJ's political skills and a liberal consensus on helping the less fortunate, medical care was now available to
millions who previously went without it because of age or
poverty, and their health and life spans improved accordingly.
Social Security benefits increased, thus raising the standard of
living of the elderly. In 1959, about 40 percent of the aged

lived below the poverty line, but by 1970 only 25 percent did, and by 1974, it was down to 16 percent. Likewise, the numbers of Americans living in poverty dropped significantly too, from 21 percent in 1959 to 12 percent in 1969. Though not there yet, LBJ and his supporters believed that America was on the path toward becoming a truly great society.

Liberalism and its Discontents: The Free Speech Movement

At the same time that two liberal presidents were trying to reform America's racial policies and attack poverty, there was a growing movement, especially among the young, to criticize and restructure the liberal state. Nationally, white youth had been supporting and emulating the efforts of black students and activists in the civil rights movement as they challenged southern segregation. Taking their cue from young African-Americans, they created a parallel political movement. Centered in various institutions – most notably the Free Speech Movement, Students for a Democratic Society, and anti-war groups – this movement would in a short time produce an effective and searing critique of American "corporate liberalism," one which would, by the end of the decade, help undermine the liberal consensus that had dominated the postwar era and, ironically, help lead to a right-wing backlash against liberalism that has grown stronger over the past generation. Collectively known as the *New Left*, this movement offered a new vision of American society. Unlike the "old left," it would not allow the ideology of anti-Communism to dominate its discourse; unlike liberals, New Leftists would not put their faith in the ability of the government and corporations to do the right thing. In this movement, young people would demand a role in making the decisions which governed their lives. Breaking down the barriers between private and public life, these young activists expected their government to act as a moral agent for change, just as individuals were supposed to act morally in their own private sphere. With such general ideas in common, and sharing a commitment to social justice, the New Left erupted into American life at the outset of a new decade.

In May 1960 – as the odious House Un-American Activities Committee (HUAC) was conducting its witch-hunts for so-called subversives in hearings in San Francisco – police attacked and arrested several hundred students from the flagship Berkeley campus of the University of California, prompting thousands to return the following day to protest the repressive law enforcement tactics. Shortly thereafter, HUAC put out a film that it hoped would show that the demonstrations were the work of radicals and Communists, but the move backfired. *Operation Abolition* was so paranoid, ham-handed, and ridiculous that it became a cult classic among college students and political dissenters – sort of a *Reefer Madness* (an early anti-drugs film) for a new political generation – and ultimately motivated thousands to travel to the Bay area, making Berkeley, as radical leader Tom Hayden described it, "the mecca of student activism" in the 1960s.[5]

The president of the University of California system, Clark Kerr, a liberal democrat, became the lightning rod for student dissatisfaction. Kerr envisioned the UC system as a "multiversity" which would educate untold numbers of students and develop stronger ties to the corporate community and the "knowledge industry," meaning more university Research and Development and contracting for big business and government, especially the Department of Defense and other agencies such as the CIA. As Kerr saw it, "the university and segments of industry are becoming more and more alike. As the university becomes tied into the world of work, the professor . . . takes on the characteristics of an entrepreneur."[6] To the Berkeley students, Kerr embodied many of the contradictions of 1960s liberalism, preventing Black Muslim activist Malcolm X from speaking on campus due to separation of church and state, for instance, but allowing evangelist Billy Graham to appear. Kerr, the angry Berkeley youth charged, represented the liberal paternalism that, on one hand, offered rhetorical support for equality and justice but nonetheless limited students' rights under the concept of *in loco parentis* ("in place of one's parents"), restricting dormitory visiting hours and curtailing their freedom of expression.

In 1963 and especially 1964, after Kerr, under political pressure, banned students from passing out leaflets and circulating petitions along Bancroft Strip, just outside the main gate of campus, the student upheaval grew and ultimately gave rise to the *Free Speech Movement* (FSM). In September 1964, various student groups – from the Socialist left to the conservative students who supported Barry Goldwater's 1964 campaign for president – protested Kerr's ban with rallies, pickets, and vigils and some directly challenged the president's edict by setting up tables and passing out literature. In turn, campus police ordered eight students to appear before a Berkeley disciplinary board. Instead of eight, however, several hundred students marched on Sproul Hall, the administration building, whereupon Kerr suspended the eight originally cited. By 1 October, UC students were in near-rebellion, again setting up tables to defy the ban. Police arrested one of them, Jack Weinberg, a veteran civil rights activist, but before they could get him into their squad car, hundreds of other students converged on the scene and prevented the police from taking Weinberg away.

Students surrounded the police car for the next 32 hours, taking turns standing on its hood (after taking off their shoes) to deliver speeches of protest, despite being taunted and pelted with foreign objects by fraternity boys and athletes. Thus was born the FSM. At that point, the administration blinked, releasing Weinberg without charges and submitting the suspension of the other eight students to an academic senate committee. But Chancellor Edward Strong would not reinstate the eight while charges were pending, and Kerr chided the protestors' "ritual of hackneyed complaints" and redbaited the FSM, claiming that about 40 percent of its participants were "very experienced and professional people . . . tied in with organizations having Communist influences." Seymour Martin Lipset, a ranking liberal intellectual, chimed in that the FSM's civil disobedience tactics were "like the Ku Klux Klan."[7] Liberals and young people had clearly come into conflict in Berkeley, not for the last time in the decade.

In any event, the tensions on campus continued to build. In mid-November, students again set up tables and passed out leaflets, and the administration began taking the names of the young people staffing the tables. At the same time, the faculty senate decided to reinstate six of the original eight demonstrators, but not Art Goldberg and Mario Savio. The FSM immediately took action, holding a rally at which 3,000 students confronted the Board of Regents and listened to Joan Baez sing protest songs, whereupon the Regents *increased* Goldberg's and Savio's punishment. As a result, Berkeley graduate students went on strike and on 2 December about 5,000 students again rallied at Sproul Hall and listened to Savio deliver one of the more compelling speeches of the era. Directly challenging Kerr's view of the "multiversity" and the impersonal liberal–corporation alliance, Savio, a working-class mathematics student, told the crowd that

> there is a time when the operations of the machine become so odious, makes you so sick at heart, that you can't take part; you can't even passively take part, and you've got to put your bodies upon the gears and upon the wheels, upon the levers, upon all the apparatus and you've got to make it stop. And you've got to indicate to the people who run it, to the people who own it, that unless you're free, the machines will be prevented from running at all.[8]

Savio's attack on the UC system and domestic containment was one of the earliest and most trenchant critiques of liberalism to emerge in the 1960s. Liberals, to FSM activists and so many others, were patronizing, impersonal, and repressive. The liberal state and liberal institutions spoke of lofty ideals like freedom and liberty, but in the final analysis the government and educational system became autonomous and impersonal, like a machine, rather than responsive to people's needs or rights. It was, to Savio and others, anti-democratic. And the Berkeley administration continued to provide the protesting students with evidence to support such arguments. After Savio's speech, over a thousand students poured into Sproul Hall, sat down, and refused to move. The Berkeley forces of order responded immediately. After several hours of occupation, at 2:00 a.m., over 600 state and local law enforcement officials ringed the building and moved inside to oust the demonstrators, twisting arms and legs and banging heads as they dragged them away, and arresting over 750 for trespassing in what had become the largest mass arrest in state history.

FSM leaders and supportive faculty fought back, calling a university-wide strike, coordinating the various protest actions, distributing handbills, and posting bail for students, while about three-fourths of Berkeley's 1,200 professors canceled classes in a show of solidarity with Savio and the others. Feeling the heat and hoping to alleviate the crisis, Clark Kerr called a campus-wide meeting to discuss the situation with the Berkeley community. The UC president, with the support of many department chairs, told over 15,000 people in the crowd that the demonstrations were "unwarranted" and he urged students to return to classes. FSM members not surprisingly jeered Kerr and other speakers and, when the meeting adjourned, Savio approached the stage to speak, but campus guards grabbed him and dragged him away. In perhaps the most overt display of liberal paternalism, the Free Speech Movement's leader was denied the right to speak freely. But the university's repressive measures backfired as the angry crowd left Kerr with no choice but to allow Savio to return to the podium to make an announcement. The next day, the faculty established new rules for student speech, basically echoing the FSM positions. The Board of Regents subsequently replaced Chancellor Strong with Martin Meyerson, who had been sympathetic to the students' agenda, and gave them access to Bancroft Strip to pass out literature, recruit members, and otherwise disseminate information. The FSM – comprised mostly of young people, 19 to 21 years old – had won, and throughout the country college students took note of the power of collective action on behalf of democratic rights.

"Democracy Is in the Streets"

In June 1962, 59 people traveled to a small town in Michigan to discuss establishing "a new kind of politics." Mostly young college students – but also union activists and Socialists – attended, and the product of their work, the "*Port Huron Statement*," came to define the oppositional politics of the decade and was a major step in the emergence of the most important dissident democratic organization of the 1960s, the *Students for a Democratic Society* (SDS). Though never organizationally strong, and not really intended to be since they were wary of centralized, bureaucratic groups, SDS would have a major role in mobilizing the anti-war movement in 1965 and its members would offer a compelling critique of liberalism that would be widely accepted and adapted by 1968.

"We are people of this generation," the Port Huron participants observed, "bred in at least modest comfort, housed now in universities, [but] looking uncomfortably to the world we inherit."[9] Hoping to shed the complacency of the 1950s and energize American politics, these young activists called for a new commitment to social justice, civil and human rights, and – in the core concept of their conceptual framework – *participatory democracy.* American democracy, as they saw it, was practiced from the top down, dominated by political and economic elites, and it offered people, in most cases at least, voting privileges and free expression, but actually discouraged popular participation in the system. In a "participatory" democracy, people would actually have a significant role, a voice, in making the decisions that affected their lives whether they be poor, young, or otherwise outside the mainstream of American life.

SDS came to life in Ann Arbor, at the University of Michigan, in early 1960. There, student activists like Al Haber, Sharon Jeffrey, Rob Ross, Tom Hayden, and others began raising awareness on campus of the southern civil rights movement, holding conferences on US democracy and human rights, and fanning out to other colleges to recruit members. That summer, Hayden, along with radical students from Berkeley, picketed the Democratic convention in Los Angeles with Martin Luther King and a year later he went south to become the SDS representative to civil rights organizations there. In Mississippi, police beat him up, and in Georgia local authorities jailed him. Hayden, a journalist, exploited his tribulations, sending out reports of his experiences which created publicity and lured new members for SDS. By mid-1962, he was emerging as the best-known young radical of the era, and his authorship of the Port Huron Statement added to his influence. Hayden's "new politics" challenged both the government–corporate establishment and the "old left." Elites had grabbed control of society's institutions and left the people apathetic and isolated. Groups that should be progressive, like labor unions, had become mainly bureaucratic entities, taking on lives of their own rather than helping the working class or the poor, and buying into the stifling politics of anti-Communism. Thus Hayden called for a movement of students to "wrest control of the educational process from the administrative bureaucracy" and for the people from all walks of life to create a system of "participatory democracy."

Though the Port Huron Statement had attracted a good deal of attention, SDS was still small and mostly marginal. In 1963, however, it began to take a new direction, releasing another manifesto, *America and the New Era,* attacking liberalism and thereafter beginning its first major grassroots organizing project. In their pamphlet, SDS theorists criticized the Kennedy, corporate liberals who conducted national affairs to ensure mainly that the "old order of private corporate enterprise shall be preserved and rationalized." SDS did, however, still see some "good liberals" in the political arena, but they were "trapped by the limitations of the Democratic Party, but afraid of irrelevancy outside."[10] SDS's job, then, would be to awaken those liberals and offer them refuge within its new politics. The first attempt to do this came with the establishment of the *Economic Research and Action Project* (ERAP). Funded with a grant from the United Auto Workers union, the program was designed to send SDS members into poor communities where they would live among and organize the residents there. This marked a shift in SDS priorities, as more activist members like Hayden and Rennie Davis – who replaced Al Haber as the head of ERAP – began to press for an "interracial movement of the poor" at the grassroots level as the key to social change rather than reform at the university level among middle-class, mostly white students. To Hayden, the "liberal posture" of campus activism led to inaction and irresponsibility. In the universities, "liberalism is defused, lacking a point of moral explosion," so only direct action could change the system. "It will take extremism to create gradualism," he advised.[11]

Coinciding with the increased awareness of the poor coming out of the Johnson administration's "war on poverty," SDS activists believed that their new project could be both relevant and effective. Their program, however, diverged sharply from the Great Society plans of the liberal establishment. SDS activists developed ERAP programs in various cities – Baltimore, Boston, Chicago, Cleveland, Louisville, Newark, Philadelphia, and others – in the summer of 1964 but often had trouble working within the established communities. Whereas the college students had an intellectual commitment to reform the corporate liberal state, poor people in ERAP areas were concerned with local issues such as sanitation, education, health care, or decent housing. In Cleveland, possibly the most successful ERAP city, activists led by Sharon Jeffrey organized a tenants' union and a welfare rights organization, but those soon faded as the local police "red squad" harassed the tenants' union and the aims of the welfare mothers were not wholly compatible with those of students trying to apply the writings of Karl Marx or Gunnar Myrdal to the near west side of Cleveland. Although the Cleveland project would last two and a half years, and Tom Hayden would work on the Newark program for three years, ERAP folded in 1965, in principal measure because SDS was devoting itself to ending the war in Vietnam.

The failures of ERAP also finally convinced SDS participants of the futility of working within the liberal system. In some areas, old-line liberal groups such as Americans for Democratic Action (ADA), the Congress On Racial Equality (CORE), the National Association for the Advancement of Colored People (NAACP), and labor unions had supported ERAP actions initially, but those institutions were outraged by the SDS program of empowerment at the local level. Rather than become a tool of the liberal establishment, ERAP leaders hoped to establish tenant unions, voter registration projects, and welfare rights organizations to give the poor a voice, per the concept of participatory democracy. But the liberals, as Hayden put it, viewed such grassroots actions "as a problem if not a danger." In Chicago, after trying to work within the structure established by the Daley machine, ERAP attitudes toward liberals "changed from . . . hope to . . . deepest hostility and contempt."[12] In 1965, then, the liberal establishment was waging its war on poverty from Washington, DC, and middle-class college students were doing it in various communities. The poor, however, were without weapons in the battle.

Vietnam and the Radicalization of the New Left

Groups such as the Free Speech Movement and SDS had actually been established to work within and reform the liberal system, but as the years passed they began to see liberalism as the enemy and often became committed to overthrowing it. To some degree, this criticism of liberalism was already evident by the earlier years of the 1960s, prompted by the paternalism of Berkeley administrators, the bureaucratic nature of labor unions, or the rabid anti-Communism of old-line liberal groups. Students derided "limousine liberals" who spoke of their concern for the downtrodden from their positions of privilege, and folk singer Phil Ochs mocked their hypocrisy brilliantly in his song "Love Me, I'm a Liberal." More than anything, however, it was the growing American commitment to Vietnam that caused so many activists to turn on the liberal establishment and become increasingly radical and militant – and occasionally violent – in the later 1960s. By the end of the decade, the New Left, which had been born as an intellectual movement to nonviolently revitalize American society, was employing the rhetoric of revolution as the besieged liberal state tried to carry on the war in Indochina and maintain control at home. In the end, New Left groups either crashed or faded away and liberalism came under a sustained backlash from the right after the frontal assault from the youthful left. Ultimately, Richard Nixon, George Wallace, Ronald Reagan, and others picked up the pieces and assumed power.

The FSM, Port Huron, SDS, ERAP, other New Left ideas and institutions, and civil rights all took a back seat to the war in Vietnam beginning in 1965. As James Miller, the best-known chronicler of SDS, explained: "fueled by the hostility of many American students to the war in Vietnam, the New Left after 1965 quickly mushroomed into a mass movement that aggressively challenged the legitimacy of America's political institutions." In turn, the earlier, "participatory democracy," phase of activism came to seem like "an irrelevant, insufficiently radical pre-history" as the movement became singularly focused on stopping the war in Vietnam by whatever means necessary. Accordingly, in 1965 SDS had sponsored the first major demonstration against the war – in April in Washington, DC – and began to wind down ERAP and set its sights on Vietnam. This new commitment also caused tension within the community groups in ERAP cities. The vehemence with which SDS members denounced the war turned off many of the local poor with whom they were working. While those communities may have been upset with the mayor or local police, they still had faith in the US mission to help the world. As Sharon Jeffrey observed, poor people still believed that the federal government "somehow is honest, moral, and good [and] if the US was involved in a war, then it must be for good reasons."[13]

Participatory democracy and an interracial movement of the poor could not be achieved in a liberal system that attacked Vietnamese peasants, so stopping the war became the prerequisite for any future New Left political action. As Paul Potter, president of SDS in April 1965, charged at the Washington anti-war rally, "the incredible war in Vietnam has provided the razor, the terrifying sharp cutting edge that has finally severed the last vestiges of illusion that morality and democracy are the guiding principles of American foreign policy."[14]

Such an analysis was becoming typical, and from that time forward SDS and other groups shifted their priorities from reform at home to anti-war activity, becoming more angry and radical in the process and giving rise to new levels of protest on campus and elsewhere throughout the country.

Once more, the universities became the flashpoint for protest. Student radicals pointed out that many of their professors were conducting research for the Pentagon and CIA, their scientists were creating napalm and herbicides, their administrators were acting like slum lords in surrounding neighborhoods where the schools owned property, and their admissions offices admitted few nonwhite applicants. "Viewed from within," as Emily Rosenberg and Norman Rosenberg observed, "the multiversity seemed to offer mind-numbing courses and senseless regimentation. Seen as part of liberal society, it appeared implicated in the war and racism."[15] From coast to coast, then, campuses began to erupt. In October 1965, tens of thousands of students nationwide participated in anti-war demonstrations; others picketed their draft boards and burned selective service cards. At a University of Colorado football game, students made a peace sign out of flash cards at halftime. In Berkeley, students staged a "peace invasion" of the Oakland Army base only to be met and attacked by the Hell's Angels, who told them to "go back to Russia, you fucking Communists." Despite such outrages, or maybe because of them, SDS became even more popular, with the number of chapters doubling to 80 that summer alone and, as the war escalated, growing even more. "I didn't go to college in 1965 expecting to become a radical," Judy Smith, a young student, related, "but I didn't expect the Vietnam War to develop the way it did either . . . For [my friends and I] it would have been immoral to just go on with college and career plans when the war was still going on. If you weren't part of the solution, you were part of the problem."[16]

At Columbia University, in one of the most painful episodes in the 1960s, students decided to attack the problem head on. Columbia had an active SDS chapter – in 1966 members had picketed military and CIA recruiters, confronted Marine representatives on campus, and demanded that their class rankings not be handed over to local draft boards – and in 1968 it shut down the university. Columbia's president, Grayson Kirk, was patrician and conservative, a member of the Board of Directors of Consolidated Edison, IBM, and the Institute for Defense Analysis. In 1967, Kirk had banned all indoor demonstrations on campus and his administration was continuing to take disciplinary actions against female students for "living with a boyfriend." The final straw, however, came as a result of Columbia's ownership of property near campus in Morningside Heights, a minority residential area near Harlem. Kirk decided to build a new gymnasium in the neighborhood, which would displace black residents from their homes, prompting SDS and other student activists to protest the further intrusion into the black community – "Gym Crow Must Go," was a frequent cry. Six SDS members, led by chapter president Mark Rudd, defied the ban on protests, holding a demonstration inside Low Library, and Kirk suspended them. Rudd, in an open letter to the Columbia president, called for the "opening shot in a war of liberation" and screamed out "up against the wall, motherfucker, this is a stick-up."[17]

While few expected the Revolution to begin on an Ivy League campus, the situation was heating up. In late April, with patience thin on all sides, the upheaval began. SDS and black students, to protest the gym construction, held a rally and marched to the library, where they occupied Kirk's office, rifling through his files, smoking his cigars, and drinking his sherry. Within days, over a thousand students had joined the protest, "liberated" three more buildings, and created communes inside. Local supporters sent food, and medical students opened up clinics. To the students it was "participatory democracy" come to life. Likening themselves to Vietnamese nationalists or Third-World revolutionaries, they too were fighting against the imperial, liberal American state and, in this case, they had shut down Columbia University. Soon, intellectuals and celebrities rushed to see the rebellion as it unfolded. Norman Mailer, Dwight MacDonald, Susan Sontag, and radical leaders Hayden, Abbie Hoffman, H. Rap Brown, and Stokely Carmichael arrived. Everywhere, one could hear the music of the Grateful Dead and, of course, Bob Dylan.

The apparent bliss would not last long, however. Kirk called in plainclothes police, who attacked sympathetic faculty with billy clubs. After a temporary truce and a series of meetings, Kirk this time called in law enforcement again. About 300 students and faculty tried to peacefully halt the police, but to no avail as they forced their way past the crowd and into the buildings. Students offered nonviolent resistance, singing "We Shall Overcome" or the National Anthem, but not fighting back. Police attacked nonetheless and, as an African-American student, Dionision Pabon, recalled, "I was called nigger [and] kicked in the head, face, back, stomach and groin. It felt like a herd of horses, instead of hooves – iron spikes."[18] Kirk had played into the students' hands. More members of the Columbia community, even conservatives, were so repulsed by Kirk's decision to call in a police attack that they too joined the strike. When the administration decided to suspend several student leaders, others again occupied Hamilton Hall. Kirk once more called in the working-class police, who again responded violently against the children of privilege. The university canceled final exams and Columbia was at a standstill. Administrators did announce that they would suspend plans for the gym construction, but the damage had been done. The Columbia uprising marked a dramatic and somewhat frightening step in the New Left's efforts to change America.

At Columbia, SDS faded away after 1968, in good measure because most of its leaders had been suspended. But the actions in Morningside Heights had a national impact, contributing to a hardening of attitudes on the right and left alike. Many moderates and conservatives, and not a few self-proclaimed liberals, turned against the youth movement, seeing it as nihilistic and extremist, and often violent. Many students, on the other hand, opted out of the liberal system and saw no hope in trying to reform essentially corrupt institutions. Many, additionally, were lured by the romance of rebellion – per Hayden's call for "two, three, many Columbias" – and students more than ever began to identify with Ho,

Mao Zedong, Ché Guevara, Fidel Castro, Frantz Fanon, Malcolm X, and other icons of revolution. As students in Paris, Prague, and Mexico City had uprisings in 1968 as well, the idea of a global youth rebellion did not seem so far-fetched. Student protests at the University of Wisconsin in Madison and at Berkeley prompted the governors to call the National Guard to campus. Black students at Cornell University – harassed by cross-burnings and bomb threats – carried shotguns and wore bandoliers on campus. At Ohio State, the National Guard appeared on campus in 1968 to discourage anti-war activity and when students in 1970 took over High Street the famed Buckeye football coach Woody Hayes rushed onto the scene to yell to students to go home. In Berkeley, police fired on protestors at "People's Park," killing one, blinding another, and wounding a hundred others. Amid the mayhem, California Governor Ronald Reagan took a hard line, announcing that "if there's going to be a bloodbath, let it begin here."

In Madison, student radicals bombed the Army Mathematics Research Center, a symbol of the military–university complex, killing a post-doctoral student who was studying inside. A group of militant SDS members splintered from the main organization and formed the Weathermen – a name taken from a line in Dylan's "Subterranean Homesick Blues": "you don't need a weatherman to know which way the wind blows" – which was committed to violent attacks on the police, legal system, and political leaders, and which conducted the 1969 "Days of Rage" action in Chicago. All told, from late 1969 to early 1970 alone, the Weathermen and other groups attempted about 250 bombings across the country, and often staged other assaults on symbols of the system, most notably the ROTC building at Kent State. The hope of participatory democracy had given way to the glamor of revolution. Spurred on by their own frustrations and the repressive nature of university administrations and politicians, many radicals saw violence, not empowerment, as the answer to state containment. But they were operating in an inherently anti-revolutionary atmosphere. Student radicals were marginalized, not identifying with or being accepted by the masses of working poor or minorities who would be essential to any large-scale action. And to those who advocated "law and order," violent activism offered proof that all dissent had to be stopped. The New Left was in disarray, organizationally and morally conflicted. "In the illumination of that bombing [at Madison]," Todd Gitlin wrote, "the Movement knew sin."[19]

Vietnam, "Corporate Liberalism," and the Shortcomings of the Great Society

Ultimately, the New Left did not create a participatory democracy, change the liberal system, or force LBJ to end the war in Vietnam. It did, nonetheless, have a tremendous impact on the politics of the 1960s. By "speaking truth to power" – as activists in that decade described it – FSM, SDS, and others forced the nation to confront many of the problems that had previously been ignored, developed a critique of the liberal order that would become powerful and widespread by 1968, and they made the nature of the war in Vietnam the dominant issue of the day. Despite outright hostility and repression from the media, law enforcement, and the political establishment, young people and committed activists exposed many of the inconsistencies of American society and demanded accountability from their leaders. But they did not overthrow the system; it was the liberals themselves who did that. By the end of the decade, the liberal hopes so eloquently pronounced at the beginning of the Kennedy years were little more than empty rhetoric. After nearly a decade of paying prices and bearing burdens, Americans were only too willing to listen to Richard Nixon, George Wallace, and others attack the liberal system. And the Great Society foundered, the victim of the commitment to Indochina and the structural limits of "corporate liberalism."

At the end of July 1965, Lyndon Johnson thought about his most recent accomplishments – including passage of Medicare, education, voting rights, and anti-poverty legislation – and proclaimed it "the most productive and most historic legislative week in Washington during this century."[20] Taking stock after he left office, LBJ pointed to further successes of his Great Society: 8.5 million jobs created; unemployment down to 3.3 percent, 40 percent less than in 1963; corporate profits and workers' pay risen by 50 percent; average working-class incomes higher by over $500; and federal revenues up by $70 billion. Federal programs covering health, education, poverty, the elderly, food stamps, AFDC, and Social Security without question had contributed to a significant improvement in the quality of life for many poor, who could be educated and afford health care and legal services for the first time. LBJ's Great Society "improved the everyday lives of millions of Americans." Looking back, the president said he "would not have changed much. I would have made the same decision to recommend a guns-and-butter budget to the congress."[21]

Despite such successes, Johnson himself lamented that nearly a million women lacked prenatal care and infant mortality rates were depressingly high, poor children still needed better educational facilities and adequate meals, and too many Americans still went without quality medical care. In large measure, such failings stemmed from the shift in national priorities away from the war on poverty and to the war in Vietnam. Indeed, during that same "productive and historic" week in July 1965, the president also noticed that the "lowering cloud of Vietnam" – he had just committed 80,000 troops to Indochina, essentially "Americanizing" the war – was affecting his political agenda. Still, LBJ was optimistic that the public would continue to support federal spending on anti-poverty programs *and* for the war. "This nation is mighty enough, its society is healthy enough," he observed in 1966, "to pursue our goals in the rest of the world while still building a Great Society here at home."[22]

Ultimately, however, Americans would not support costly "wars" on two fronts. Although liberals in the House of Representatives and Senate had secured passage of the major Great Society bills, there were still significant political groupings – conservatives, Republicans, southerners – opposed to the federal expansion of and spending on "welfare" programs. And, economically, Vietnam was siphoning away resources that LBJ had hoped to commit to his anti-poverty crusade. Indeed, the war was calling into question America's post-World War II hegemony in the global political economy. Because of Vietnam, an already existing deficit in the country's balance of payments – the amount of American dollars being sent abroad in investment, tourism, and, especially, military spending – grew much worse. In connection with that, America's gold reserves began to decline dramatically as well. At the end of World War II, the United States had created the so-called Bretton Woods system in which the US dollar was established as an international currency within the gold standard. Foreign currencies could be traded for gold at fixed rates of $35 per ounce, thereby ensuring stability in world financial markets.

By 1965–6, however, the war was destabilizing both the American and foreign economies. At home, the payments deficits grew as spending on the war approached $25 billion per annum. Gold stocks, which already had dropped from $23 billion in 1957 to $16 billion in 1962, dwindled as well. Because foreign central banks could not adjust their currencies – Bretton Woods demanded fixed rates pegged to the dollar – they were paying higher prices for American goods because the war was causing inflation in the United States. Thus foreign banks began to cash in their dollars for gold as a hedge against inflation, withdrawing $1.7 billion in specie in 1965 alone. The situation worsened as American spending in Vietnam grew; US Treasury Department officials estimated that balance-of-payments deficits would soar due "entirely to our intensified efforts in Southeast Asia," while another $200 million in red ink was likely in 1967 due to the war. By late 1967, there was a full-blown monetary crisis as Britain devalued its pound sterling and European nations, especially France, began to call for a change in the US-dominated world economy. French President Charles De Gaulle warned of an "American takeover of our businesses" resulting from the "exportation of inflated dollars." At the same time, deficits in 1967 rose to $7 billion, triple the rate for the previous year.

By 1968, at the same point as the Tet Offensive, the world economy verged on crisis. Deficits grew by over $300 million a week and gold losses amounted to almost $600 million in the first weeks of March 1968 alone. Should European banks continue to trade their dollars for gold, it could trigger a devaluation of the dollar, which in turn could ignite a series of foreign currency devaluations. A situation like the world depression of the late 1920s and 1930s seemed wholly possible. Finally, LBJ stepped in to stop the bleeding. He temporarily froze all payments of gold and, more importantly, began to take measures to slow down the war in Vietnam and military spending; as a first step he rejected the request for 200,000 more troops, which would have cost another $25 billion. As Arthur Okun, the president's principal financial officer, explained, unless world markets had confidence in the dollar American prosperity was at great risk, and Vietnam was at the root of such considerations. American leaders, for the first time since 1945, had discovered the limits of its economic strength and liberal system. After World War II, the United States had been able to create jobs and opportunity at home while being active, and often interventionist, abroad due to its consistent economic growth, and in the process it established an effective and profitable liberal order at home and internationally. But the war exposed the difficulties involved in the American mission, as the costs of a major military effort abroad cut into LBJ's plans to wage war on poverty in the United States. With deficits going up and gold going out, liberal Keynesian economics came under assault and the conservative counterattack on the Great Society grew more vigorous while, globally, America could not direct world economies as it previously had. Maybe the *Pax Americana* had not ended, but it was surely on the wane.[23]

Clearly, the war had a significantly negative impact on LBJ's plans to help the poor, but even without the US intervention into Vietnam there were a good many structural obstacles to effective reform in the 1960s. The American system of "*corporate liberalism*," as leftist scholars and activists described it, made it unlikely if not impossible for the government to address the basic problems facing its people. Originally developed and discussed by theorists associated with the journal *Studies on the Left*, the radical scholars Gabriel Kolko and William Appleman Williams, student activists, and especially SDS, the concept of corporate liberalism became the key analytical idea within the New Left and offered a comprehensive explanation for both the Vietnam War and the shortcomings of the Great Society. By 1968 establishment figures like Martin Luther King and Robert Kennedy were addressing this concept as well. To critics on the left, the real barrier to democracy was not the right wing, but in fact the liberals, namely corporate liberals. Wholly supportive of large corporations and defensive of America's unequal class structure, liberals believed in the primacy and importance of big businesses and pursued policies to extend their influence. The goal of liberal reform, therefore, was to create a stable business environment and enable the biggest firms to withstand competition and stave off all but mild labor demands for better wages and conditions. As JFK admitted to an audience of corporate leaders, the government's tax revenues and "thus our success are dependent upon your profits and your success – and . . . far from being natural enemies, Government and business are necessary allies."[24]

Like the president, movement leaders too recognized the convergence of state and corporate interests, but did not share Kennedy's optimism about the arrangement. Dick Flacks, an SDS leader in the early 1960s, explained that "the people who are running society are the corporate liberals. They want to stabilize, not repress. . . . 'Corporate liberalism' meant reforms made by the power elite in the interests of social stability [not] redistribution and social equality." Even liberal groups, especially labor, bought into this system as their leadership was brought into the halls of Democratic Party power and divorced from the rank-and-file. "These groups," to Flacks, "had been separated from the real base of power."[25] Paul Potter developed the concept further and introduced it to a mass New Left audience at the April 1965 anti-war rally. There Potter denounced the "system" that waged war against the Vietnamese, denied fundamental human rights to minorities at home, allowed millions to remain impoverished, created "faceless and terrible bureaucracies . . . where people spend their lives and do their work," and "consistently puts material values before human values" yet "still persists in calling itself free and still persists in finding itself fit to police the world."[26]

"We must name that system . . . describe it, analyze it, understand it, and change it," Potter thundered, in order to stop the war in Vietnam and end oppression and violence at home. Carl Oglesby, SDS president, built upon Potter's critique at the next major anti-war action in Washington in October 1965. Oglesby denounced those officials – LBJ, McNamara, Dean Rusk, the Bundy brothers, Arthur Goldberg, and others – responsible for the war, but also reminded the crowd that "they are not moral monsters. They are all honorable men. They are all liberals." These corporate liberals, the SDS leader pointed out, "can send 200,000 young men to Vietnam to kill and die in the most dubious of wars, but it cannot send 100 voter registrars to go into Mississippi"; were cutting funding to anti-poverty programs while offering huge contracts to aerospace firms to build new planes; and talking about democracy while overthrowing Third World nationalist governments. Corporate liberalism, Oglesby concluded, "performs for the corporate state a function quite like what the Church once performed for the feudal state. It seeks to justify its burdens and protect it from change." Instead of an Inquisition, however, McCarthyism and redbaiting were used to weed out so-called enemies, and it was all "made possible by our anti-Communist corporate liberalism." The liberals, Todd Gitlin added, believed that "a bigger and better welfare state," not economic restructuring and redistribution of wealth, could solve problems of social inequality, an approach which he likened to applying "aspirin to cancer."[27]

The New Left, however, ultimately did not offer a popular critique of the liberal order, as SDS and other groups often became more rigid, strident, and violent. But the concept of corporate liberalism remained a highly useful analytical tool for examining the shortcomings of LBJ's programs. The Great Society, as the New Left charged, was inhibited by its own liberalism. While LBJ wanted to offer lower-income Americans "opportunity, not doles," the Great Society tended to be run, as Ted Morgan explained, "from the top down by an elite realm of decision-makers cut off from the world of their subjects, by insiders righteously unaware that their own subjectivity distorted the object of their analysis and policy."[28] The Johnson administration, like Clark Kerr or the clueless Grayson Kirk, thought that it knew what was best for the poor and would only work within established political structures, so it essentially was carrying out another form of liberal paternalism. Nor did its spending on social programs, though markedly expanded, reach the levels needed to address fundamental problems of poverty. Funding under the 1965 Education Act, for instance, usually went to local school boards – usually run by middle-class white conservatives or bureaucrats – who had their own agenda, namely taking care of the children from families like theirs. In a 1966 survey, about 70 percent of school district superintendents *opposed* allocating education funds on the basis of poverty, even though that was the basic intent of the program. In addition, local districts decided which schools would receive federal monies, and, not surprisingly, appropriations did not arrive at those institutions which were the poorest and most needed aid. By maintaining such a system, though, the administration did not alienate important liberal constituencies like the teachers' unions or working-class, but not poor, whites.

Similarly, the establishment of Medicare represented an accommodation between reformers and vested interests, namely the medical community. The American Medical Association (AMA), alarming Americans that "Socialized medicine" was on the way, was paying lobbyists $5,000 a day to defeat the Medicare bill. Though it did not achieve that, the AMA did pressure Congress to create a system that would work to doctors' advantage. Medicare thus contained no price controls; the government would reimburse physicians and hospitals caring for the elderly for their usual fees, in effect causing medical inflation to soar as doctors and hospitals raised their prices because federal insurance was paying the bill.

Medicaid had its problems as well: too few physicians participated in the system because of the paperwork involved and
because the government reimbursed those doctors caring for
the poor at fees below their customary level. The states, moreover, controlled benefits, so the quality of care varied widely;
in Missouri, the average recipient got $214 worth of care, but
in Minnesota it amounted to $911. Americans living in pov-
erty but not on welfare – about 40 percent of the poor – were
not eligible for Medicaid. And, as with any program of that
magnitude, fraud was not uncommon.

Perhaps the best example of the failure of Great Society
liberalism to address the needs of the poor came with the
Community Action Program (CAP), part of the 1964 Economic Opportunity Act. The CAPs would develop "maximum
feasible participation" among the poor. Rather than establish
a bureaucracy to make decisions and administer funding, pov-
erty-stricken communities themselves would determine where
the money would be spent and organize their own programs
to better their lives. Activists and residents in various poor
urban areas thus set up community boards to fight their own
"wars" against the local political structure. CAP boards thus
began to form tenants' unions, conducted rent strikes against
slum lords, called for police review boards composed of citizens, lobbied for educational facilities for their youth, registered the poor to vote, and engaged in other political activity
that challenged the status quo. In Syracuse, New York, for
instance, the famed radical community organizer Saul Alinsky
helped establish a CAP which bailed out protesting welfare
mothers and became involved in the mayoral election in hopes
of defeating the incumbent William Walsh. When the director
of the local Housing Authority learned of such CAP actions,
he warned that "we are experiencing a class struggle in the
traditional Karl Marx style in Syracuse, and I do not like it."

In Philadelphia, to avoid the threat of participatory democracy, local political officials stacked the CAP boards with their
political cronies, who would be sure not to rock the boat. In
New York the noted black psychologist Kenneth Clark had
devised HARYOU – Harlem Youth Opportunities Unlimited

– to provide services to young African-Americans and establish neighborhood boards to educate the poor and foster institutional reform. But allies of Congressman Adam Clayton Powell took control of HARYOU and used millions of federal dollars to make sure that no community boards ever developed into political forces independent of Powell.[29] In major cities throughout the country, despite pleas to "let the people decide," that pattern repeated itself. Time and again local political officials and the federal government saw community programs as a threat to their control, not as an opportunity for empowerment and progress.

Empowerment and independence were never LBJ's purpose. Vice-President Hubert Humphrey, a liberal icon, told Sargent Shriver, whose agency ran the CAPs, to suppress the citizenry's demands for maximum participation. But Shriver himself bluntly admitted that "we have no intention, of course, of letting . . . the poor themselves . . . 'run the programs.'"[30] Big city Democratic mayors such as John Shelley of San Francisco and Sam Yorty of Los Angeles attacked the CAPs as well, claiming that they were "fostering class struggle" by empowering the poor. And no-one attacked the community programs more than Chicago's mayor Richard Daley, who called CAP a "prize piece of political pornography." Daley would not tolerate the poor making decisions in "his city" but he also used the program to his advantage, taking federal monies and creating jobs for friends and political allies. When representatives of a local housing group in one of Chicago's slums (where a Chicago politician and Daley supporter owned property) criticized the mayor's actions, Daley contacted LBJ, who put an end to the experiment in popular democracy in Chicago. Daley and Johnson were never willing to tolerate a situation in which the government would pay community organizers who turned around and criticized the local political system. Liberal politicians thought it was far more important to maintain patronage among established constituencies than to politicize the poor and underclass, who would almost certainly have a different agenda. To the president and Daley, then, reform essentially meant buying off established liberal elites, not empowering the poor. When the "kooks and sociologists" in the CAPs, as LBJ called them, tried to redistribute wealth or power, they had exceeded the limits that corporate liberalism had established.

The failure of the CAPs illustrated the structural shortcomings of the Great Society. Though many Americans' lives, education, and health may have improved, far too often federal funding did not reach those who really needed it and was too limited to make a substantial difference. Despite LBJ's commitment and billions of dollars, never did the War on Poverty effectively address the structural needs of the poor. It tried to fix poor people rather than a system of poverty. Many critics – on the political right, in the "vital center," and among blue-collar Democrats – moreover believed that the government was simply giving money away to people too lazy to work, even though then, as now, the majority of welfare recipients held jobs. Indeed, one of the greatest failures of the War on Poverty was its inability to help the working poor. Almost half of black families still earned less than $5,000 a year; 18 percent of all families continued to live in poverty; and three out of every four Americans below the poverty line never received any assistance. Structural factors such as the decline in America's coal and industrial sectors, foreign competition, agricultural mechanization, or northward migration from Mexico had created economic dislocation for millions, but LBJ's plans did not include them. "Unwilling to back programs that challenged local political bosses, administration officials never even considered undertaking the struggle with major corporations to address the structural causes of poverty." The president's "unconditional war on poverty," in the end, "turned out to be not much more than a skirmish."[31]

Sundown for the Liberals – 1968

The legacy of the Great Society – mixed at best – by 1968 posed a great challenge to Lyndon Johnson in part and liberals nationally as well. Within the course of that year, the

American political landscape would be rocked by a series of upheavals and crises that would shatter the liberal order and alter the political context of American society. To be sure, the liberal reforms of the JFK and LBJ years did not disappear and indeed continued and in some part grew into the 1970s. But just as certainly, the heyday of liberalism had ended. Economic crisis, the Tet Offensive, political assassinations, labor problems, a grassroots movement of the poor, infighting among liberal groups, and a tumultous presidential campaign all contributed to the anguish of that year and led to a backlash against liberals. After 1968, American life would be much different than it had been earlier in the decade.

The first indications that the year would bring new problems came early. In January 1968 the Viet Cong began its Tet holiday Offensive, creating a political crisis in Washington, DC as LBJ had to scramble to explain how the enemy could conduct such widespread operations just months after the American military commander had assured the country that things were going well and there was "light at the end of the tunnel." At that same point, the balance of payments and gold crises erupted, forcing the president to take measures to reform the world financial structure and alter American hegemony. Adding insult to injury, North Korea seized a US Navy ship, the *Pueblo*, took the crew hostage, and charged them with espionage. America's leadership in the world, militarily and economically, was under attack. Vietnamese peasants could attack American installations and forces apparently at will, and European nations were demanding US action to prevent economic collapse and depression. Liberalism, the defining principle in the western war against fascism, in the restructured global political economy after 1945, and in the containment of radicalism abroad and at home, no longer seemed so effective a way to run the world.

At home, the crisis was more grave. The traditional liberal alliance between labor, blacks, Jews, and progressives came undone, the victim of attacks from New Left and right. Earlier in the decade, activists had envisioned a strong labor movement as the key to democratic reform, and unions had supported the earliest efforts to organize SDS and ERAP programs. But by the latter 1960s, labor and the left were at odds. Culturally, many working-class Americans were turned off by the angry rhetoric and lifestyles of the young; hardhats in New York City, for instance, even attacked an anti-war demonstration at one point. To many blue-collar and middle-class Democrats, the New Left and civil rights movements were a threat to their own livelihoods and security. "Yeah, I helped the War on Poverty," critics would joke, "I threw a hand grenade at a bum."[32] Institutionally, the left began to view labor as a static, bureaucratic giant, beholden to the Democratic Party and afraid of the rank-and-file, and the American Federation of Labor – Congress of Industrial Organizations continued to strongly support the war in Vietnam. Ironically, many white voters bolted from the Democrats because they saw liberalism as a tool to provide handouts to minorities at the expense of hard-working Caucasians.

Labor's own internal racial divisions became more public and troublesome as well. Indeed, the major labor issues of 1968 involved nonwhite workers in nonindustrial economic sectors. In March, Cesar Chávez, head of the United States Farm Workers Organizing Committee (USFWOC), began a hunger strike to gain recognition of his union, consisting mostly of Mexican- and Filipino-Americans, by grape growers in California. When the farmers began to negotiate with the USFWOC, Chávez and his associates still had to contend with the Teamsters Union, which, in its typical fashion, offered "sweetheart contracts" to the grape growers that did little for the workers. Nationally, liberals, labor, and religious leaders supported a Chávez-led boycott of grapes, and later lettuce, as a way to force the growers to deal with the FWOC, but national liberals, with the exception of Robert Kennedy, did not join the fray, thereby allowing the reactionary Governor Reagan, the growers, and the Teamsters to intimidate and bully the farm workers. African-Americans had their issues with organized labor and liberals as well. Black leaders would often charge that unions were protecting the jobs and incomes of white workers at the expense of blacks, while labor, a big

supporter of Martin Luther King and the civil rights movement in the early 1960s, was diverging from the black community later in the decade. When the Keynesian economy was
growing, it was easier for labor to support expanded rights
for minorities; but by 1968, the economic pie was shrinking
and unions were not feeling so charitable about expanding
opportunities for blacks or the poor.

As if the possibility of a mass of disaffected workers and
poor people protesting liberal inactivity and witholding support to the Party did not upset liberals enough, the Democrats themselves were involved in a kind of civil war in early
1968. During the previous fall, a liberal activist from New
York, Allard Lowenstein, began to seek a liberal candidate to
run for president in the coming election. His first choice to be
the "dump Johnson" candidate was a senator from New York
and brother of LBJ's predecessor, Robert F. Kennedy (RFK).
But Kennedy was reluctant to enter a race that he seemed
unlikely to win, so Lowenstein kept looking. Finally, Eugene
McCarthy of Minnesota, a critic of Johnson's Vietnam policies and the Senate's greatest wit (when Michigan Governor
George Romney changed from supporting the war to opposing it, claiming he had earlier been "brainwashed," McCarthy
suggested that "a light rinse would have done"), entered the
contest. Johnson and the Democratic establishment did not
really take McCarthy's candidacy seriously, but the senator
and an army of young activists who were "clean with Gene"
– they had shaved and began wearing more traditional clothing – undertook an impressive grassroots effort throughout
New Hampshire, the site of the first presidential primary in
March 1968. Because of their efforts, and the shock of Tet,
McCarthy made an unusually strong showing, garnering 42
percent of the vote against the sitting president. Kennedy, sens-
ing Johnson's vulnerability, then jumped into the race. With
the war raging and his political career crumbling, Lyndon
Johnson made a televised address to the nation on 31 March
and ended on a stunning note, withdrawing from the presidential race. LBJ, like so many others, had become a casualty
of the war in Vietnam and the War on Poverty.

Bobby Kennedy, who earlier in life had redbaited with Joe McCarthy and served as his brother's "ruthless" lieutenant on political matters, by 1968 was the last best hope of the liberals. Distraught by Vietnam and disillusioned by the elite nature of reform, RFK sought a new kind of politics himself. To Kennedy, the Democrats had to forge a new political co-alition. Organized labor and the south were no longer reli-able, but blacks, working-class whites, and "the kids" were. "Poverty," he came to believe, "is closer to the root of the problem than color," so the liberals needed to show that the "Negroes and the poor whites . . . have common interests."[33] Bobby Kennedy, like the New Left, Chávez, King and others, was talking about *class*, a concept usually ignored or repressed in political discourse in the United States. And he began to practice what he preached. Though it alienated big growers and gained him little support, Kennedy went to California to meet with Chávez and express his solidarity with the migrant (and thus nonvoting) farm workers. RFK, as Chávez saw it, looked at life "through the eyes of the poor . . . It was like he was ours." He reached out to inner-city blacks – lamenting that "today in America, we are two worlds" – and, upon hearing of King's death, deeply moved a crowd of African-Americans in Indiana with his heartfelt plea for racial coop-eration to "remove the stain of bloodshed from our land." Vine Deloria, a Native American activist, believed that "spir-itually, he was an Indian!"[34] Even "radicals" who had given up on the system were being drawn to his campaign. Perhaps participatory democracy could be realized after all!

In early June, after winning the California primary and promising a fight for the nomination at the Democratic con-vention, Kennedy spoke of such dreams: "What I think is quite clear, is that what has been going on within the United States over a period of the last three years . . . the divisions, whether it's between blacks and whites, between the poor and more affluent, or between age groups or on the war in Vietnam – is that we can start to work together." Looking ahead, RFK ral-lied his supporters with what would be his final words: "On to Chicago and let's win there." As he left the stage, he was

gunned down by Sirhan Sirhan, a Jordanian nationalist an-
gered by Kennedy's pro-Israel positions. Coming on the heels
of the King killing and other crises of that year, RFK's assassination plunged Americans into despair. Blacks, the poor, and
youth now had no-one to turn to for leadership. Even Tom
Hayden, who had little faith in the liberal system, was shaken,
lamenting that Kennedy's coffin held "all that remained of
last night's hopes of the poor." Sitting in the back of St Patrick's
Cathedral clutching a Cuban cap at the Kennedy funeral mass,
he wept openly.[35]

While it was not likely that Kennedy could have seized the
nomination from Hubert Humphrey – for the Vice-President
had the support of organized labor and the party's establishment – he probably would have done much more to prevent
the fiasco in Chicago in early 1968. Only Kennedy could speak
the language of equality, justice, and public morality that had
moved liberals in the 1960s. With Kennedy, and King, gone,
no leader who could unify the nation appeared on the scene.
The old Democratic coalition was tearing at the seams and
the schism would worsen in the latter part of the year, helping
to further daze liberals and create a political vacuum that the
right wing would fill. That fall, in a preview of future conflicts among traditional liberal constituencies, blacks and Jews
associated with the Ocean Hill-Brownsville school district in
New York City engaged in a virulent dispute over community
control of local schools. Ocean Hill-Brownsville was derided
as a "tiny piece of urban blight" and the schools were a mess.
Beginning in 1966, black activists demanded more control
over local education, arguing that they had a vested interest
in reforming a system in which the majority of students were
black but over 50 percent of the teachers were Jewish. John
Lindsey, the WASP ("White Anglo-Saxon Protestant") mayor
of New York, sided with the black activists while the liberal
United Federation of Teachers (UFT) and its president Albert
Shanker opposed plans to decentralize and restructure the
schools to accommodate African-American complaints. Inevitably, blacks and Jews were at odds. When the UFT went on
strike in 1967, many black teachers crossed the picket lines

and taught classes as a way of showing that they were in control of their own schools. Throughout the fall of 1968, all of New York's public schools were on strike and the labor conflict turned into a racial conflict as blacks and Jews grew increasingly bitter toward each other. By the time the dispute ended, with blacks in control of the local schools and Shanker and the UFT still representing the teachers, the old liberal coalition was badly damaged.

The various crises of 1968 to that point served as prologue to the presidential election. The Democrats' nominee was Vice-President Humphrey, a traditional liberal who was similar politically to LBJ. Another Democrat, the segregationist governor of Alabama, George Wallace, was also running. Disgusted with liberal attempts to help blacks and the poor, Wallace was challenging the Democratic establishment from the right. And for the Republicans, Richard Nixon was their standard-bearer. Eisenhower's Vice-President for eight years and the candidate who barely lost to JFK in 1960, Nixon cleverly exploited the liberals' crises that year and won the election with a little over 40 percent of the vote in the three-man race. But if Wallace's votes were added to Nixon's, conservatives gained well over half the vote, a huge renunciation of the liberals just four years after LBJ had won nearly two-thirds of the national vote. Humphrey received only 35 percent of the white vote and 30 percent of whites who had voted for LBJ in 1964 did not vote Democratic this time around. Both Wallace and Nixon were responsible for this political transformation. The Alabama governor attacked both parties, complaining that "there's not a dime's worth of difference" between the two but especially promising that the "intellectual morons" and the "theoreticians" in the Democratic Party were "going to get some of those liberal smiles knocked off their faces."[36]

Nixon likewise took advantage of the Democratic-liberal identification with blacks, the poor, and youth. Basing his campaign on a "secret plan" to end the war in Vietnam and restoring "law and order" at home – a thinly veiled use of racial buzzwords which implied a crackdown on blacks – Nixon reached out to disaffected white voters. His campaign ads flashed images of angry youth and other disaffected Americans while Nixon, in a voiceover, promised to "rebuild respect for law across this country." The Democrats, with Vietnam, their half-hearted efforts at reform, and the disastrous Chicago convention behind them, only made it easier for their opponents to attack successfully. Nixon, who had been one of liberalism's biggest enemies as a redbaiting representative and vice-president, now held the highest office in the land. Though as president, Nixon did not dismantle the liberal state, his election did signify that the high hopes of JFK's inaugural, the dreams of a Great Society, and the federal War on Poverty were ending, giving way to the blunt realities of the liberals' failures in Vietnam and at home. Ironically, the groups that had done so much to expose those failures – youth, blacks, disaffected working-class whites – were now looking at a sworn enemy of the liberal state enter the White House, and they were further outside the mainstream than ever before in that decade.

Concluding a moving eulogy to his brother in St Patrick's Cathedral, Senator Edward Kennedy repeated one of RFK's favorite sayings: "some men see things as they are and ask why. I dream things that never were, and say why not?" Those eloquent words could serve as a requiem for the 1960s as well. Throughout the decade, liberal politicians and intellectuals saw poverty, inequality, and racial conflict and asked why; others dreamed of a new politics of democracy and inclusion and wondered why not. Neither question was ever satisfactorily answered. Taking advantage of the nation's great wealth, liberals had tried to create a Great Society, but did not provide adequate funding or channel aid to those who needed it most. Johnson's War on Poverty, in the end, consisted more of "poor laws" than real welfare. But liberal ideology would allow no more that that. Participatory democracy and empowerment – the mantra of the New Left – threatened the established order. Maintaining the status quo, along with trying to contain a growing and grueling war in Vietnam, dominated the liberal political agenda and ultimately undermined effective reform. People's lives had improved in the

1960s, legislation to improve health care and education and measures to reduce poverty had made an impact, but those who needed help most were most likely to be excluded, and the social and economic structure that had created the problems in the first place was not being addressed. Critics of the liberal state thus attacked it firmly and effectively, and by 1968 few people even mentioned the "Great Society" any more.

Those critics of liberalism were stifled as well. Rhetoric about, and experiments in, participatory democracy finally crashed as students in the New Left could not identify with the poor and could not survive political repression, and, most importantly, had shifted priorities to fight the war in Vietnam, becoming far more militant and alienated along the way. Their "new kind of politics," involving popular democracy and community empowerment, could not survive the bureaucratic assault of liberal institutions or the Vietnam War. Though the New Left had done much to delegitimize liberalism, when that ideology was rocked in 1968 the fragmented left was not there to offer alternative leadership, but George Wallace and Richard Nixon were. The great hope and promise of a liberal world had all but evaporated by then, though liberal reforms hung on. Robert Frost could not have known about the eventual scope of Vietnam or the Great Society, but he had presciently described the coming decade on that cold January day in 1961: "the deed of gift" was indeed "many deeds of war."

7

The Struggles at Home: Civil Rights and Women's Liberation

By themselves, Vietnam and the War on Poverty created grave problems and began to transform American society in the 1960s. But, exacerbating such conditions, the American people also witnessed the most monumental struggles for African-American Civil Rights (CR) and justice and for women's liberation in modern US history. Though both movements had long histories of their own, they were particularly well mobilized and effective in the 1960s and, because of the war in Vietnam and domestic reactions to it, became increasingly militant as the decade moved forward. Thus, what began in 1960 as political reform within the liberal system became a fundamental challenge to the structure of the liberal state. Along with other groups such as Mexican-Americans, Native Americans, gays, and environmentalists, to name a few, blacks and women gained a measure of empowerment and equality and, like the New Left, challenged and helped transform life in the United States, creating opportunities and engendering opposition along the way.

Morality and Politics: The Modern Civil Rights Movement

From the moment that slaves from Africa arrived in Virginia in 1619, the United States had a racial problem. Over three centuries later, despite a Civil War, constitutional amendments, and federal laws, an apartheid system still existed in which African-Americans in the south were legally denied the fundamental rights to accommodation, transportation, public education, the franchise, and other aspects of life that white people took for granted. Blacks themselves, since the founding of the Republic, had been pointing out the illegal, immoral, and hypocritical nature of such racial division in a self-proclaimed democracy, but without a great deal of success. Beginning in the mid-1950s, however, black activists and everyday people would make a revolution in racial politics in America. Driven by moral outrage and keen political instincts, politicians, ministers, working people, housewives, students, and children would conduct a frontal assault on southern segregation and successfully dismantle legal apartheid in the states of the old Confederacy. But once that was accomplished, African-American leaders shifted their sights on northern, *de facto*, segregation, where the movement would founder. By the late 1960s, conditions for black Americans would be considerably better than a decade earlier, but well short of the democratic ideals of equality that had inspired the movement early on.

The first major crack in the southern segregation system came in October 1954, when the US Supreme Court, in the famous *Brown v. Board of Education of Topeka, Kansas* case, ruled that separate schools for black and white students were "inherently unequal." Throughout the south, local districts had established different public schools for Caucasian and African-American students, with the white kids naturally receiving much more funding and better resources. The Court, unanimously, held that educational facilities would have to be integrated, but, rather than set a specific date for schools to comply with the ruling, only ordered that desegregation occur with "all deliberate speed" – an ambiguous concept that would cause more problems. In 1957, in a major national test of *Brown*, the segregationist governor of Arkansas, Orval Faubus, ordered the National Guard out to prevent nine black students from enrolling at Central High School in Little Rock. After a few weeks of negotiations and court injunctions failed to settle the issue, President Eisenhower ordered the Army's 101st Airborne Division into Little Rock to safeguard the students' entry into Central High. If the *Brown* decision was going to be effective, the federal government was going to have to provide the means of enforcement.

At the same time, African-Americans were taking matters into their own hands, especially in Montgomery, Alabama. On 1 December 1955, the secretary of the local NAACP chapter, *Rosa Parks*, refused to give her seat on a city bus to a white man and was promptly arrested. Local black leaders, led by E. D. Nixon, thought that her arrest could be used as a test case against the bus system and decided to rally the community behind Parks, even though her husband was quite uneasy, warning her that "those white folks will kill you, Rosa." More importantly, the Women's Political Council at the Dexter Avenue Baptist Church, which had only recently been organized by a young minister new to Montgomery, put out a flyer "asking every Negro to stay off the buses on Monday [Parks's court date] in protest of the arrest and trial" – thus began the *Montgomery Bus Boycott*. The minister at Dexter Avenue Baptist, *Martin Luther King, Jr*, became the leader of the boycott movement and, for over a year, he coordinated the effort by Montgomery's blacks to walk and organize car pools in defiance of local segregation practices. Despite injunctions and arrests, the African-American community did not bend and, on 20 December 1956, after local negotiations and a Supreme Court case desegregating bus transportation was decided, blacks won the right to sit wherever they wanted on city buses. That combination of local action and federal support would become a keystone of the early CR years. While Supreme Court cases and government laws would help dismantle southern apartheid, it was the grassroots mobilization and organization of the black community itself that kept the issue in the public eye and put pressure on politicians and the media to do something about the segregated race system in the south.[1]

By 1960, on the heels of *Brown*, the Montgomery boycott, Little Rock, and numerous local actions throughout the south,

CR had clearly become a major issue on the national agenda. The American response, however, was ambivalent. Southern racists still forcefully opposed any attempt to desegregate their communities, while northern politicians offered support to the African-American movement, but only to a point. To many northerners and liberals, the southern system was an anachronism and the open discrimination against blacks a blight. As America waged Cold War against the Communist nations, it was imperative to have its own house in order before criticizing the "Reds" for their own violations of civil and human rights, so dealing with the African-American question was a political necessity. In addition, liberals believed that the key to America's continued global leadership was constant economic growth, and thus it was important to them to bring the southern states into the modern liberal system, and segregation and economic deprecation of a significant portion of the population made that task impossible. Liberals, to paraphrase a famous scholar of the old south, were trying to create "middle-class whites in black skin." For a time, the strategy worked, as the federal government, after wavering and handwringing, would enact moderate measures to dismantle segregation and place some black groups within the mainstream of American politics. When African-Americans wanted to do more than that, however, the movement would face a crisis.

The First Thing We Did Right, Was the Day We Started to Fight

In late 1959, in a speech to fellow pacifists, Martin Luther King (MLK) predicted that southern blacks would engage in "direct action against injustice without waiting for other agencies to act . . . We will not obey unjust laws or submit to unjust practices."[2] He was right. On 1 February 1960, four black students from North Carolina A&T went to a Woolworth lunch counter in Greensboro, took seats and asked for service, and were refused. They finally left when the store closed. A few days later, hundreds of A&T students held a demonstration in Greensboro and marched on the lunch counters. When white mobs asked "who do you think you are?" the A&T football team responded "we are the Union Army" and formed a wedge for the black demonstrators to rush the counter. From such spontaneous acts of defiance emerged one of the largest protest movements in American history. Word of the initial Greensboro action, termed a *sit-in*, filtered through black communities and students throughout the south began to do likewise. Soon, sit-ins occurred in various cities in North Carolina, spread to Virginia and then into Tennessee, Kentucky, and Maryland. By mid-April, black activists, especially students, had conducted sit-ins in all the southern states, with about 50,000 blacks and whites participating. In some cases, white onlookers physically assaulted blacks sitting at lunch counters, and even when they did not, they verbally attacked and threatened them. Still, the students, in line with King's philosophy, renounced violence and their behavior impressed some in the white community. Even James Kilpatrick, a segregationist columnist in Richmond, wrote about the contrast between the "colored students in coats, white shirts, and ties" and the white hecklers – a "ragtail rabble, slack-jawed, black-jacketed, grinning fit to kill" and waving the Confederate flag.[3]

Despite their appearance and demeanor, the students had a hard time getting mainstream support. Many northern liberals and even national black organizations like the NAACP feared that the sit-ins were too militant and could provoke an even greater attack on southern blacks. King and his organization, the Southern Christian Leadership Conference (SCLC), thought otherwise. They threw their support and resources behind the sit-ins, helping to coordinate them and raise bail for those demonstrators, nearly 4,000, arrested for trying to desegregate lunch counters. Most importantly, an SCLC officer, *Ella Baker*, organized a conference of young black activists that would give rise to the most important protest group in the CR era, the *Student Nonviolent Coordinating Committee* (SNCC, or "Snick"). Out of SNCC would come many of the leaders of the African-American struggle in the

1960s, including John Lewis, Diane Nash, Julian Bond, James Lawson, Marion Barry, and many others. SNCC would take a different approach to CR than older, established groups. Articulate and confrontational, SNCC activists would have a hand in all the major CR actions of the decade. SNCC members became the prime target of southern hatred and violence, but to other young activists across the country they held a special place and served as role models for other movements. Tom Hayden believed that SNCC activists "lived on a fuller level of feeling . . . because by risking death they came to know the value of living each moment to the fullest . . . I wanted to live like them."[4]

Most establishment black leaders and white liberals, however, feared that the sit-ins and SNCC were too militant and aggressive and would provoke an even greater white backlash. But MLK continued to back the movement and agreed to join a protest, albeit reluctantly, in Atlanta in mid-October. Arrested, King and 36 others chose "jail, not bail" in line with their Gandhian principles of civil disobedience – willfully breaking unjust laws and accepting the consequences. While waiting trial, the Reverend received a sentence of four months of hard labor for violating the terms of an earlier arrest for a traffic offense. His wife, Coretta, six months pregnant, contacted an old friend and member of JFK's campaign staff, Harris Wofford, and cried "they are going to kill him, I know they are going to kill him" – a fate not uncommon to jailed blacks in the south. Immediately, Kennedy called Mrs King to express his concern and his brother Bobby used the family's connections to arrange bond for MLK and get him released from jail. That Sunday, King's father, "Daddy King," one of the better-known ministers in the south, and scores of other African-American clergy endorsed Kennedy for president during their sermons. Up to that point the Republican candidate, Richard Nixon, was enjoying fairly large black support, but Kennedy eventually received over 75 percent of the black vote, a decisive amount in a close victory over Nixon. King was grateful and optimistic that he could work with JFK and envisioned a relationship with the president like that of Frederick Douglass with Abraham Lincoln during the Civil War, serving as a moral voice to pressure national action on race issues. Like Douglass, King would face challenges at every step along the way.

While the Kennedy administration would offer support to CR, it also valued traditional southern support and did not want to alienate loyal Democratic segregationists, so JFK's behavior on racial issues would be ambivalent and tentative. African-Americans generally were enthused by Kennedy's victory and the new president made symbolic overtures to the black community as well; many of the same Hollywood celebrities that had celebrated JFK's inaugural – including Frank Sinatra, Sammy Davis, Count Basie, Dean Martin, Tony Bennett, Nipsey Russell, and others – had a gala fundraiser for King a week afterwards and raised over $50,000 for the SCLC.

During the first CR crisis of his presidency, however, Kennedy wavered. In the summer of 1961 the national director of the Congress On Racial Equality (CORE), James Farmer, organized a series of *"freedom rides."* The rides involved a challenge to laws that segregated interstate travel, by having black and white activists travel together by bus throughout the south. CORE's approach was admittedly confrontational. "Our intention," Farmer proclaimed, "was to provoke the Southern authorities into arresting us and thereby prod the Justice Department into enforcing the laws of the land." Rather than arrest the riders, however, authorities in South Carolina and Alabama simply looked the other way as white mobs attacked and beat the CORE members. The original riders, battered and injured, then flew to New Orleans, but SNCC activists, led by John Lewis, traveled to Montgomery to resume the rides. They too were immediately savaged as they stepped off their bus. No police were in sight as the white mob grew to nearly a thousand. Finally, after three weeks of wavering, Attorney-General Robert Kennedy sent 400 marshalls to Montgomery to protect the riders, but also called on CORE and SNCC to end the rides and "cool off." They refused, with

Farmer explaining that blacks "had been cooling off for a hundred years. If we got any cooler, we'd be in a deep freeze."[5]

So the rides continued. Over 1,000 Americans – northern and southern, black and white – participated, over 300 were arrested, and countless others were intimidated and attacked. Their sacrifice finally paid off, though. In late 1961, the Interstate Commerce Commission banned segregation in interstate travel and most southern communities began to comply with the laws in 1962. If whites could be provoked into violent responses to CR demonstrations, the freedom riders proved, then the media would report on it and politicians would have to act. That scenario would only become more common as the struggle continued. Indeed, blacks continued to defy authority and fill jails in 1962. In Albany, Georgia, the main CR theater in 1962, one out of twenty African-Americans spent time behind bars, much to the satisfaction of Police Sheriff Laurie Pritchett, who was fond of saying that he followed a policy of "mind over matter" because whites "didn't mind" and blacks "didn't matter." Southern governors such as Ross Barnett of Mississippi and George Wallace of Alabama believed likewise, and made defiant public stands against the admission of black students into state universities.

Enemies North and South

Racist southerners, however, were not the movement's only enemies at the time. Northern liberals, as the mixed Kennedy response to the freedom rides had shown, were wary of the confrontational nature of the CR actions in 1961–2. The Department of Justice did little to investigate the myriad cases of police brutality and lynchings against blacks, while the FBI did less because it was afraid of being seen as "a crusader on civil rights." Other liberals redbaited the movement, claiming that it had been infiltrated and taken over by subversives. Militants, the liberal journalist James Wechsler wrote, were "staging an uprising against the major civil rights blocs . . . encouraged by a fragment of Communists."[6]

In particular, liberals attacked King's relationship with Stanley Levinson, an SCLC adviser with past ties to the US Communist Party. Though the Atlanta office of the FBI found no evidence of Red influence over the SCLC, the reactionary head of the Bureau, J. Edgar Hoover, rejected their conclusion and, with Kennedy's approval, began conducting surveillance on King and other movement leaders, reporting on all facets of their public and private lives. At one point the Bureau suggested to King, who was having extramarital affairs, that he should commit suicide to avoid embarrassing the movement if word of his dalliances got out – as if the FBI supported CR in the first place. In fact, Hoover publicly called King the "most notorious liar" and "one of the lowest characters" in America, and another FBI official considered the Reverend "the most dangerous Negro . . . in this nation from the standpoint of Communism . . . and national security."[7]

King's southern foes were, of course, even less tolerant of the CR struggle. In April 1963, in one of the epic battles of the era, King began a campaign to desegregate Birmingham, Alabama businesses at Eastertime, traditionally one of the busiest and most profitable times of the year. Eugene "Bull" Connor, who fit the image of the "redneck" sheriff better than anything Hollywood could have invented, used attack dogs and fire hoses to disperse marchers, and jailed hundreds of black protestors – including King. Various Protestant, Catholic, and Jewish clergy criticized the demonstrations as untimely, provocative, and illegal. *Time* magazine called it a "poorly timed protest"; the *Washington Post* sneered at its "doubtful utility"; and the *New York Times* gushed that a "warm sun was shining" on Birmingham under the leadership of a new mayor, while the "giggles of little girls" at his inaugural was a welcome relief from the "sounds of demonstrations" of black protestors.

King responded with his classic "Letter from a Birmingham Jail" in which he confessed to being "gravely disappointed with the white moderate." Not unlike Frederick Douglass's oration on "What to the Slave is the Fourth of July?" King attacked southern racism and northern liberalism, wondering

whether whites who claimed to support CR were more committed to "order" than to justice and might be a greater barrier to racial progress than the Ku Klux Klan. King was tired
of northern calls for him to go slowly:

> For years now, I have heard the word "Wait!" . . . This "wait" has
> almost always meant "Never." We have waited more than 340 years
> for our constitutional and God-given rights . . . Perhaps it is easy for
> those who have never felt the stinging darts of segregation to say
> "Wait." But . . . when your first name becomes "nigger," your middle
> name becomes "boy" . . . when you are harried by day and haunted
> by night by the fact that you are a negro . . . when you are forever
> fighting a degenerating sense of "nobodiness" – then you will under-
> stand why we find it difficult to wait.[8]

King's powerful letter, however, did not end the protests in
Birmingham. That would be up to the local African-American population, especially the children. With so many blacks
jailed or awaiting trial, the movement was running out of demonstrators, so King made one of the more controversial decisions of his career, approving of a plan to let Birmingham
schoolchildren march in protest. On 3 May 1963, with nearly
a thousand black children inside the Sixteenth Street Baptist
Church, Bull Connor had police bar the doors. Hundreds of
kids escaped, however, and joined a crowd in a park across
the street. Incredibly, Connor ordered his troops to attack.
The ensuing scenes – police swinging clubs, German Shepherd dogs lunging at children, water hoses knocking young
protestors down – shocked Americans as they turned on network news that evening, while newspapers throughout the
world ran the Birmingham story and photos on the front page
the next day. The Kennedy administration was finally forced
to act, dispatching representatives to Alabama to mediate a
settlement and pressuring both Birmingham's white businessmen and black leaders to reach a compromise. In the meantime, the demonstrations continued, with Connor still using
dogs and water hoses and Governor Wallace sending in armed
state troopers to reinforce the Birmingham police. But the
boycott was working and Birmingham commerce was suffering heavy losses. Finally, on 10 May, both sides reached a

settlement to end the protests in return for desegregating public facilities and making jobs available to blacks. The combination of aggressive nonviolence, media attention, and especially the persistence and sacrifice of Birmingham's blacks had paid off and created the greatest CR triumph to that point.

We Shall Overcome

Connor, Wallace, and other segregationists had unwittingly given JFK an opening. Their violent responses so sickened the nation that the president felt secure enough politically to finally seek federal CR legislation to prevent further Birminghams. Speaking to the nation in early June, Kennedy asserted that "now the time has come for this nation to fulfill its promise . . . The fires of frustration are burning in every city, North and South, where legal remedies are not at hand. Redress is sought in the streets, in . . . protests which create tensions and threaten violence and threaten lives." The president would thus ask Congress for laws "giving all Americans the right to be served in facilities which are open to the public – hotels, restaurants, theaters, retail stores, and similar establishments."[9] Southern senators – including J. William Fulbright, soon to be a hero of the anti-war movement and the New Left – blocked the legislation, however, and by late summer the chances for passage were not good. King thus resurrected an old strategy, first posed by the black labor leader A. Philip Randolph during World War II: a huge rally in Washington, DC to agitate for CR laws. The president, still fearing southern backlash, told King that the demonstration was "ill-timed," to which the Reverend replied that "I have never engaged in any direct-action movement which did not seem ill-timed. Some people thought Birmingham ill-timed."[10]

The subsequent demonstration, the famous *March on Washington* of August 1963, drew over 300,000 Americans of all races and from all regions to express their support for CR legislation. Joan Baez and Peter, Paul, and Mary sang "Blowin' In The Wind" and Dylan himself performed for the first time

"Only a Pawn in Their Game," a haunting ballad about the murder of Mississippi CR leader Medgar Evers. Odetta, Harry Belafonte, Sammy Davis, Jr, James Garner, Dihann Carroll, Sidney Poitier, Marlon Brando, Ossie Davis and Ruby Dee, and Charlton Heston were among the dozens of celebrities on the stage supporting the march. Bayard Rustin, labor leader and demonstration organizer, announced the movement's demands, including passage of the CR bill, a $2 an hour minimum wage, school desegregation, a federal jobs program, and federal laws against employment discrimination. Without doubt, however, the highlight was King's stirring "I Have a Dream" oration, one of the greatest speeches in US history. King dreamed of the United States becoming an "oasis of freedom and justice" in which all Americans would "not be judged by the color of their skin but by the content of their character," and he concluded with words from an old Negro spiritual, "Free at last, free at last: thank God almighty, we are free at last."[11]

The March on Washington put great moral force behind the CR bill and presented the nation with an indelible image of the dignity and strength of King and other African-American leaders. But the legislation was stalled in a Congress which, despite the public's horror at the scenes from Birmingham and its support of King's speech, could be quite hostile to CR. In fact, in September 1963, after a tragic bombing of a church in Birmingham which killed four young black girls, only a handful of senators would even write a resolution proclaiming the Sunday after the bombing as a national day of mourning, and then they did not even present it to their colleagues because of lack of support. In late November, with Kennedy's shocking assassination in Dallas, the future of CR was uncertain at best. With a southerner, Lyndon Johnson of Texas, entering the White House, black leaders who had only won over JFK after years of vacillating were wary about the future of racial progress. But LBJ, who considered himself open-minded on racial matters and wanted to emulate FDR's appeal to the downtrodden, vowed to carry on Kennedy's work, pledging his support for the bill and even concluding a televised speech on CR with words from the old spiritual that served as an anthem for the movement, "We Shall Overcome." In 1964, then, Johnson used his considerable political skills to secure passage of the *Civil Rights Act*, which outlawed segregated public accommodations such as restaurants, restrooms, or businesses; authorized the federal government to take legal action on behalf of discriminated individuals; established a federal Equal Employment Opportunities Commission (EEOC) to investigate racially harmful hiring practices; and barred racial discrimination in federally funded programs. The militant nonviolence of Birmingham and moral force of Washington had worked magic in 1964, it seemed.

On the Fourth of July, 1964, the headline of the Columbia, South Carolina *State* read "Southern Segregation Falls Silently, Without Violence" after passage of the CR Act. That message did not make it to Mississippi that summer, however. SNCC and other CR groups organized "*Freedom Summer*" to showcase segregation in Mississippi and force the government to act. Black and white students poured into the state to organize local African-Americans and register them to vote. Only about 7 percent of eligible blacks were registered at that time and in many rural counties, no blacks were even on the voting lists. In return, Mississippi whites, mostly associated with the "Mississippi State Sovereignty Commission" – a quasi-official racist group with close ties to the state government – began a reign of terror. They burned 35 black churches and bombed 30 buildings; shot 35 people, severely beat 80 others, and murdered six, all with little national attention, probably because the victims were black.

In August, however, when Andrew Goodman and Michael Schwerner, CORE workers from New York, along with CR volunteer James Chaney of Mississippi were found dead in a swamp near Philadelphia, Mississippi, the media took notice, likely because Goodman and Schwerner were white. Again, events forced the federal government to act, and the Justice Department sent the FBI to Mississippi to investigate the murders. At the same time, however, the Johnson administration refused to seat a delegation from Mississippi – the Mississippi

Freedom Democratic Party, or MFDP – at that summer's Democratic convention, instead authorizing the official racist white delegates to vote on the convention floor. Indeed, when Fanny Lou Hamer, a sharecropper who headed the MFDP, offered moving testimony about life as a black woman in Mississippi, LBJ hastily called a press conference to pre-empt her appearance at the convention. Even after that evening's news showcased Hamer nonetheless, the Democrats would only designate the MFDP as "honored guests" – a compromise the delegates rejected as "evidence of liberal hypocrisy and pervasive racism" within the party, and they then left the convention. One activist, connecting the major issues of the day, explained that the president's refusal "to negotiate with the Viet Cong is like the power structure of Mississippi not wanting to negotiate with the MFDP."[12] The whole affair harmed LBJ little at the time – he won well over 90 percent of the black vote that November – but the relationship between African-Americans and liberals was sure to be revisited later.

In 1964, blacks were encouraged by LBJ's landslide victory, believing that he now had a national mandate to follow through with his commitment to desegregation and build on the success of the CR Act. At the grassroots level, however, African-Americans still held the key to effective action. In March 1965, King – who had just returned from Norway where he had received the 1964 Nobel Peace Prize – moved into Selma, Alabama to work on a SNCC voter registration project. Again the movement was met with violence by southern whites as Sheriff Jim Clark called together a posse and Governor Wallace deployed 500 state troopers, all of whom met the black marchers at the Edmund Pettus Bridge and beat them with clubs, cattle prods, and bullwhips while white onlookers cheered the assault. The events on "Bloody Sunday," as it became known, and the subsequent murder of a white CR volunteer, Viola Liuzzo of Detroit, shot to death by Klansmen on her way out of Selma, again shocked the nation. LBJ thus went on television just days later to denounce the mobs at Selma and announce plans to secure voting rights for southern blacks. The resulting legislation, the *Voting Rights*

Act, would mark the denouement of the movement. Passed in August 1965, the Act barred literacy tests as a requirement for blacks to vote, and sent federal officials to register African-Americans wherever they were being denied the right to vote. After a decade of struggle, the legal barriers to segregation had been eliminated. Court decisions and federal initiatives such as the Civil and Voting Rights Acts now offered blacks rights and opportunities they had not enjoyed before. The resistance and sacrifice of King and so many others had paid off.

But the movement was now at a crossroads as well. King and others were not content to rest on their success and wanted the struggle to continue, not just in the south but throughout the United States, and not just for blacks but for all poor people. They would soon discover the limits of reform.

Civil Rights and the Vietnam War

Selma and the Voting Rights Act came at the precise time that LBJ was committing the first US ground forces to Vietnam and then "Americanizing" the war, and from that point onward Vietnam and CR would be intricately linked in American life. The war would ultimately overshadow the African-American struggle, end the sense of liberal hope that had opened the decade, and create great splits in the movement itself. King, the moral voice of desegregation, would become an angry critic of Vietnam, and CR would not again have the same levels of public support that it enjoyed earlier in the decade. King especially saw the connections between the war and racial justice, telling a Howard University audience in early 1965 that "the war in Vietnam is accomplishing nothing," and in July calling for a negotiated settlement with the VC. When challenged by reporters about his authority to speak out against the war, the Reverend told them that he was "much more than a civil rights leader" and that Vietnam did indeed affect domestic political issues.[13]

Younger and more radical blacks went further. Eldridge

Cleaver pointed out that "those who most bitterly oppose Negro progress are also the most ardent advocates of a belligerent foreign policy"; and Stokely Carmichael of SNCC warned blacks that when LBJ "talks all that garbage about he's sending boys over there to fight for the rights of colored people, you ought to know that's a lie. 'Cause we live here with them, and they don't ever do a thing for us." The war, as he brilliantly described it, was a case of "white people sending black people to make war on yellow people to defend the land they stole from Red people."[14] By the mid-1960s, then, Vietnam was becoming the dominant issue in American life, as King's powerful speech in April 1967 indicated. The war also radicalized the CR movement and brought it into convergence with the anti-war movement. Students involved in the struggles to end segregation and the war, as the radical journalist I. F. Stone explained, "compare the one rebellion with the other and are doubly revolted." In Vietnam the United States had 150,000 soldiers in 1965, but in the south there were fewer than 150 voting registrars.[15] Even as some mainstream black groups such as the NAACP and CORE were reluctant to take a public stand on Vietnam, many other African-Americans were furious over the commitment to Indochina at their expense. Within a few years, as they feared, Vietnam would transform and help destroy the movement.

Critics from Within

Even before the national emphasis on Vietnam began to affect CR, the movement had to address criticism from other black representatives. Indeed, King, the Nobel Prize winner who had worked with JFK and LBJ on CR legislation, came under attack from some quarters for his alliances with white liberals. The black nationalist and spokesman for the Nation of Islam, *Malcolm X*, was King's most vocal critic. Where King came from an educated and relatively prosperous background and spoke for southern blacks fighting legal segregation, Malcolm, an ex-convict familiar with the streets, represented the rage of urban and young blacks who believed that the reality of African-American life in the north – where discrimination was based on economic power and a *de facto* condition rather than the law – was little better than below the Mason–Dixon Line. Indeed, he was fond of saying that the US South was "everything below Canada." Malcolm rejected cooperation or accommodation with white America and dismissed claims of improvement in black life – "you don't stick a knife in a man's back nine inches," he explained, "and then pull it out six inches and say you're making progress." Instead he called on blacks to reject white society and work for their own liberation "by any means necessary." The August 1963 demonstration was "The Farce on Washington" as he saw it, and its leaders were "Toms" who had been bought off or hoodwinked by JFK's people. Even many who disagreed with his views respected Malcolm X. "His early rhetoric," as the philosopher Cornel West described it, was "too honest, too candid, precisely the things black folk often felt but never said publicly due to fear of white retaliation, even in the early 60s. In fact, his piercing rhetoric had primarily a cathartic function for black people; it purged them of their deferential and defensive attitudes toward white people."[16]

Younger activists especially followed Malcolm's approach. At the 1963 march, for instance, SNCC Chair John Lewis was prepared to deliver a fiery denunciation of Kennedy's CR bill as "too little, and too late," the product of "cheap political leaders who built their careers on immoral compromises," and to attack the administration for its slow response to white assaults on southern blacks and movement workers and its appointment of "racist judges." SNCC and the black "masses," Lewis vowed, would take matters into their own hands and, nonviolently, "crack the South into a thousand pieces and put them back together in the image of democracy." "The Revolution," he declared, "is at hand!" But Lewis did not deliver that speech. King and other black leaders, afraid of insulting the Kennedys and killing the CR bill, forced the SNCC leader to take out his militant message, while two of JFK's aides were ready to "pull the plug" on the public address system if Lewis's message was too radical. Other activists, such as Cleveland Sellers of SNCC and James Forman of CORE, were also disillusioned by the march and what they saw as the "take-over" by the white liberal establishment. To Forman, "fancy productions" like the August 1963 demonstration gave blacks a sense of satisfaction "when, in fact, nothing had been changed."[17]

Burn, Baby, Burn!: Northern Rage

Malcolm X too believed that CR legislation had not come near solving America's race problems. As he saw it, so long as whites controlled social institutions – banks, companies, politics – black progress would be minimal. Blacks, he urged, should own businesses and run their own neighborhoods and cities. "Once you gain control of the economy of your own community," he pointed out, "then you don't have to picket and boycott and beg some cracker downtown for a job in his business." To Malcolm, the CR movement, while ending legal discrimination in the south, did not speak to the concerns of northern blacks such as lack of jobs and low wages, inadequate housing, no health care, or poor education. Blacks, he argued, were being denied their human rights, not just civil rights, and the African-American crisis in the United States was part of a worldwide system of white domination of people of color. "The same man" oppressing the people of Vietnam or the Congo, he noted, was "the same man, the same enemy, opposing the black people in Detroit."[18]

Malcolm X, however, never had the opportunity to bring his message to the black masses as King had. In February 1965 – as he was softening some of his militant nationalist views and reaching out somewhat to King and other CR groups – he was assassinated by rival Black Muslims. African-Americans had been deprived, again, of a powerful spokesman for radical change. Others, however, would follow through on Malcolm's mission, and white liberals would discover that northern blacks had their own critique of American society.

In early 1965, King's own position had been moving toward Malcolm's. Still an "apostle of militant nonviolence," King was also broadening his own analysis of US society to include the north. "Some of our most nagging problems in the future will be in the big cities of the North on the areas of jobs and schools and housing," he understood at the time of Malcolm's death.[19] Indeed, King was advocating a system in which, as in many countries of Western Europe and Scandinavia, the government would provide free health care, create jobs, and more equally distribute wealth. America "must move toward a democratic socialism," he announced.[20] To a large degree, King's views were being shaped by the visible anger of northern blacks, and he was being led by grassroots blacks as much as leading. In August 1965, in the most destructive racial uprising prior to the 1992 Rodney King rebellion (riots after an unpopular court case acquitting police of beating a black man), blacks in the Watts section of Los Angeles, following a case of police brutality, rebelled. Over 30 African-Americans were killed, over 100 injured, and over $40 million in property was destroyed.

To King, the LA uprising was tragic and counterproductive; "fewer people have been killed in ten years of nonviolent demonstrations across the South," he pointed out, "than were killed in one night of riots in Watts." Nor did the rebellion lead to jobs or housing, and, in fact, most whites blamed African-Americans for the destruction and found them "ungrateful" for the progress of previous years. In one poll, 75 percent of whites thought that blacks were gaining too many rights too soon. King recognized that the movement had entered a new phase and "the paths of Negro–white unity . . . began to diverge." The "first phase" of CR, 1954–65, had been a struggle "to treat the Negro with a degree of dignity, not of equality." When blacks looked for a "second phase, the realization of equality," they discovered that many white allies had "quietly disappeared."[21]

King's liberal allies had not disappeared so much as shifted their attentions to Vietnam at the expense of race relations. Indeed, Vietnam was exacerbating the divide between

American blacks and whites. Twice as many blacks fought and died in the war, in proportion to population, as whites, while the United States spent over $300,000 per each enemy killed in Vietnam, vastly more than the amount spent on jobs and education combined for blacks. The war in Indochina, moreover, alienated and angered many blacks who charged the government with racism and hypocrisy for attacking nonwhite peoples (not just in Vietnam but Africa as well) and for praising the passive resistance of the CR movement but then sending, as King put it, "black young men to burn Vietnamese with napalm, to slaughter men, women and children." The Reverend wondered "what kind of nation it is that applauds nonviolence whenever Negroes face white people in the streets . . . but then applauds violence and burning and death when those same Negroes are sent to the field in Vietnam."[22] Indeed, King's increasing public criticism of Vietnam in the mid-1960s marked his transformation from a CR leader only to a radical spokesperson for all marginalized Americans. King even suggested that Vietnam was in large part responsible for much of the urban tumult of the era. The racial implications of a war against "gooks" was not unnoticed by people of color in the United States, and the behavior of the forces of order, politicians and police forces, was analogous to America's military response in Vietnam. Little wonder, then, that white leaders, who had praised King's passivism, were now, as the Reverend charged, jumping ship. In the summer of 1966, for instance, King decided to bring the movement to the north, to Chicago, where he would agitate for decent housing in the ghettos and advocate the formation of tenant unions against the slum lords, many allied with Mayor Daley, who controlled black communities.

The Chicago campaign, however, was far from successful. As one of King's close associates, Andrew Young, explained, "genuine school integration, housing integration, and employment opportunity for poor blacks was going to require real sacrifices," and white people were not as accommodating to such goals as they had been to southern desegregation.[23] Moreover, King, as Malcolm had earlier charged, did not really understand the depths of urban black rage and his non-violent, albeit aggressive, approach was called into question. Combined with a hostile media, court injunctions, and Daley's ability to upstage King and provide favors to black leaders in Chicago, the movement was constantly on the defensive. King also saw that northern whites could be quite similar to their southern brethren: during one demonstration, thousands of whites threw rocks and bottles at King and his associates, burned cars, wore Klan attire, and waved Nazi and Confederate flags. Later, the Reverend would tell reporters that he had "never seen – even in Mississippi and Alabama – mobs as hostile and hate-filled as I've seen in Chicago."[24]

To avoid further violence, Daley and King negotiated a settlement in which the city and white realtors "promised" to make housing available to Chicago blacks, a move denounced by many local African-American activists as a "sellout" to the white power structure. King, lucky to have survived, left Chicago bitter and more radicalized. His rhetoric was sounding like that of the New Left as much as that of a baptist minister as he began to link southern CR, northern racism, economic injustice, and the Vietnam War in a comprehensive critique of corporate liberalism. Throughout 1966–7, then, he began to more stridently attack the war, call for a guaranteed annual income for all Americans, support union registration and strikes, and consequently frustrate, if not infuriate, his white allies. Ironically, even as King was becoming more militant, younger blacks were moving far beyond the Reverend, further complicating the CR struggle in America.

Black Power!

Even during the heyday of southern desegregation, many black leaders such as Malcolm X, John Lewis and his SNCC comrades, Jim Forman, and others sought a more militant posture. By 1966, with memories of Watts and Chicago still fresh and the war in Vietnam growing and taking up resources that were earmarked for anti-poverty programs, younger African-

Americans began to abandon the earlier bi-racial coalition that had worked on the Civil and Voting Rights Acts and, instead of settling for laws to prevent segregation, now demanded *Black Power*. Stokely Carmichael, new president of SNCC in 1966, described Black Power as a "call for black people . . . to unite, to recognize their heritage, to build a sense of community . . . to define their own goals, to lead their own organizations . . . [and] to reject the racist institutions and values of this society."[25] Black Power became more than that though, developing into a militant political ideology that would markedly alter the nature of race discussions in America. King, already being abandoned by white supporters for being too radical, would also come under attack by African-Americans for being too compromising. The movement's best days, it seemed, were behind it.

SNCC and CORE were more radical than ever in 1966. Both organizations kicked out white members that year and began pressing a more militant agenda. Carmichael insisted that blacks needed to empower themselves as other ethnic groups – the Irish in Boston, Poles in Chicago, Italians in New York – had done so that they could control their own communities and not depend on the gratitude of supportive politicians. "We don't need white liberals," he announced, "we have to make integration irrelevant." Floyd McKissick of CORE went further, telling his supporters that non-violence had "outlived its usefullness." To Carmichael, American blacks were part of a global struggle against white colonialism; he thus made common cause with revolutionaries in Vietnam and Cuba, carried VC flags at anti-war rallies, and urged resistance to the draft. Dorm rooms throughout the country had posters of Stokely with the words "Hell No, We Won't Go" written on them. "From Mississippi and Harlem to . . . Vietnam," he explained, "a powerful few have been maintained and enriched at the expense of the poor and voiceless colored masses." Within the United States, he added, the main barrier to black progress was "a federal government that cares far more about winning the war on the Vietnamese than the war on poverty . . . which is unwilling to curb the misuse of white power but quick to condemn Black Power."[26]

Carmichael had a point. Up to that time most Americans could support the CR movement as a simple matter of justice. Legal desegregation, they believed, did not fundamentally challenge the structure or ideology of US society. But Black Power militants – with their advocacy of defensive violence, revolution, and separatism and their solidarity with the Vietnamese, Cuban, and African revolutionaries – terrified white Americans and many established African-American leaders as well. More so, the government intensified its surveillance of so-called black subversives. The FBI revived "*Operation Cointelpro*" (Counterintelligence Program), orginally set up in the 1950s to repress the US Communist Party, to "expose, disrupt, misdirect, discredit or otherwise neutralize" groups such as the SCLC, SNCC, CORE, and the Nation of Islam. King himself, especially after publicly denouncing the Vietnam War, came under growing attack from the FBI. J. Edgar Hoover "was quite aware of how hostile the Johnson White House was toward King" and monitored and harassed him more than ever in 1967 and 1968, continuing to try to smear him as a Communist and blackmail him with reports on his personal life.[27]

The emergence of Black Power marked a distinct turning point in the CR struggle. In addition to alarming whites, radicals such as Carmichael, H. Rap Brown, Julius Lester, and others stood in stark contrast to King and the mainstream movement leaders. By 1966–7, then, there were in effect two movements, with the younger and more militant blacks increasingly rejecting racial accommodation and cooperation with liberals in favor of separatism, black nationalism, and the rhetoric of violence. Indeed, the most publicized black group of the day was the *Black Panthers*, an organization of angry and armed blacks dramatically different from the SCLC or SNCC in its early days.

The Panthers grew out of the Lowndes County (Alabama) Freedom Organization, an African-American political party started in 1966 to run in local elections, whose symbol was a black panther. Urban blacks in Oakland, California led by Huey Newton and Bobby Seale subsequently formed the Black Panther Party (BPP) for Self-Defense in late 1966 and became immediate media sensations. Wearing black berets and bandoliers, carrying weapons in public, shooting it out with police, and rejecting King's methods – violence was "as American as cherry pie" according to H. Rap Brown – the Panthers offered the rhetoric and romance of revolution. The BPP, however, contributed more to the backlash against CR than to black empowerment. Though the party never had a significantly large membership and it did sponsor breakfast programs and black history classes for schoolchildren, its behavior terrified whites. The media and FBI and other law enforcement groups – which ultimately killed about 30 Panthers – convinced Americans that the party was representative of black thought and thus effectively smeared the entire African-American movement. By 1967, when Muhammad Ali refused induction into the army to protest Vietnam, and blacks in Detroit, Newark, New Jersey, and dozens of other cities staged violent uprisings to protest local cases of police abuse and racial discrimination, whites were only too willing to believe the worst about black America.

Adding to the distance between the races was the emergence of *cultural nationalism* and internationalism. "Black Power" became not just a political movement but a statement of racial identification and pride as well. African-Americans, as soul singer James Brown would express it, should "Say It Loud, I'm Black and Proud." Black men and women started wearing their hair in natural "afros" and often were clad in African-style dashikis. Universities, often pressured by African-American activists and students, established Black Studies Programs. Musicians, actors, and athletes reflected this cultural ideology too, with even mainstream artists like Stevie Wonder and Marvin Gaye eventually incorporating political themes into their songs; black writers like James Baldwin being read more widely; sports figures Cassius Clay and Lew Alcindor converting to Islam and become internationally famous as Muhammad Ali and Kareem Abdul-Jabbar; and medalists Tommie Smith and John Carlos being removed from the 1968 US Olympic team because they had raised their gloved fists in a Black Power salute on the victory stand as the National Anthem played.

Young black activists also began to connect their own cause to that of other nonwhite peoples. Malcolm X went to the United Nations to charge the United States with violations of *human* rights, not just civil rights, and compared America's racial conditions to those of South Africa. African-American radicals seriously engaged global, especially leftist, political ideas, identifying with and studying Ho, Mao, Fidel, and even Kim Il-Sung of Korea and Enver Hoxha of Albania. Just as SDS members carried and quoted Mao's *Little Red Book*, SNCC activists referred to *The Wretched of the Earth* by Frantz Fanon, a black French psychiatrist and Algerian freedom fighter. To increasing numbers of blacks, CR was part of a larger global struggle being waged by the nonwhite peoples of the world against Caucasian imperial powers.

Race and Class

Martin Luther King was deeply conflicted by the emergence of Black Power and cultural nationalism. As his April 1967 attack on the war showed, he was terribly frustrated and militant himself, but he could not support the extremism of the radicals, no matter the legitimacy of their grievances. Many blacks were moving in a different direction, however, looking to the Panthers and other radicals for examples of African-American resistance. But King was not unsympathetic to the militants. "Black Power, in its broad and positive meaning," he wrote, "is a call to black people to amass the political and economic strength to achieve their legitimate goals. No one can deny that the Negro is in dire need of this kind of legitimate power." Black Power was also "a call for the pooling of black financial resources to achieve economic security." While the federal government held primary responsibility to help the poor, to develop "a kind of Marshall Plan for the disadvantaged," the black community itself had an annual income of $30 billion, and King believed it could use such buying power as an instrument for social change.[28]

King, however, still fought to make common cause with white allies and retained many of the mannerisms of the elite gentleman that he was – still using the term "Negro," for instance, when younger activists were referring to themselves as "blacks" or "Afro-Americans." The biggest difference, however, was on the question of aggression and violence. The Panthers, quoting Mao, believed that "all power flows from the barrel of a gun." King, as his associate Jesse Jackson noted, "talked about the futility of violence, just in terms of strength." To take arms against the forces of order in America was "more suicidal than militant." King had no illusion about the will and ability of the military and police to crush black dissent, having witnessed it personally too many times.[29]

Despite such distinctions between King and the Black Power advocates, many African-American leaders were beginning similarly to focus on the structural economic causes of racial inequality. The Vietnam War, most CR activists agreed, had highlighted the shortcomings of liberalism, daily taking away more resources and attention from needs at home. America had not just a race problem, black leaders pointed out, but a significant *class* problem as well, and after 1965 such issues dominated African-American discourse. Americans had paid little notice to the masses of blacks who did not require legal desegregation. They lived in ghettos, sent their kids to inferior schools, had higher crime and mortality rates, and disproportionately experienced violence. "The right to vote, eat at a lunch counter, sleep in an integrated motel, or move into an all-white neighborhood had not altered their marginal existence."[30] Black Panthers, in their party program, included class-based demands for jobs, housing, education, and "an end to robbery by the CAPITALIST of our black community" as well as racial justice. King, less militantly but just as firmly, agreed. He called on Americans to "honestly admit that capitalism has often left a gulf between superfluous wealth and abject poverty, has created conditions permitting necessities to be taken from the many to give luxuries to the few, and has encouraged small hearted men to become conscienceless."[31]

Examinations of class also caused division within the CR community. Already in the late 1960s many lower-income and working-class blacks were pointing out the shortcomings of anti-discriminatory measures. Kenneth Clark, a prominent black sociologist, noted in 1967 that "the masses of blacks now realize . . . that they haven't really benefitted significantly from the civil rights movement"; only "a relatively small percentage of middle class and educated blacks" really gained anything from the struggle. Kathleen Cleaver, a Black Panther leader and later an honors graduate of Yale Law School, agreed, observing that the CR movement's goals "were essentially goals for easier assimilation for middle class people, and that working class people and poor people weren't going to get too much out of this." The NAACP, Cleaver joked, could have stood for the National Association for the Advancement of *Certain* People. Perhaps such developments should have been expected, however. King and most other black movement leaders came from the African-American bourgeoisie and, unlike Malcolm X, Panthers, or younger militants, did not really grasp conditions in the urban north for most blacks until after 1965. On top of that, as Jesse Jackson observed, "as little as Americans talk about race, they talk about class even less."[32]

The Death of a Dream

King, however, was talking about class in 1968 and thus began to organize the "*Poor People's Campaign*." The Reverend by this point was sounding like a partisan of the New Left, offering a comprehensive analysis of race, poverty, and the Vietnam War and indicting corporate liberalism in the process. Thus King sent out a call to the poor and ethnic minorities to join him in a march on Washington, DC to demand fair employment practices and jobs, housing, health care, justice for immigrants, union rights, and higher wages for the working poor. Cesar Chávez, dirt poor Appalachian whites, Native Americans, women, and Chicanos were among the groups that joined the cause. Linking racism, poverty, and the war, King was trying to create a mass movement based on class to restructure American society. Widely praised as a "Negro" leader in the early 1960s, he was becoming a "radical" spokesman in 1968 – and much of white America was nervous about it.

King, by planning the Poor People's Campaign, forced liberals to confront the limits of their own privileged thought by calling for a "radical redistribution of economic power" along with an end to the Vietnam War. Like younger radicals, he was attacking the paternal, liberal state at its base, the unequal class system that left millions without adequate employment, housing, health care, or education. If successful, the Poor People's movement could have constituted the greatest challenge to entrenched liberal power in national history; but that would not be the case. In the early years of the CR movement, white liberals and labor had been crucial and effective supporters of King's efforts, but, as Andrew Young – one of the organizers of the new campaign – put it, they "were less enthusiastic when it came to social justice for the poor." The Johnson administration felt great consternation as well. This class-based movement, Young explained, "had the potential of unifying protest across a wide spectrum of ethnic and underprivileged groups [and] it could also raise massive civil disobedience to a new level in American life." In the Senate, Robert Byrd called King a "self-seeking rabble-rouser"; John Stennis told the "colored people" in his home state of Mississippi to stay away from the campaign since "nothing good for them or for anyone else can come from" joining it; the White House tried to stop the march; and Harry McPherson, one of LBJ's closest aides, complained in a moment of liberal candor that "the Negro . . . showed himself to be, not only ungrateful, but sullen, full of hate and the potential for violence."[33]

With such formidable opposition from the Washington political establishment, the Poor People's chances for success were not great to begin with, and they virtually disappeared during the first week of April 1968. King, working feverishly on the march on Washington, traveled to Memphis, Tennessee that week to show his support for striking sanitation workers. On the night of 3 April, the Reverend, in an eerily prophetic sermon, told a huge crowd at the Masonic Temple:

> Well, I don't know what will happen now. We've got some difficult days ahead. But it really doesn't matter with me now, because I've been to the mountaintop. And I don't mind. Like anybody, I would like to live a long life. Longevity has its place. But I'm not concerned about that now. I just want to do God's will. And He's allowed me to go up to the mountain, and I've looked over, and I've seen the promised land. I may not get there with you. But I want you to know tonight, that we, as a people will get to the promised land.[34]

The next evening, while standing on a balcony at the Lorraine Motel, he was assassinated by a sniper.

Ironically, the death of the nonviolent King sparked the worst urban uprisings in US history. Violence wracked nearly 200 cities, with scores dead and hundreds of millions of dollars of property destroyed. In Chicago, Daley gave his police "shoot to kill" orders to deal with rioters; in Maryland, Governor Spiro Agnew – who once referred to the slain Muslim leader as "Malcolm the Tenth" – blamed "Black Power advocates and known criminals" for the crisis. But Stokely Carmichael took a different lesson from the Memphis assassination. "When white America killed Dr. King last night, she declared war on us. We have to retaliate for the death of our leaders," he warned. "The only way to survive is to get some guns ... We are going to stand on our feet and die like men. If that's our only act of manhood, then goddammit, we're going to die." Rap Brown called the uprisings a "rehearsal for Revolution."[35] Fortunately, the violence stopped and racial battles were averted, but King's dream of racial equality and justice for the poor had died in Memphis just the same. Though the Poor People marched on Washington, they were demoralized and dismissed, the name of their encampment, "Resurrection City," ultimately reflecting only wishful thinking.

White America, it seemed, no longer had to care about blacks. After the progress of 1954–65, the movement foundered as the war in Vietnam and questions of class entered into the CR equation. In 1954, Thurgood Marshall, who had successfully argued the *Brown* case and would later become the first black Supreme Court Justice, turned to his colleagues and said "in five years it will all be over . . . because there won't be a race problem. We will be integrated into American society."[36] And, for a time, Marshall's vision seemed possible. The sacrifice of the black masses and the powerful moral leadership of King and others had created new opportunities for African-Americans. Through direct action and federal legislation, the apartheid system below the Mason–Dixon line had been abolished. Blacks could eat and work in white-owned restaurants, ride buses, stay in hotels, and vote. Because of CR laws, the black middle class grew and gained economic power; and politically, blacks gained more clout than ever before, proving to be a vital segment of the Democratic Party's base and even being elected to office themselves.

Just over a decade after *Brown*, however, urban America seemed to be in chaos, with police brutality and rioting becoming a common occurrence. Many African-Americans did not identify with King so much as Malcolm X or younger militants who did not share the Nobel Prize winner's faith in integration. And, after 1965, the war in Vietnam replaced CR as the dominant national issue. Resources that might have been used to address problems of race and poverty were now going to Indochina; young black men were dying disproportionately in the war; and African-American leaders began to link their own struggle with that of other nonwhite peoples throughout the world. The liberal coalition that had so impressively worked on early CR legislation fell apart as King and other "ungrateful" blacks publicly decried the war. By 1967–8, as Black Power emerged and questions of America's class system began to dominate the discourse over African-American rights, the white backlash was in force. King's assassination and the failure of the Poor People's Campaign signalled the end of the dream that had been so movingly announced in August 1963. By the 1970s, as black inmates at

Attica Prison in New York were slaughtered by state troops and white mobs in Boston attacked black kids who were desegregating the schools there, Americans felt little sympathy and less outrage. To be sure, the early movement had made its mark on American society. Blacks were integrated economically and politically like never before and gained access to jobs and elected offices in significantly higher numbers. But, just the same, the war came along at the very time that black leaders were beginning to raise issues of poverty and opportunity for the black masses, and the commitment to Vietnam thus made it impossible to address the larger needs of the African-American community. As King lamented, "despite feeble protestations to the contrary, the promises of the Great Society have been shot down on the battlefield of Vietnam. The pursuit of this widened war has narrowed the promised dimensions of the domestic welfare programs, making the poor white and negro bear the heaviest burdens, both at the front and at home."[37]

Women and the Movement

While Civil Rights and the New Left constituted the most notable movements of the early to mid-1960s, by the end of the decade they would be attacked by the forces of order and divided from within. Amid the general sense of frustration and anger, however, another movement would emerge to challenge and transform American life, namely *Women's Liberation*. An amorphous movement with little formal organization, "Women's Lib" had no elected leaders, membership dues, or bureaucratic requirements. The 1960s Women's Movement mostly consisted of thousands of local groups and individuals, connected by word of mouth and newsletters. Declaring that "the personal is political," Women's Lib followers spoke to a large range of issues, both public and private, such as job and pay discrimination, educational access, health care, sexual double standards, media images of females, abortion, militarism and the Vietnam War, workplace harassment, and domestic violence. By the 1970s, women's issues were thus at the forefront of American political life.

The first indication that women would be included in the political dialogue of the 1960s came when JFK, right after his election, appointed a *Presidential Commission on the Status of Women* to assess women's places in the economy, family, and legal system. The Commission's report, issued in 1963, documented problems like job discrimination, unequal pay, lack of child care, and legal inequities in divorce and credit, and led to the Equal Pay Act of 1963, which required that women and men receive the same wages for the same work. Just as importantly that year, Betty Friedan, a writer and labor activist, produced her classic *The Feminine Mystique,* which hit the best-seller list. Friedan compared suburban domesticity to a "comfortable concentration camp" and argued that women's problems were "a problem of identity – a stunting or evasion of growth that is perpetuated by the feminine mystique." To millions of women – especially educated, middle-class housewives – Friedan's book seemed to describe their lives and legitimize and foster a shared experience, and the issues she raised would remain central to the Women's Movement throughout the decade.

The next year, women's issues got an unexpected boost when Congress passed the 1964 CR Act. Southern congressmen, in an effort to kill the bill, put forth an amendment in *Title VII* that would prohibit "sex" as well as "race" discrimination. The bill nonetheless passed and women had gained, or so they thought, federal protection for equal pay, hiring, and promotions. The government, however, did not seriously examine cases of sex discrimination, thus prompting female political figures like Representative Martha Griffiths to denounce federal inaction and leading many women in October 1966 to form the *National Organization for Women* (NOW). NOW was a political organization aiming to bring women into a "truly equal partnership with men . . . [to] mobilize the political power of all women and men intent on our goals." In its first victory, NOW pressured LBJ to include women in government affirmative action programs that were originally designed for African-Americans. By the mid-1960s, then, the "founding mothers" of the Women's Movement had put their issues onto the national agenda. Millions of others would pick up the struggle, often more militantly, in the coming years.

Grassroots Feminism

While the first measures to address women's concerns – federal laws, best-selling books, NOW, and the like – came from the top down, Women's Lib in the 1960s was mass-based and decentralized. Indeed, many of the women who brought issues of sex inequality into the national debate of the 1960s had experience in other major issues of the era, particularly in CR and anti-war activity, and formed their own groups to escape the discrimination and patriarchy they felt within those movements. Women had played a vital role in the early CR years. Many northern, white women had traveled to the south to work with SNCC and CORE on various projects. In SDS women were effective community organizers in the ERAP projects and performed crucial anti-war work. Within these organizations, however, women had second-rate status. Instead of being officers and policymakers, females disproportionately did clerical work and often were expected to be sexual partners of men in the movement. Indeed, many sexual liaisons did occur in the early CR and New Left days. Men would often accuse women of being "uptight" if they did not sleep with them. In addition, interracial dating was not uncommon, which could cause conflict between white and black women. As for the men, they had traditional attitudes, often referred to as "male chauvinist," that they should lead and women should follow.

Finally frustrated by such attitudes, women in the movement responded. In a memo written for a SNCC conference in late 1964, activists Casey Hayden, Mary King, and other white women – writing anonymously because they expected ridicule from their brethren – described "Women in the Movement" in stark terms. Women in SNCC, despite their skills and experience, were usually assigned secretarial work and were expected to "defer to a man . . . for final decisionmaking." Men, Hayden and others charged, simply expected to be leaders: "assumptions of male superiority are as widespread and deep rooted and every much as crippling to the woman," they explained, "as the assumptions of white supremacy are to the Negro." Men in the movement, the women in SNCC seemed to be saying, were no different from the hypocritical liberals they had all decried. Hayden and King had hoped at best to generate a discussion, "amidst the laughter" they expected, on sex issues, but they were ignored for the most part. Indeed, many African-American women in SNCC also believed that the organization needed a strong centralized administration and "considered the issue of women to be a diversion . . . [or] as disruptive and divisive."[38]

Slowly, however, women involved in various groups – SNCC, SDS, the National Student Association, the Student Peace Union, and others – began to discuss their own conditions within the movement and more openly raise the issue of sex discrimination. By 1965, then, Hayden and King were willing to go further. Hayden had been working on a Chicago ERAP project – where one of her major goals was to prevent the women she was organizing from being attacked by the men Rennie Davis was working with – and King was still with SNCC when they produced "Sex and Caste: a Kind of Memo" in November 1965. This time, the women signed their names to the document and acknowledged authorship. Again, Hayden and King compared male treatment of women to white attitudes toward blacks, and added that women in the movement had become a "caste," in a "position of assumed subordination" in both organizational and personal situations. Women still did most clerical work, cooking, and cleaning, and held few leadership positions. But Hayden and King were not optimistic that their manifesto would get much attention. "Objectively," they predicted, "the chances seem nil that we could start a movement based on anything as distant . . . as a sex-caste system. Therefore, most of us will probably want to work full time on problems such as war, poverty, race."[39] They were only partly right – many women did continue to work for racial equality and to end the war, but untold others formed the largest mass women's movement in US history.

"The Personal Is Political": The Emergence of an Independent Women's Liberation Movement

Women's Lib thus grew out of the CR and New Left movements of the 1960s. "Most of us," feminist activists and scholars Linda Gordon and Ann Popkin explained, "came through the male-dominated New Left." Working in CR, community organizing, and anti-war activities, "we kept forgetting about ourselves." Within those movements, women were "relegated to positions of typists, office clerks, janitors, and flunkeys . . . Our opinions were seldom asked for and rarely heard."[40] Such conditions, already noticeable during the early 1960s, became more pronounced in the later years of the decade because, as Sara Evans pointed out, "the student movement grew most spectacularly . . . in reaction to the Vietnam War."[41] The primacy of anti-war activity, along with the growth of black nationalism and the departure of whites from many CR organizations, brought significant numbers of women into the New Left in 1965 and 1966, and thus exposed females, again, to discrimination within the movement. Women began to see a distinction between *sex*, a biological condition, and *gender*, a socially constructed set of identifications and relations between females and males. Men in the New Left had thus subordinated women as a secondary gender – with traditional and less respected roles. Indeed, at the December 1965 SDS convention, acrimony over the Hayden–King memo broke up the conference and motivated many women to break off and form their own caucus. Men in the movement could critique the white power structure for its racial and class attitudes, but could not tolerate women who pointed out that male behavior in the New Left was quite similar to that of the "enemy."

As women involved in the movement began to communicate with each other, they unearthed common experiences – strong and self-respecting mothers and supportive and politically active families, and "they shared stories about the opposition they had met in school or SNCC or SDS." Many saw their own experiences on the left as part of a larger social system which discriminated against women, hence the admonition that "the personal is political." Toward that end, women began to focus on the questions of both their identification and their social roles. They held "*consciousness-raising*" sessions to discuss common problems and plan collective action and to take a political role on women's issues. Intensifying that process was Vietnam. As the war took over center stage on the left, radicalizing the CR agenda and turning SDS into almost exclusively an anti-war group, women found themselves outside the mainstream still. In the CR struggle or ERAP, women could be on the front lines – marching, desegregating public places, registering voters, organizing the poor, facing arrest and violence. But women were auxiliary to anti-war activity. "Men were drafted, women were not. Men could resist the draft; they burned draft cards; they risked jail." And women were supposed to support and nurture anti-war men. The "action and awareness of a *mother or young lover* who hides or protects her man from the draft" was highly valued, and "Girls Say Yes to Guys Who Say No" was a common slogan of the movement.

Many women, however, began to balk at such secondary roles. In 1967, in the movement journal *New Left Notes*, Francine Silbar called on women to organize separately from men. "Let's define our own roles," she advised. "We don't have to be secretaries to be useful. What's the matter with men's hands anyway?" By mid-1967, male–female acrimony was rampant in SDS. Female activists, building on the Hayden–King 1965 analysis, found "that women are in a colonial relationship to men and we recognize our roles as part of the Third World," like Vietnamese or blacks. They called on New Left men to recognize and deal with their male chauvinism "in their personal, social, and political relationships" and for women to demand child care, birth control and abortion rights, and equal sharing of housework. With their "Resolution for Women's Liberation," females in SDS had struck a nerve and men within the organization were furious, refusing to debate the issue and drowning out those who wanted to speak with derisive jeering and catcalls. In the next issue of *New Left Notes*, an article about the debate appeared "alongside a cartoon of a girl – with earrings, polkadot minidress, and matching visible panties – holding a sign: 'We Want Our Rights and We Want Them Now.'" SDS, as Sara Evans pointed out, "had blown its last chance."

Sisterhood Is Powerful

By 1968, the radical movement in general was foundering. Martin Luther King and Kennedy were dead; SDS, after Columbia, was on the defensive; Nixon was entering the White House. Women's Lib, however, was growing. Once huge numbers of women left the CR and New Left struggles to go out on their own, American's gender landscape changed forever. Engaging in both personal and political actions, female activists, mostly white and middle-class, not only confronted Americans about their gendered attitudes but engaged in effective political reform. By the mid-1970s, women would break through and achieve more opportunities than at any time in US history.

The first time many Americans heard of Women's Lib was in September 1968 when the "Radical Women of New York" crashed the Miss America Pageant that year. They set up a "freedom trash can" where they discarded, but never burned, bras, girdles, wigs, false eyelashes, and anti-woman magazines. They held signs comparing the pageant to a "cattle auction" and had a poster of a naked woman with body parts labeled "loin" and "rump" as if she were just a side of beef. And they chanted "Atlantic City is a town with class. They raise your morals and they judge your ass." Using guerrilla theater, these women wanted to introduce their agenda to a national crowd. They criticized not only sexism but racism, commercialism, and war. Miss America was a "Military Death Mascot," they claimed, a "cheerleader" for US troops; "last year she went to Vietnam to pep-talk our husbands, fathers, sons and boyfriends into dying and killing with a better spirit."[42]

Other women struck out on their own and conducted similar protests. *WITCH* – the Women's International Terrorist Conspiracy from Hell – held a "Halloween Witches' Dance" on Wall Street to hex the stock market, which fell five points the next day. Women at the University of Chicago seized a building to protest the firing of a radical feminist professor. In 1970 Women's Liberation–Seattle took over the Applied Physics Laboratory at the University of Washington and demanded that scientists there stop working on nuclear submarine weapons and that the lab be turned into a daycare center. Two years later, the "February Sisters" took over the Asian Studies Building to highlight grievances over the lack of health care and day care at the University of Kansas, and shortly afterwards the administration acted on these issues and established a Women's Studies department as well. Women's publications like *Off Our Backs* and, later, *Ms. Magazine* appeared, and essays like "The Myth of the Vaginal Orgasm" and "Why I Want a Wife" were widely read and discussed.. Feminists such as Gloria Steinem, Angela Davis, Germaine Greer, Robin Morgan, and others wrote best-selling books and became nationally known. An underground group of Chicago health care activists, calling themselves "Jane," made safe abortions available to thousands of women who, before the procedure was legalized, could not control their reproductive lives and who had illegal "backalley" abortions at great risk. In Boston, a group of women appalled at the lack of knowledge and care given to female health issues by male doctors published a self-help pamphlet, *Our Bodies, Ourselves* which became an internationally recognized guide for women's health care. Testing the movement's limits, *SCUM*, the Society for Cutting Up Men, produced a virulently anti-male manifesto written by Valerie Solanas, later to become a radical feminist icon after shooting pop artist Andy Warhol. While such behavior did gain media attention, it did not reflect mainstream thought and, like college takeovers or the Poor People's Campaign, probably turned off as many Americans as it attracted. Women's issues, however, were in fact being taken more seriously by the late 1960s and both their cultural images and political agenda were shifting.

Jeannie versus Samantha

Even before Women's Lib exploded into the public sphere in the latter part of the decade, images of women in pop culture were changing.[43] Two of the more highly rated TV shows of the mid-1960s featured female leads who explored the changing roles of women in US life – *I Dream of Jeannie* and *Bewitched*. "Jeannie," though a "real" genie living in a bottle, was more traditional, always looking to please her "master," an astronaut with NASA (symbolic of Cold War technological progress). "Samantha" on *Bewitched* also had magical abilities but often used them to assert her power as a woman, frequently bailing out her befuddled husband Darrin and, along with her mother Endora, letting him know about it. *The Munsters* and *The Addams Family* too featured strong female characters who seemed to live in a different world from Lucille Ball, June Cleaver, or Donna Reed. More likely to cook frog-eyeball stew than bake cookies for the PTA, they were assertive and independent and could be sexy – traits generally not attributed to women by the media in the early 1960s. By the end of the decade and into the 1970s, the depiction of women reflected the success of the movement. "Ann Marie," *That Girl* played by Marlo Thomas, was the first female to star in a sitcom who lived independently and (gasp!) did not need or want to get married and got along quite well on her own in New York City (apparently proving the accuracy of Gloria Steinem's quip that "a woman needs a man like a fish needs a bicycle"). "Mary Richards," Mary Tyler Moore's character on her show, also remained single by choice and brought feminist issues like equal pay and sexual harassment to the screen. On *All In the Family*, Archie Bunker's daughter Gloria constantly called him on his chauvinist views while their cousin *Maude*, played by Bea Arthur, broke new ground on TV by choosing to have an abortion. In less than a decade, Women's Lib had transformed the way females were being portrayed.

Politically, women were gaining ground as well. In 1968, NOW had decided to get involved in electoral politics by backing candidates who supported feminist issues and by calling for ratification of the *Equal Rights Amendment* (ERA) to the Constitution which would outlaw any discrimination based on sex. In 1971, NOW, along with feminist leaders like Steinem, Friedan, and Representatives Shirley Chisolm and Bella Abzug, supported the establishment of the *National Women's Political Caucus*, a bipartisan group formed to increase women's participation in politics. By 1972 – as Helen Reddy's "I Am Woman" was becoming an anthem for the movement and moving to number 1 on the pop charts – women were playing a vital role in the political process. During the national conventions that year, 40 percent of Democratic and 30 percent of Republican delegates were female, up from 13 and 17 percent in 1968. That same year, Shirley Chisolm, the first black woman elected to Congress, ran for president. Congress also passed the ERA in 1972 and by the end of the year 22 states had ratified it. The Higher Education Act of 1972 also passed, which included *Title IX* outlawing sex discrimination in schools that received federal funding. Despite opposition from alumni groups and male athletes, Title IX was the catalyst for the tremendous growth in women's intercollegiate sports in the 1970s.

Along with Title IX, a 1973 Supreme Court decision legalizing abortion, in the *Roe v. Wade* case, constituted the greatest successes of the first phase of the Women's Liberation Movement. Millions of American women had been illegally terminating pregnancies for years (in the 1940s Alfred Kinsey found that nearly one-fourth of American women had had an abortion) with great risks to their health, so *Roe v. Wade* not only decriminalized that practice but helped women's health. By giving females control over their own bodies, it also enabled women to pursue the types of educational opportunities and jobs that they could not gain if pregnant or raising children. Into the 1970s, the movement continued and grew more accepted. Women were depicted more realistically in the media. Female sports gained credibility, especially after Billie Jean King defeated Bobby Riggs in the tennis "battle of the sexes." Women were elected to office in larger numbers and became a vital part of the political process. An anti-feminist backlash, however, began as well. Led by a reactionary female lawyer, Phyllis Schlafly, conservatives prevented the ERA from being ratified. Images of unhappy, single women continued to populate TV shows and movies. Abortion rights came under attack. The number of women living in poverty, which was far greater than men, or raising children by themselves did not decline. And black women, who often felt like outsiders in the Women's Movement, continued to suffer disproportionate rates of poverty. As with CR or the New Left, women had discovered the limits of reform in American political society.

People's Movements in the Sixties and the Vietnam War

Civil Rights and Women's Lib demonstrated both the power of ordinary Americans to seek social change and the difficulties inherent in 1960s reform movements. While the movements successfully broke through the political landscape of the early 1960s, internal division and state opposition limited their gains. The biggest factor in this regard was surely the Vietnam War. Beginning in 1965, CR passed the baton, as it were, to Vietnam as the nation's most important concern. Funding and attention was now given to the war rather than to America's racial or gender problems, thereby making activists more frustrated and militant. The result, an angry movement to end the war and restructure American society, helped prompt the Women's Movement as females in the movement found New Left men to be often as discriminating and paternal as the white male elite that they all claimed to oppose. The war had seriously impeded CR, given rise to a mass Peace

Movement, caused a radicalization of youth politics, and led to division along ideological, strategic, race, and gender lines.

Other movements developed out of this process as well. More than a labor leader, Cesar Chávez was representative of a growing movement of Mexican-Americans and Chicanos for dignity and equality. In New Mexico, Chicanos called for the return of lands taken from Mexico. In California, Texas, and elsewhere, they formed their own political party, *La Raza Unida*, while militant young Chicanos formed the "Brown Berets," modeled on the Black Panthers. Mexican-Americans and Chicanos were also active in the anti-war movement, pointing out the similarities between the US war on Asian peasants and conditions for people of color at home. Similarly, the *American Indian Movement* (AIM) attempted to start a national debate on the plight of Native Americans, who suffered tragic rates of poverty and alcoholism on government reservations. In 1968, militant Indians fought with Washington state officials over fishing rights, and the following year Native Americans in San Francisco invaded and occupied Alcatraz Island. Vine Deloria's *Custer Died for Your Sins* and Dee Brown's *Bury My Heart at Wounded Knee* helped propel an Indian cultural renaissance and more militancy. In 1972, AIM occupied the offices of the Bureau of Indian Affairs in Washington, DC and in 1973 staged a 71-day protest at Wounded Knee, South Dakota – the site of an 1890 massacre of hundreds of Sioux by the US Army – until driven off by government forces. Indeed, political ferment was widespread throughout the decade. In 1969, rather than tolerate continued police brutality, gay patrons at the *Stonewall Inn* in Greenwich Village fought back, prompting a more radical and public "gay power" movement than ever before. Environmentalists – many appalled by the American ecological destruction of Vietnam and copying many of the tactics of the anti-war movement – likewise emerged in the late 1960s to form an effective mass movement.

The issues of CR, women's inequality, Chicano and Indian discrimination, gay politics, and environmentalism of course preceded the 1960s, but all grew significantly and publicly in that decade. All occurred, too, with Vietnam as the backdrop. The war was central to the militancy of the era, creating a mass movement by bringing together people from disparate causes – participatory democracy, racial justice, women's rights – to oppose the US intervention in Vietnam. But the war created a paradox as well; Vietnam created a political left but the emphasis on anti-war activity overshadowed other causes and frustrated and alienated large segments of that left as well. By decade's end, blacks, women, and others had a much different place in American society, in good measure because of the grassroots activism of millions of women and men – black, white, and brown, gay and straight. Fighting for social justice and against a war, they led the movement to create a new society.

8

"One, Two, Three, What Are We Fightin' For?" Cultural Politics in the Vietnam Era

Perhaps the greatest transformation in American life in the 1960s was cultural. Liberalism waned, civil rights suffered under a backlash, people's movements were suppressed or they faded away, but American cultural life is distinctly different after the Vietnam War and other upheavals of the sixties. During that decade, the foundations of American life were challenged, and often rocked, to their core. Dissent, youth culture, music, sex, film, and other media – indeed the very politics of culture – all changed markedly because of the war and attendant movements, and today, as we remember the 1960s, it is such cultural images that constitute our most public history of the era.

Make Love, Not War: From the Beats to the Hippies

In the 1950s, conformity reigned, or so it seemed. The "man in the grey flannel suit" went to work and came home to his mate, who was a "housewife," and his kids in their suburban home. *I Love Lucy*, sock hops, hula hoops, and Beaver Cleaver seemed to be the cultural paradigms of the day. Beneath the acceptable surface, however, beyond where politics and the media examined American life, there was a cultural revolution developing. By the end of the 1960s, the way Americans dressed, talked, played, loved, entertained, and thought would all be dramatically different. The movements of the 1960s, layered on top of the Vietnam War, would create a new political culture.

Signs of the coming tumult were already visible in the 1950s. "Hipsters" listened to jazz, smoked marijuana, and went out in interracial groups. The Women's Strike for Peace and Bertrand Russell's "Ban the Bomb" movement publicly criticized America's Cold War military policies. Most notably, a group of poets and literary figures directly confronted the conformity of American life and helped usher in a new youth culture. Jack Kerouac, Gregory Corso, Lawrence Ferlinghetti, Gary Snyder, William Burroughs, and, of course, Allen Ginsberg – collectively known as *beatniks* – were appalled by McCarthyism, the arms race, the Cold War, elite institutions and universities, corporate America, and racism. All authority should be questioned and conformity was a disease. Ginsberg, in the famous collection of his peyote-induced poems, *Howl*, and Kerouac in *On the Road* mocked consumerism and suburbia. To Ginsberg, it was a generation "destroyed by madness" because of the conformity and hatred. Instead of going along with the crowd, the beatniks urged personal and sexual freedom. And in the 1960s, as the war in Vietnam grew, many took an active role in the Peace Movement.

By the mid-1960s, the beatniks were replaced, in the media at least, by the *hippies*, a loose, unorganized collection of young people who developed their own way of life. Some took drugs, others got high on Jesus. Most wore their hair longer than usual, but did not have to. Some participated in sex orgies, or lived in communes, and almost all listened to rock music. There were no hippie organizations, meetings, age limits, or membership requirements – just a commitment to personal freedom and peace. The hippies constituted the most public group in what came to be known as the *counterculture*, the 1960s movement in general that challenged the traditional values of US society. Often caricatured as nothing more than advocates of "sex, drugs, and rock and roll," counterculture youth indeed had a political awareness and engaged in cultural political activity. Andrew Kopkind, a leftist journalist, described this "new culture of opposition" which "grows out of the disintegration of the old forms, the vinyl and aerosol institutions that carry all the inane and destructive values of privation, competition, commercialism, profitability and elitism."[1] As with other movements, the war was an essential aspect of hippies' lives.

Many young people in the early 1960s were already disturbed over America's racial policies and would become even more disenchanted by the Vietnam War. Some joined civil rights groups to try to change American society, and at least hundreds of thousands protested the war actively. But even more expressed their resentment culturally, by rejecting the look and the values of a society that had attacked black children in the south or peasants in Vietnam. John Kenneth Galbraith – eminent economist, policymaker, and liberal icon – explained that the youth of the 1960s "were in general retreat from the values of the consumer society. One manifestation was the rejection of its manners and dress. Nothing caused my generation such discontent as the sudden abandonment by the young of razors, haircuts and regular bathing and the seeming satisfaction in shabby clothes. But in the United States the Vietnam war and the hot breath of the draft boards were probably more important."[2] All over America – in New York's Greenwich Village, San Francisco's Haight-Ashbury, and countless smaller and less famous locations – hippies and other countercultural and antiwar movements came into existence. They may not have had a political program like SDS or SNCC but, through their politics of personal expression, bucked the system just the same. Men broke down gender lines by wearing their hair long, often in ponytails. Students no longer wore the traditional clothing of a previous generation: ironed pants, oxford shirts, full-length skirts that fell below the knee, bobby socks and saddle shoes. Now they wore bell-bottomed jeans, tie-dyed shirts, and short skirts. Some, such as the San Francisco Bay Area "Diggers," rejected the system of private property and money and lived communally, recycling surplus goods procured from local stores to hand out to the public for free. Instead of writing their congressman to express their opinions, the counterculture acted outrageously or staged guerrilla theater, as when Abbie Hoffman and Jerry Rubin threw dollar bills onto the floor of the New

York Stock Exchange or women demonstrated at the 1968 Miss America pageant. Indeed, Hoffman became something of a hippie superstar with his antics. Dressing in a shirt that looked like the American flag; protesting traffic in New York by calling for a rally and transforming the streets into a dance stage and pedestrian mall; stopping traffic to "plant" a tree in the street because he wanted more green space; bringing a duck onto a television interview in a spoof of Groucho Marx's "You Bet Your Life," he never failed to gain attention.[3]

Such cultural outrages were being conducted on a national scale by the mid-1960s. As Vietnam raged, hippies urged Americans to "make love, not war" and in 1967, a time of death in Indochina, celebrated a *"Summer of Love"* in San Francisco. Thousands of young people poured into Haight-Ashbury, some in psychedelic vans, others hitchhiking. They protested the war, meditated, took large amounts of LSD, and daily listened to the best music around: the Grateful Dead, Jefferson Airplane, Jimi Hendrix, Country Joe and the Fish, and so many others. They held "be-ins" and "love-ins" to give off peaceful vibes and protest the war and to celebrate individual freedom. Alas, the Summer of Love, good intentions notwithstanding, also included numerous drug overdoses, sexual exploitation of teenaged girls and runaways, soaring rents, and even violence. Indeed, the Diggers became so distraught they announced a "Death of the Hippie" ceremony at the end of the summer. "Hippiedom," however, did not end. Thousands of youth returned home from San Francisco in 1967 to bring new values to their own communities and campuses. They continued to listen to rock and roll, take drugs, have sex, and question and reject "mainstream" values. And they continued to protest the war in Vietnam. The counterculture, as it were, was making a clear mark on American society.

The Sounds of Protest: From Folk to Rock

Music has always had a political aspect to it, and never more so than in the 1960s. In that decade both traditional folk music and the newer rock and roll began to reflect political themes such as civil rights and pacifism. By decade's end, music was a vital part of the national cultural rebellion and of the anti-war movement. Folk singers like Woody Guthrie, Huddie Ledbetter, and Pete Seeger had been singing protest songs throughout the twentieth century, challenging racism, attacking bankers, decrying conformity. By the early 1960s a full-blown folk revival was in bloom. The arms race, segregation, and commercialization all became targets of folk singers. "A person shouldn't have more property than he can squeeze between his banjo and the outside wall of his banjo case," was Pete Seeger's advice.[4] During the monumental civil rights struggles and anti-Vietnam rallies, Seeger and others such as Peter, Paul, and Mary or Joan Baez or Phil Ochs were always present, protesting US policies while entertaining the demonstrators. A new musical culture was being born.

A young man from Minnesota, however, would define the musical politics of the era. Robert Zimmerman of Hibbing had listened to the early rockers of the 1950s and African-American blues musicians. His biggest influence, however, was Woody Guthrie, and he imitated his folk style and shared his progressive beliefs. Adopting the stage name *Bob Dylan* (from the poet Dylan Thomas) he embodied the musical and political changes of the 1960s. He first emerged in 1961 with the album *Bob Dylan*, which paid homage to Guthrie. Within the next few years, Dylan assumed a central place in the nascent counterculture and political opposition. He wrote about the horrors of nuclear war in "A Hard Rain's a Gonna Fall"; the military-industrial complex in "Masters of War"; the violence of racism in "The Lonesome Death of Hattie Carroll" and "Only a Pawn in Their Game." He touched upon the national sense of anxiety and hope in the anthemic "Blowin' in the Wind" and the alienation of youth in "Like a Rolling Stone" or "Gates of Eden."

On 25 July 1965, Dylan entered a new phase. Appearing at the Newport, Rhode Island, Folk Festival, he came out in black leather and boots instead of the traditional folkie jeans and flannel workshirt. More shockingly, he plugged in an electric guitar – eschewing the acoustic version that was a staple of folk music – and lit into a raucous rendition of "Maggie's Farm." Though Seeger and other purists were furious and Dylan himself was booed off the stage, the conversion to rock symbolized the power of the new music, the new generation, and the new culture.

Rock had been around since the early 1950s when artists such as Bill Haley, Buddy Holly, and especially Elvis Presley had adapted older African-American blues songs and sanitized them for middle-class white audiences. In the early 1960s, rock took off like a rocket, especially with the emergence of The Beatles. Singing simple and sometimes silly love songs like "I Wanna Hold Your Hand," "She Loves You," or "Love Me Do," the group – like Frank Sinatra or Presley in earlier decades – captured the national imagination and announced another progression in the new youth culture, full of energy and imagination and, especially, fun. Rock soon took a more serious turn, however. Musicians began to incorporate larger social themes – race, alienation, the war – into their songs and both educated and created a shared experience for their listeners. Indeed, the music became a defining characteristic of the counterculture. In the Bay Area alone, the Dead, Airplane, and Janis Joplin embodied hippie lifestyles and urged nonconformity and drug use. The Rolling Stones used Mick Jagger's overt sexuality to challenge traditional values, though not without a backlash. Before appearing on the "Ed Sullivan Show" the band had to change the lyrics of "Let's Spend the Night Together" to "Let's Spend Some Time Together." Similarly, The Doors, featuring the brooding poet Jim Morrison, disturbed listeners with haunting songs about the hostility of modern life, and their music would become intricately linked to the Vietnam era through Francis Coppola's use of "The End" as a theme song in *Apocalypse Now*. Even The Beatles got into the new culture, moving away from simple love songs to experiments with Eastern music and religions and, with 1967's *Sgt. Pepper's Lonely Hearts Club Band*, into the hippie and drug worlds.

Vietnam obviously had a tremendous impact on this musical transformation as various artists began to protest the war through song. Folkies like Dylan, Ochs, Baez, and others either indirectly criticized the war through pacifist songs like "Where Have All the Flowers Gone?" or more directly, as with Ochs's "Talkin' Vietnam Blues." By 1965, as Barry McGuire's "Eve of Destruction" became one of the fastest-selling, and most banned, songs of the era, Vietnam had a central place in counterculture music. When The Animals sang "We Gotta Get Out of This Place," who could not think of Vietnam? Their "Sky Pilot" moved listeners with its tale of a military chaplain sending pilots off on bombing missions. Motown, best known for its ballads and dance music, got into the act. Marvin Gaye's pathbreaking album *What's Going On?* included songs about the war, ecology, and urban violence, included despite CEO Berry Gordy's fears that such political music would bring on commercial disaster, while The Temptations made listeners think about American society with their song "Ball of Confusion."

The Beatles, especially John Lennon, became vocal critics of the war too. In 1966, the original album cover for *"Yesterday" . . . and Today* pictured the group with slabs of raw meat and decapitated dolls, but Capitol Records forced them to change it. To Lennon, the cover was a comment on American butchery in Vietnam and The Beatles announced at a press conference that "we think of it [the war] every day. We don't like it. We don't agree with it. We think it's wrong."[5] Other artists surely agreed. Joe McDonald and his band Country Joe and the Fish sang what is probably the best-known anti-war song of the era, the "I-Feel-Like-I'm-Fixin'-to Die Rag," a tirade against the war, Wall Street, and the military. Creedence Clearwater Revival condemned the class nature of the war in "Fortunate Son," decrying the ability of the rich to avoid service. Crosby, Stills, Nash, and Young contributed "Chicago" – a tribute to the 1968 anti-war movement – and "Ohio" – a memorial to the students killed at Kent State. And Lennon, with songs like "Give Peace a Chance," "Power to the People," and "Imagine," was a visible symbol of the political power of the music.

Liberating Minds and Bodies

While rock and roll spoke to a new-found cultural freedom on a society-wide scale, millions of young people looked for personal liberation through the use of drugs or a new sexual morality. Though drug use and premarital sex had not been uncommon in the 1950s, they were covered up by the media and polite society, which gave off the impression that mainly "delinquents, blacks, hipsters or bad girls" took part in such hedonistic acts. By the 1960s, however, drugs and sex would be part of the countercultural revolution, endorsed and practiced openly as part of the larger generational struggle of the Vietnam era. Students on college campuses began to use marijuana with some frequency, a trend that grew especially in the later 1960s as drug use associated with the Vietnam War spiralled. Drugs in fact became a major part of hippie lifestyle. No "be-in" or anti-war rally was complete without easy access to weed or psychedelic drugs. The drug culture even had its own "guru" – Timothy Leary, an ex-Harvard professor who sang the praises of LSD and urged youth to "turn on, tune in, drop out."

Dope was also seen as an agent of sexual liberation, releasing youth from traditional morals and anxieties over their bodies. In fact, sexual activity among young, unmarried partners was far more common in the 1960s, but that reflected many factors. Sexual standards had already begun to change in the aftermath of World War II, when women, many of whom had worked during the war, became more economically and sexually independent. In 1953, the first issue of *Playboy*, published by Hugh Hefner and featuring nude photos of Marilyn Monroe, further highlighted the growing sexual freedom. Hefner told his readers that sex should be a pleasure, for men and women both, and that they should not be afraid to express themselves physically. Still, millions of young people remained chaste, for either moral reasons or fear of pregnancy or disease, into the 1960s. The first effective oral contraceptive for females, *the Pill*, began to break down even those barriers, however. Following its introduction in 1960, millions of women would use the Pill in the following decade, giving themselves levels of sexual liberation not imagined earlier. The Pill seemed to be a "panacea for reproduction control" and was so easily used that it "allowed consumers to adopt this method without examining . . . their sexual behavior."[6]

Though it was soon discovered that the Pill had many side effects dangerous to women's health, the new contraceptive had created the scientific basis for a sexual revolution. Morally and politically, sex was changing as well. Young people, no longer so respectful of a generation whose values had brought on segregation and Vietnam, rejected their parents' sexual beliefs. Indeed, pleasures of the body became a vehicle for dissent, with speakers at political rallies often calling for "free love" as well as an end to the war. Politico-cultural groups like the "Neo-Naked Noisy Committee for Peace and Love" or the "Bare Breasts for Peace Brigade" emerged to link sex and anti-war thought in guerrilla theater. The "Sexual Freedom League" attacked "the double standards between the sexes . . . and the . . . hypocritical morality and diseducation on the subject of sex." Timothy Leary also explained the politics of sex: "the key energy in our revolution is erotic . . . The sexual revolution is not just part of the atmosphere of freedom that is generating with the kids. I think it is the center of it." And the "revolution" took in all comers. Orgies, oral sex, sodomy, gay and lesbian practices, and casual sexual activity all became more common and accepted as the decade progressed. Janis Joplin reflected on the new attitudes toward sex, observing that "my music isn't supposed to make you riot. It's supposed to make you fuck."[7] Women in particular were given license to engage in and enjoy sex as many, but by no means all, double standards disappeared. Still, however, sexual abuse of women remained high and many hippie men had the misogynist values typical of male society.

Hollywood and the Sixties

Marlon Brando and James Dean – in *The Wild One* and *Rebel Without a Cause* – had brought a new image to film. Outsiders, free, sneering, they reflected a new youth culture in the 1950s. By the 1960s, again with the Vietnam War as backdrop, Hollywood would even more symbolize the growing counterculture. Though films such as *Where the Boys Are* and *Beach Blanket Bingo* were popular, cinema with a social conscience emerged as well. Many young filmmakers began producing low-budget 16 and 8 mm films about current affairs and showing them in art galleries and on campuses. Soon, major studios were producing movies with countercultural themes and influenced by the war. Though the most notable Vietnam films such as *Go Tell the Spartans*, *The Deer Hunter*, *Apocalypse Now*, or *Coming Home* would not be made for another decade, Vietnam was already making an impact on films in the 1960s. In 1967's *Bonnie and Clyde*, director Arthur Penn offered a raw and brutal depiction of the famed criminal couple, with the movie ending in a slow-motion shot of bullets ripping into the stars, Warren Beatty and Faye Dunaway, making clear connections for a public used to seeing war scenes on the nightly news. And leftist critics often raved about Bonnie and Clyde – the outlaws made revolution look like fun. That same year *The Graduate*, a Mike Nichols film, derided the conformist, corporate culture and urged personal and sexual liberation.

Perhaps the movie most associated with the 1960s counterculture was *Easy Rider*, a film in which Peter Fonda and Dennis Hopper were hippies traveling by motorcycle, taking drugs, and celebrating individual liberation until blown away by rifle-carrying, truck-driving patriotic Americans. *The Wild Bunch*, a brutal western directed by Sam Peckinpah, also appealed to a society accustomed to the violence of Vietnam. It was a "revolutionary film," according to radical Stew Albert, because it showed how "to pick up the gun."[8] Such films also appealed to a generation whose icons – JFK, Malcolm X, King,

Bobby Kennedy – had been victims of violence or had become "doomed outsiders" like Bonnie and Clyde or Hopper and Fonda. As a result of this new cultural era, Hollywood shifted markedly, making films such as *Catch-22* or *M*A*S*H* that may have been set in World War II or Korea but were, indeed, "about" Vietnam and the futility of wars.

The "Other" 1960s

Images of hippies, sex, drugs, and protests often dominate our memory of the Vietnam era, but it would be a mistake to assume that the counterculture was the only significant movement of the decade. Many, probably most, Americans, including the young, viewed hippie culture with revulsion, while corporate America took steps to use the cultural images of the decade for its own purposes. "Mainstream" political, entertainment, and media figures attacked the counterculture. Richard Nixon spoke of them as "bums." Country singer Merle Haggard condemned hippies and drugs in "Okie from Muskogee." Anita Bryant, a past Miss America and anti-gay crusader, led "rallies for decency." Many fast-food joints banned young customers with long hair, beads, beards, flowers, or sandals. Police often harassed or arrested "freaks" for vagrancy or idleness. New Orleans cops arrested a female hippie in jeans for "wearing the clothes of the opposite sex." Long-haired students were routinely hassled and even assaulted. Americans told pollsters that the three groups they most feared were "Communists, prostitutes, and hippies."[9]

Some opponents of the counterculture organized politically. The right-wing John Birch Society, seeing JFK and LBJ as little better than Communists, had thousands of members. Mothers, businessmen, and professionals in towns throughout the United States organized against the "red menace" in local communities and schools, trying to weed out "unAmerican" teachers or arguing for school prayer. Every major protest rally was sure to include right-wing demonstrators as well, carrying signs with slogans like "America – Love It or Leave It" or "Go Back to Russia, You Communists." On various campuses, chapters of the Young Americans for Freedom popped up. Clean cut, conservatively dressed, wearing short hair and long skirts, these young people honored traditional values, rejected the hippies, and worked for conservative causes like the 1964 Barry Goldwater campaign or other anti-Communist issues, or against sex education or pornography.

The counterculture was also commercialized and commodified during the 1960s. Images of hippies and "flower power" – prevalent in advertisements in the 1980s and 1990s – were already common in the Vietnam era. Despite the counterculture's disdain for conformity and commercial society, its main symbols could be used to enhance the market. Corporate music companies rushed to San Francisco to sign and promote rock bands. Middle-of-the-road magazines and television specials focused on the antics of the Summer of Love, portraying its carnival atmosphere rather than discussing its political protest element. Big-city boutiques began to sell huge volumes of highly priced bell-bottoms, tie-dyes, and miniskirts, turning such clothing into a fashion rather than a political statement. This was a period when "record companies, clothing manufacturers, and other purveyors of consumer goods quickly recognized a new market," the counterculture.

Co-opting the language of youth, an automaker boasted of the "Dodge Rebellion." AT & T ads featured the line "The Times, They Are A-changing." 7-Up ran ads featuring one of its bottles surrounded by psychedelic images and called itself the "unCola" to consciously identify its product in opposition to the establishment, namely Coke. Virginia Slims Cigarettes tried to convince females that smoking was part of Women's Lib with the slogan "You've Come a Long Way, Baby." Warren Hinckle, a left journalist, saw the connection between hippies and sales as early as 1967, writing that "in this commercial sense, the hippies have not only accepted assimilation . . . they have swallowed it whole . . . If the people looking in from the suburbs want change, clothes, fun, and some lightheadedness from the new gypsies, the hippies are delivering – and some of them are becoming rich hippies because of it."[10] Little surprise then that the Diggers lamented the death of "Hippie, devoted son of Mass Media."

Celebrating the Counterculture: *Hair* and Woodstock

As the sixties drew to a close, the counterculture became a recognized segment of American life. Not only had Madison Avenue found ways to make the new culture marketable to a mass audience but virtually every high school yearbook included photos of class hippies and "freaks." The sounds of the new generation, which seemed raw and dangerous in the early 1960s, now constituted pop music. Perhaps the best examples of the new culture and its growing acceptance were the Broadway play *Hair* and the 1969 music festival at *Woodstock*, in upstate New York. Though both *Hair* and Woodstock were stridently anti-war spectacles, their message was diluted by the media. Rather than focus on the political statements made in both, mainstream cultural commentators talked about hippies, long hair, and nudity. The movement, as it were, had lost its teeth amid a co-optive and homogenizing media culture that ignored real politics and substituted image and sensationalism.

Hair told the story of Claude Bukowski, a Nebraska farmboy headed to New York to be inducted into the service and presumably fight in Vietnam. Upon arrival, he meets a group of hippies led by George Berger, and they collectively introduce him to drugs and the counterculture. Anti-war themes and music pervade the play; Vietnam is a "dirty little war," according to one of the songs. LBJ is mocked as a warmonger. The draft board is ridiculed in a brilliant homoerotic satire. Most powerfully, Berger, at the play's end, takes Claude's place on the plane headed to Vietnam. His headstone indicates that he was killed in action there. Not as bleak, but just as important, Woodstock signalled the merger and ambivalence of the counterculture and protest. The festival was billed as "three days of peace and love," in contrast to the war and hatred in Vietnam. Festival organizers pointed out that anyone buying a ticket was contributing to a united front against the Vietnam War. Scores of acts played and made anti-war speeches, with Country Joe exhorting the crowd that "if you want to stop this fucking war, you'll have to sing louder than that." "Movement leaders" and other activists took their turns at the mike and "some of the young men destroyed their draft cards in protest of the Vietnam War."[11] Yet, the media images and memory of Woodstock focus on the celebrative aspects of it: the rain, the music, nudity, drugs, free love.

Obviously, the counterculture's political message was too dangerous and had to be sanitized and softened for the American public. Like the New Left, the counterculture developed a critique of and alternative to the society in which they were raised. Where the political youth joined SDS or took over campus buildings, the cultural opposition dressed differently and dropped acid. Often, the two movements convered. Many hippies were indeed political and counterculture behavior was endemic in the anti-war movement. But often, the New Left saw hippies as apolitical, and hippies saw the political youth as bureaucratic and uptight. In the end, though, the challenge they both posed to American society was resisted, or channeled into acceptable avenues.

Epilogue: At War With Vietnam . . . Still

By the mid-1970s, America, it seemed, wanted to forget the previous decade. The memories of Vietnam, the Civil Rights Movement, Kent State, drugs, hippies, and other symbols of the 1960s were painful and searing, reminders of an era when hope, anguish, love, and death were a daily part of life on a grand as well as personal scale. Around 1980, however, the 1960s re-emerged, this time as the scapegoat and bogeyman for a new conservative generation. To be sure, there was already a backlash against the Vietnam generation in place, as Richard Nixon's famous charge that liberals stood for "acid, amnesty, and abortion" would attest. But it was the rise of Ronald Reagan and other conservatives that made the sixties the political and cultural centerpiece of their oppositional program. The Vietnam generation was unpatriotic, immoral, angry, they contended. Youth were disrespectful, blacks were ungrateful, women were too ambitious. Cherished values – paternalism, the nuclear family, patriarchy, deference, obedience – had been uprooted by too many young rebels without a cause, or with the wrong cause. To Robert Bork, failed conservative Supreme Court nominee, the 1960s had sent America *Slouching Towards Gomorrah,* as his polemic on American life was titled. Allen Bloom, a right-wing scholar, likened the Woodstock generation to the Nazis and saw the sixties as an "unmitigated disaster" for American educational life. To Newt Gingrich, the Speaker of the House of Representatives, "countercultural McGovernicks," like Bill Clinton, had destroyed family values. Fred Barnes, a reactionary political commentator, saw the "counterculture [as] a momentary aberration in American history that will be looked back upon as a quaint period of Bohemianism brought to the national elite."[12]

Popular culture also reflected such antagonistic and patronizing themes. Sylvester Stallone's "Rambo" complained that American soldiers "weren't allowed to win" in Vietnam; cowardly politicians and drugged-out protestors had ruined the war effort. Television shows such as *Family Ties* or *The Wonder Years* also rekindled interest in a safe version of the sixties. In the former, Michael J. Fox played a conservative youth amused by his hippie parents' values of peace and love. Indeed, hippie parents became a staple on TV sitcoms like *Dharma and Greg* or *Murphy Brown. The Wonder Years* also weekly demonstrated the strength and triumph of the bourgeois, nuclear family amid the upheavals of the 1960s. Self-absorbed hippies, like the Arnolds' daughter (who ultimately chose the traditional path of marriage and motherhood), were exposed as inane and silly, all against the backdrop of songs from that era. *The Big Chill* featured old college friends from the 1960s who had reunited to agonize over, and in large measure renounce, their radical pasts. *Austin Powers,* the "international man of mystery," saw the 1960s as little more than a time of good music, hot sex, and drugs.

"Classic Rock" radio stations popped up in every major market, introducing, and depoliticizing, songs of the sixties for a new generation. MTV likewise emerged, championing corporate rock but dubbing it "revolutionary" with memories of the sixties at the forefront. In fact, the MTV generation even tried to recreate Woodstock, holding a 25th-anniversary concert in 1994 that was a tribute to commercialism rather than the counterculture. Advertisers exploited the images of the 1960s too. Commercials featured rock music – The Beatles and Gil Scott-Heron for Nike, Sly and the Family Stone for Chevy, Janis Joplin for Mercedes Benz, War for Nissan – to market their products to a generation nostalgic for the good old days of the sixties. But ads which used memories of the sixties to sell products did so selectively. Television and print media made frequent use of hippies, minivans, sandals, beards, wardrobe, or slogans from the counterculture, but consciously avoided any reference to America's racial struggles or Vietnam, which were clearly the two greatest legacies of the era. In one of the more ironic displays of such co-optation, the Washington, DC Lottery Board "celebrated the dream" of Martin Luther King by invoking his name to encourage more people to play the lottery, an institution which exploited poor people and one which King almost certainly would have found repugnant.

Perhaps the most notable example of this cultural attack on the sixties came in the Academy Award-winning movie *Forrest Gump* in 1994. Hailed for its technological breakthroughs and simple messages, *Gump* actually was a reactionary assault on the 1960s. Young and mentally slow, Forrest was raised in segregationist Alabama, and his mother had to sleep with the school principal to get him enrolled into public school. His best friend, Jenny, was a negative symbol of the women's movement of the era; she was variously a hippie, a slut, a drug-user, a disco queen, and, ultimately, an early victim of AIDS. An anti-war leader, a caricature of Abbie Hoffman, used the "f-word" frequently and had no respect for authority. Gump, though simple, always succeeded and became rich, simply by doing what he was told to do and not thinking about the rules governing society. The 1960s, the movie suggested, was a dangerous time and the true heroes of that generation were obedient and nonpolitical.

While such caricatures of the 1960s can be appealing and amusing, they present an ahistorical and inaccurate historical record of the era. The 1960s, for all its shortcomings, was a decade in which masses of Americans tried to claim, or reclaim, their democratic rights as citizens, end a bloody war, create racial and gender equality, and liberate themselves from often repressive values. Millions of people – crossing class, racial, and gender lines – opposed the war in Vietnam, creating the largest political movement in US history. Others, frustrated by the limited promise and abortive reforms of liberalism, took to the streets and campuses to call for a new kind of politics, one in which people had a voice in the decisions affecting their lives. African-Americans, women, Chicanos, gays, environmentalists, and other groups demanded recognition and rights of their own, creating a new America in the process. And countless numbers challenged the traditional US culture, using music, dress, love, film, and other media to protest what they saw as the dangerous conformity inherent in society.

And they collectively left a legacy that cannot be ignored into the twenty-first century. Because of the Vietnam War, American citizens are now far more likely to question their government's behavior. No longer does the public accept the "my country right or wrong" principle. National leaders are expected to explain and justify their actions and national debates precede military action, as with the Gulf War of 1991. The government too is less likely to get involved in larger-level wars as a result of Vietnam. Since the 1970s, US military action has been confined to smaller engagements in which American success against weak enemies such as Libya, Grenada, Panama, or Iraq was certain. Likewise, the domestic movements of the 1960s have left their mark. Despite the use of the term "liberal" as a political slur, many of the reforms of the 1960s – Medicare, Medicaid, welfare programs, environmental programs, safety agencies, and others – are still around and functioning. Many of the student activists of that generation are still engaged today, serving as professors, politicians, community activists, and businessmen, bringing the consciousness of the 1960s to their workplaces. Blacks and women, despite the prevalence of racism and sexism in American society, have made great strides. African-Americans and females have served as big-city mayors, representatives, even senators and business leaders.

When Martin Luther King spoke out against Vietnam in April 1967, he could not have imagined how the next decades would play out. He simply saw the intersection of the war in Vietnam and the other movements of the decade. The war had come along at a time of hope and promise and shattered the national sense of hope. It had become a spectre that was haunting American life. In many ways it still is today. The historical legacy of Vietnam continues to transform American life. The war, the movement against it, the radicalization of politics on both the left and right, the inclusion of outside groups, the exclusion of inside groups, the emergence of new cultures all came about because of the whirlwind put into motion by the Vietnam War. The war exposed America's liberal world mission, made clear the contradictions between foreign intervention and domestic reform, energized millions, especially the young, to become involved in the affairs of their country, and led to distinct and often dramatic new social relations and ways of thinking. Because of Vietnam and the 1960s, America is a vastly different place.

Notes

Note to Introduction

1   "A Time to Break the Silence," Speech by Dr Martin Luther King, Jr, delivered at Riverside Baptist Church, 4 April 1967, from Catholic Worker Home Page, Worldwide Web, http://www.cais.com/agf/mlkvnam.htm; "I Have a Dream," Speech by Dr Martin Luther King, Jr, delivered at the March on Washington, 28 August 1963, Worldwide Web, http://www.students.uiuc.edu/~rosanina/King.html.

Notes to Chapter 1

1   On American policy toward Third World countries, see, among others, Walter LaFeber, *Inevitable Revolutions* (New York, 1983); George McT. Kahin and Audrey Kahin, *Subversion as Foreign Policy* (New York, 1995); Thomas Paterson, *Contesting Castro* (New York, 1994); Richard Immerman, *The CIA in Guatemala* (Austin, TX, 1983); Piero Gleijeses, *Shattered Hope: The Guatemalan Revolution and the United States, 1944–1954* (Princeton, 1991); Robert J. McMahon, *The Cold War on the Periphery: The United States, India, and Pakistan* (New York, 1994); Mark Lytle, *The Origins of the Iranian–American Alliance* (New York, 1987).

2   *Doonesbury* strip of 21 July 1985, from *Doonesbury Flashbacks: 25 Years of Fun*, CD-Rom (Mindscape, Inc., 1995).

3   There are scores of books which express this type of revisionist viewpoint. Among the more important and well-known are Richard Nixon, *No More Vietnams* (New York, 1985); William Westmoreland, *A Soldier Reports* (Garden City, NY, 1976); Harry Summers, *On Strategy* (Novato, CA, 1982); Guenter Lewy, *America in Vietnam* (New York,

1978); and U. S. G. Sharp, *Strategy for Defeat* (San Rafael, CA, 1978).
4   Bush in *Washington Post*, 17 January 1991.
5   Statistics from *The Nation*, 18 February 1991, 184; Vietnam is 127,000 square miles large while New Mexico is 121,000 square miles. By comparison California – 156,000 square miles – is a bit larger, and Arizona – 113,000 square miles – slightly smaller.

Notes to Chapter 2

1   David G. Marr, *Vietnamese Anticolonialism, 1885–1925* (Berkeley, 1971), 11–12; see also Neil L. Jamieson, *Understanding Vietnam* (Berkeley, 1995), 8–10; John K. Fairbank, Edwin O. Reischauer, Albert M. Craig, *East Asia: Tradition and Transformation* (Boston, 1973), 266–7.
2   Ngo Tat To, "When the Light's Put Out," in Ngo Vinh Long, ed., *Before the Revolution: The Vietnamese Peasants Under the French* (New York, 1991), 161–75.
3   Marr, *Vietnamese Anticolonialism*, 46.
4   Marr, *Vietnamese Anticolonialism*, 108, 118–19.
5   Jean Lacouture, *Ho Chi Minh: A Political Biography* (New York, 1968), 71–2.
6   "Appeal Made on the Occasion of the Founding of the Communist Party of Indochina," 18 February 1930, in Bernard Fall, ed., *Ho Chi Minh on Revolution: Selected Writings, 1920–1966* (New York, 1967), 129–31.
7   William J. Duiker, *The Communist Road to Power in Vietnam* (Boulder, CO, 1981), 31–3; Idem, *Sacred War: Nationalism and Socialism in a Divided Vietnam* (New York, 1995), 33–4.
8   Duiker, *Sacred War*, 36; Idem, *The Communist Road to Power*, 48–9.
9   "Letter from Abroad," 1941, in Fall, *Ho Chi Minh on Revolution*, 132–4.
10 Lacouture, *Ho Chi Minh*, 82.
11 "Instruction to Establish the Viet-Nam Propaganda Unit for National Liberation," December 1944, in Fall, *Ho Chi Minh on Revolution*, 138–9; Lacouture, *Ho Chi Minh*, 89.
12 Huynh Kim Khanh, *Vietnamese Communism, 1925–1945* (Ithaca, NY, 1982), 238.
13 "Appeal for General Insurrection," 16 August 1945, in Fall, *Ho Chi Minh on Revolution*, 138–9.
14 Devillers in Lacouture, *Ho Chi Minh*, 104; for an extended list of the various areas of Viet Minh insurrection in the latter part of August 1945, see Huynh Kim Khanh, *Vietnamese Communism*, 326.
15 "Declaration of Independence of the Democratic Republic of Viet-

Nam," 2 September 1945, in Fall, *Ho Chi Minh on Revolution*, 141–3.

16 In Stanley Karnow, *Vietnam: A History* (New York, 1983), 153. I would like to thank Amy Blackwell for bringing Ho's quote to my attention.

17 In Lacouture, *Ho Chi Minh*, 147.

18 In Marilyn Young, *The Vietnam Wars: 1945–1990* (New York, 1991), 16.

19 In Lacouture, *Ho Chi Minh*, 162–3.

20 "Appeal to the Entire People to Wage the Resistance War," 20 December 1946, in Fall, *Ho Chi Minh on Revolution*, 162.

21 In Lacouture, *Ho Chi Minh*, 175–6, 171.

22 In Gary R. Hess, *Vietnam and the United States: Origins and Legacy of War* (Boston, 1990), 38, and in George McT. Kahin, *Intervention: How the United States Became Involved in Vietnam* (Garden City, NY, 1987), 24.

23 In Duiker, *Sacred War*, 67.

24 In Duiker, *Sacred War*, 74; see also Bernard Fall, *Street Without Joy* (Harrisburg, PA, 1961), 35–8.

25 Gallagher in Gareth Porter, ed., *Vietnam: The Definitive Documentation of Human Decisions* (Stanfordville, NY, 1979), I:77–8; Marshall in Ibid., I:145–6 and 176–7; JCS 1992/4, "U.S. Policy Toward Southeast Asia," Record Group [RG] 319, National Archives, Washington, DC.

26 In US Department of State, *Foreign Relations of the United States* (*FRUS*), 1952–4, 13:496–503.

27 In Lloyd C. Gardner, *Approaching Vietnam: From World War II to Dienbienphu* (New York, 1988), 65.

28 Andrew Rotter, *The Path to Vietnam* (Ithaca, NY, 1987), 205; I would like to thank Jennifer Morales for explaining this concept to me in laymen's terms.

29 Vo Nguyen Giap, *People's War, People's Army* (New York, 1962), 18.

30 Collins in US Department of State, *FRUS*, 1950, 3:1696; JCS 1992/57, 23 February 1951, RG 218, National Archives; Army P & O Report, 25 February 1950, RG 319, National Archives.

31 Cabell in *FRUS*, 1952–4, 13:366–9.

32 Davis in *Pentagon Papers: Senator Gravel Edition* (hereafter cited as *PP–Gravel*), I:89–90; information on Ridgway and Gavin in Robert Buzzanco, *Masters of War: Military Dissent and Politics in the Vietnam Era* (New York, 1996), 42–9; JCS 1992/334, 7 June 1954, RG 218, National Archives.

33 Matthew B. Ridgway, *Soldier: The Memoirs of Matthew B. Ridgway* (New York, 1956), 278.

34 In Lacouture, *Ho Chi Minh*, 194.

35 JCS 1992/287, 11 March 1954, RG 218, National Archives.

36 Lansdale in *PP–Gravel*, I:573–83; Army study, 2 November 1954, RG

319, National Archives; Collins in *FRUS*, 1955–7, I:200–370, passim; JCS 1992/367, 3 August 1954, RG 218, National Archives; Gavin and Adams to Ridgway, 10 August 1954, RG 319; JCS to Secretary of Defense, 22 September 1954, RG 218.

37 Frederick Reinhardt to State Department, 14 October 1955, *FRUS*, 1955–7, 1:562–3.

38 The best treatment of this controversial episode is Gareth Porter's *The Myth of the Bloodbath: North Vietnam's Land Reform Reconsidered* (Ithaca, NY, 1972).

Notes to Chapter 3

1 Nguyen Thi Dinh, *No Other Road to Take* (Ithaca, NY, 1976), 70. (Cornell University Southeast Asia Program.)

2 "Committee for the South" statement, in Porter, ed., *Vietnam*, 59–67.

3 NLF statement in Kahin, *Intervention*, 114–15.

4 In United States, Government Printing Office, *Inaugural Addresses of the Presidents* (Washington, DC, 1961), 267–70; Kennedy in Young, *Vietnam Wars*, 58–9.

5 Kennedy in Arthur Schlesinger, *A Thousand Days* (Boston, 1965), 391; Rostow, 24 April 1961, in Laurence Chang and Peter Kornbluh, eds, *The Cuban Missile Crisis* (New York, 1992), 16–19; McGarr, 10 May 1961, *FRUS*, Vietnam, 1961, 129.

6 In David Halberstam, *The Best and the Brightest* (New York, 1972), 167.

7 Kennedy, 14 November 1961, in Kahin, *Intervention*, 137–9, see also *FRUS*, Vietnam, 1961, 601–3; McNamara in Notes of Colonel Howard Burris, Ibid., 746–7.

8 Harkins in Roger Hilsman, *To Move a Nation* (Garden City, NY, 1967), 16; *PP–Gravel*, 2:162–4; *FRUS*, Vietnam, 1962, 546–60.

9 Kennedy interviews with Cronkite, 2 September 1963, in Roger Hilsman Papers, box 4, JFK Library; with Huntley, 9 September 1963, *PP–Gravel*, 2:827–8.

10 In addition to Stone's film *JFK*, see Schlesinger's *A Thousand Days*, and John Newman's *JFK and Vietnam* (New York, 1992); Thomas G. Paterson, ed., *Kennedy's Quest for Victory* (New York, 1989), 23; for an effective refutation of the Stone–Schlesinger–Newman argument, see Noam Chomsky, *Rethinking Camelot* (Boston, 1993).

11 Lyndon B. Johnson, *The Vantage Point: Perspectives of the Presidency, 1963–1969* (New York, 1971), 42; Tom Wicker, *JFK and LBJ* (Baltimore, 1973), 205.

12 In Kahin, *Intervention*, 193.

13 Taylor, 27 November 1964, *Declassified Documents Reference*

System (DDRS), 83, 557; Johnson in Halberstam, *Best and Brightest*, 430.

14 Johnson in Doris Kearns, *Lyndon Johnson and the American Dream* (New York, 1976), 252– 8.

15 Karnow, *Vietnam*, 371–5.

16 *PP–Gravel*, 2:311–14.

17 McNamara and Bundy to Johnson, 27 January 1965, National Security Council (NSC) History, "Deployment of Major U.S. Forces to Vietnam," microfilm edition, University Publications of America, emphasis in original.

18 In James S. Olson and Randy Roberts, *Where the Domino Fell* (New York, 1996), 128; Bundy in Halberstam, *Best and Brightest*, 646.

19 Harold K. Johnson in Military History Institute Senior Officer Oral History Program, used at Center of Military History, Washington, DC.

20 Larry Berman, *Planning a Tragedy* (New York, 1982), 124.

21 Decker, 29 April 1961, in House Committee on Armed Services, *U.S.– Vietnam Relations*, 11:62–6; Neil Sheehan, *A Bright Shining Lie: John Paul Vann and America in Vietnam* (New York, 1988); officers' report, August 1962, in Krulak to Army, Navy, and Air Force Chiefs, 27 December 1962, John Newman Papers, JFK Library.

22 Greene in tape #6276, Marine Corps Historical Center (MCHC), transcribed by the author; Taylor memoranda of 6 January, 1 February, 22 February, 16 March 1965 in NSC History, "Deployment."

23 Taylor to State Department, 4 September 1964, *DDRS*, 84, 737; Westmoreland Question and Answer Report, November 1964, Westmoreland Papers, box 4, LBJ Library; Westmoreland in Taylor to Johnson, 5 January 1965, NSC History, "Deployment."

24 In Berman, *Planning a Tragedy*, 8–9.

25 In Douglas Pike, *Viet Cong* (Cambridge, MA, 1966), 174.

26 In Duiker, *Sacred War*, 148.

27 Frances FitzGerald, *Fire in the Lake* (New York, 1972), 272–80.

28 In Robert J. McMahon, ed., *Major Problems in the History of the Vietnam War* (Lexington, MA, 1995), 302–3.

29 Krulak to Robert Baldwin, 20 April 1966, Victor Krulak Papers, box 2, MCHC.

30 In Thomas G. Paterson, J. Garry Clifford and Kenneth J. Hagan, *American Foreign Relations*, vol. 2 (Lexington, MA, 1995), 384–5.

31 Harold G. Moore and Joseph L. Galloway, *We Were Soldiers Once . . . and Young* (New York, 1992), 16, 57.

32 In Andrew Krepinevich, *The Army and Vietnam* (Baltimore, 1986), 190–1.

33 Wheeler to Westmoreland, 9 March 1967, *Westmoreland v. CBS*, DA/ WNRC Files, box 2, Washington National Records Center (WNRC), Suitland, MD.

34 White House Report, *DDRS*, 85, 002248.

35   Harold K. Johnson to Creighton Abrams, 22 November 1967, Creighton Abrams Papers, box: Cables, June 1967–June 1972, Military History Institute.

36   Victor H. Krulak, *First to Fight* (Annapolis, MD, 1984), 221–6; Krulak, December 1965 report, FMFPac Trip Reports, MCHC; Krulak, "A Strategic Appraisal – Vietnam," Victor H. Krulak Papers, box 2, MCHC.

37   Greene's notes, Wallace M. Greene Papers, box 415, MCHC; Greene and Krulak in tape #6278, MCHC, transcribed by author.

38   Phillip Davidson, *Vietnam at War* (New York, 1991), 410–11; PROVN Report, Center of Military History, Washington DC.

39   Sheehan, *Bright Shining Lie*, 537–58; in Olson and Roberts, *Where the Domino Fell*, 79.

40   Unless otherwise noted, the information in this section is derived from Robert Buzzanco, "The Myth of Tet: American Failure and the Politics of War," in Marc Jason Gilbert and William Head, eds, *The Tet Offensive* (Westport, CT, 1996), 231–57.

41   In Clark L. Clifford with Richard Holbrooke, *Counsel to the President* (New York, 1991), 473–4.

42   McGarr to Lemnitzer, 12 October 1961, *FRUS*, Vietnam, 1961, 347–59; NMCC to White House, 13 June 1965, NSC History, "Deployment"; McDonald in Richard K. Betts, *Soldiers, Statesmen, and Cold War Crises* (Cambridge, MA, 1971), 11; Johnson in Military History Institute Oral History Program interview, 10.

43   Karnow, *Vietnam*, 461–4.

44   Christian Appy, *Working-Class War* (Chapel Hill, NC, 1993), 6.

45   In Richard Moser, *The New Winter Soldiers* (New Brunswick, NJ, 1996), 63.

46   Ibid., 65–6.

47   See Wallace Terry, *Bloods: An Oral History of the War by Black Veterans* (New York, 1984); Stanley Goff and Robert Sanders, *Brothers: Black Soldiers in the Nam* (New York, 1982); William King, ed., *A White Man's War*, special issue of *Vietnam Generation* (spring 1989).

48   Donald Duncan in *Ramparts* (February 1966), 12–24; see also his book, *The New Legions* (New York, 1967).

49   In Moser, *New Winter Soldiers*, 69–72; see also David Cortright, *Soldiers in Revolt* (Garden City, NY, 1975).

50   In McMahon, *Major Problems in Vietnam War*, 468–70.

51   Shoup speech of 14 May 1966, in David Shoup Biographical File, MCHC.

52   Chomsky, "The Responsibility of Intellectuals," in *American Power and the New Mandarins* (New York, 1969), 323–66.

53   Morgenthau, "Truth and Power," November 1966, in *Truth and Power: Essays of a Decade, 1960–1970* (New York, 1970), 26.

54   Address by Walter B. Wriston, 17 January 1968, Henry Fowler Pa-

pers, box 82, folder: Domestic Economy: Gold, 1968 (1 of 2), LBJ Library; "Hope and Trouble," Report by Goldman, Sachs and Company, 8 May 1968, Fowler Papers, box 78, folder: Domestic Economy: Economic Data, 1968 (2 of 2).
55 Martin to Pamela Graham, 2 May 1968, William McChesney Martin Papers, box 81, folder: Miscellaneous Appearances, FRB, April–May 1968, LBJ Library.
56 Charles DeBenedetti with Charles Chatfield, *An American Ordeal* (Syracuse, NY, 1990), 228; Personal Papers of the President, LBJ, 1968, vol. I, v.

Notes to Chapter 4

1 In Rostow to Johnson, 28 November 1966, Confidential File (CF), ND19/CO312, box 72, LBJ Library.
2 In Young, *Vietnam Wars*, 239.
3 In Hess, *Vietnam and the United States*, 119.
4 In Young, *Vietnam Wars*, 235.
5 In Al Santoli, *Everything We Had* (New York, 1981), 111–12.
6 Henry Kissinger, *The White House Years* (Boston, 1979), 1010.
7 *Public Papers of the President: Richard Milhous Nixon*, 1970, 470–1.
8 Richard M. Nixon, *RN: The Memoirs of Richard Nixon* (New York, 1978), 558.
9 In Tom Wells, *The War Within* (Berkeley, 1994), 424–5.
10 In DeBenedetti and Chatfield, *An American Ordeal*, 280.
11 Kissinger, *White House Years*, 1032.
12 In Seymour Hersh, *The Price of Power: Kissinger in the Nixon White House* (New York, 1983), 516.
13 In George Herring, *America's Longest War* (New York, 1986), 247.
14 Wells, *The War Within*, 370–9.
15 Ibid., 391–4.
16 John Kerry and Vietnam Veterans Against the War, David Thorne, George Butler, eds, *The New Soldier* (New York, 1971), 12.
17 Vietnam Veterans Against the War, *The Winter Soldier Investigation* (Boston, 1972), 12.
18 Kerry and VVAW, *The New Soldier*, 24.
19 In Karnow, *Vietnam: A History*, 652.
20 Hess, *Vietnam and the United States*, 132.
21 Roger Morris, *Uncertain Greatness* (New York, 1977), 190.
22 In Gabriel Kolko, *Anatomy of a War: Vietnam, the United States, and the Modern Historical Experience* (New York, 1985), 442.
23 In Arnold Isaacs, *Without Honor* (Baltimore, 1983), 58; Hersh, *Price of Power*, 634.

24 William Shawcross, *Sideshow: Kissinger, Nixon and the Destruction of Cambodia* (New York, 1987), 264–5.
25 In Ibid., 331.
26 In Noam Chomsky, "Cambodia," in James Peck, ed., *The Chomsky Reader* (New York, 1987), 290.
27 Jamieson, *Understanding Vietnam*, 359.
28 Ngo Vinh Long, "The Tet Offensive and Its Aftermath," in Gilbert and Head, *The Tet Offensive*, 119.
29 In Olson and Roberts, *Where the Domino Fell*, 256.
30 In Young, *Vietnam Wars*, 298.
31 Ibid., 250; Pham Van Dong in Karnow, *Vietnam*, 9.
32 In *New York Times*, 25 March 1977, 10.
33 The best treatment of this issue is Bruce Franklin, *M.I.A., or Mythmaking in America* (New Brunswick, NJ, 1993).
34 In Kolko, *Anatomy of a War*, 570.
35 Reagan in *New York Times*, 19 August 1980; Weinberger in *Washington Post*, 12 November 1984; Bush in *Washington Post*, 20 January 1991, and in Paterson et al., *American Foreign Relations*, 578.

Notes to Chapter 5

1 In Jim Heath, *Decade of Disillusionment: The Kennedy–Johnson Years* (Bloomington, IN, 1975), 62; Richard Slotkin, *Gunfighter Nation* (1992), 499-500.
2 Heath, *Decade of Disillusionment*, 24.
3 Johnson, *The Vantage Point*, 322–5.
4 In Edward P. Morgan, *The '60s Experience* (Philadelphia, 1991), 22.
5 Minutes of Meeting in Cabinet Room, 9 January 1967, Reference File, box 1, LBJ Library.
6 In Robert Mullen, *Blacks and Vietnam* (Washington, DC, 1981), 13.

Notes to Chapter 6

1 In Allen Matusow, *The Unraveling of America: A History of Liberalism in the 1960s* (New York, 1984), 50.
2 Johnson, *The Vantage Point*, 206; in Matusow, *Unraveling*, 222.
3 Johnson, *The Vantage Point*, 213.
4 *Public Papers of the President: Lyndon B. Johnson*, 1965, 813–14.
5 In David Farber, *The Age of Great Dreams: America in the 1960s* (New York, 1994), 194.
6 In Morgan, *The '60s Experience*, 115.

7   In David Burner, *Making Peace with the Sixties* (Princeton, 1996), 140; and Morgan, *The '60s Experience*, 114.

8   In Farber, *Age of Great Dreams*, 196.

9   James Miller, *Democracy Is In the Streets: From Port Huron to the Siege of Chicago* (New York, 1987), 13.

10 In Matusow, *Unraveling*, 314.

11 In Miller, *Democracy Is In the Streets*, 189.

12 In Matusow, *Unraveling*, 316.

13 Miller, *Democracy Is In the Streets*, 15–16, 214.

14 In Massimo Teodori, *The New Left: A Documentary History* (Indianapolis, IN, 1969), 246.

15 Norman L. Rosenberg and Emily S. Rosenberg, *In Our Times: America Since World War II* (Englewood Cliffs, NJ, 1995), 171.

16 In Terry Anderson, *The Movement and the Sixties* (New York, 1995), 141, 160.

17 In Todd Gitlin, *The Sixties: Years of Hope, Days of Rage* (New York, 1987), 307.

18 In Anderson, *Movement and the Sixties*, 198.

19 In Farber, *Age of Great Dreams*, 211.

20 Johnson, *The Vantage Point*, 322–5.

21 Rosenberg and Rosenberg, *In Our Times*, 132; Johnson, *The Vantage Point*, 342.

22 In Merle Miller, *Lyndon: An Oral Biography* (New York, 1980), 563.

23 Robert Buzzanco, "The Vietnam War and the Limits of Military Keynesianism," Paper delivered at 1997 conference of the American Historical Association, New York.

24 In Matusow, *Unraveling*, 33.

25 In Miller, *Democracy Is In the Streets*, 172.

26 In Teodori, *The New Left*, 246–8.

27 In Teodori, *The New Left*, 182–8; in David Steigerwald, *The Sixties and the End of Modern America* (New York, 1995), 136.

28 Morgan, *The '60s Experience*, 29.

29 Matusow, *Unraveling*, 248–60.

30 In Robert Fisher, *Let the People Decide* (Boston, 1984), 117.

31 The American Social History Project, *Who Built America?* (New York, 1992), 2:555.

32 In Rosenberg and Rosenberg, *In Our Times*, 131.

33 In Steigerwald, *The Sixties and the End of Modern America*, 31.

34 In Douglas T. Miller, *On Our Own: Americans in the Sixties* (Lexington, MA, 1996), 224–5.

35 In Miller, *On Our Own*, 237–8.

36 In Rosenberg and Rosenberg, *In Our Times*, 179.

Notes to Chapter 7

1   Taylor Branch, *Parting the Waters: America in the King Years, 1954–1963* (New York, 1988), 128–205.
2   In James A. Colaiaco, *Martin Luther King, Jr.: Apostle of Militant Nonviolence* (New York, 1993), 29.
3   In Clayborne Carson, *In Struggle: SNCC and the Black Awakening of the 1960s* (Cambridge, MA, 1981), 14.
4   In Farber, *Age of Great Dreams*, 78.
5   In Colaiaco, *Martin Luther King*, 34–7.
6   I. F. Stone, *In a Time of Torment, 1961–1967* (Boston, 1967), 147; in Andrew Kopkind, *The Thirty Years' War* (New York, 1995), 5.
7   In William Chafe, *The Unfinished Journey* (New York, 1991), 363–6.
8   "Letter from a Birmingham Jail" was reproduced that year in Martin Luther King, Jr, *Why We Can't Wait* (New York, 1963).
9   JFK Civil Rights announcement of 11 June 1963, on PBS website for "The American Experience" show "The Kennedys."
10 In Colaiaco, *Martin Luther King*, 71–2.
11 In David Garrow, *Bearing the Cross: Martin Luther King, Jr. and the SCLC* (New York, 1986), 284.
12 In Anderson, *The Movement and the Sixties*, 158.
13 In Garrow, *Bearing the Cross*, 394, 429–30.
14 Eldridge Cleaver, *Soul on Ice* (New York, 1968), 166; Carmichael in "The Home Front" episode of PBS series "Vietnam: A Television History," transcript on PBS website, and in Anderson, *The Movement and the Sixties*, 159.
15 Stone, *In a Time of Torment*, 363.
16 In Cornel West, "Malcolm X and Black Rage," in Joe Wood, ed., *Malcolm X in Our Own Image* (New York, 1992), 48–58; Cornel West, "The Paradox of Afro-American Rebellion," in Sohnya Sayres et al., eds, *The 60s Without Apology* (Minneapolis, 1985), 44–58.
17 Lewis in Garrow, *Bearing the Cross*, 281–3; James Forman, *The Making of Black Revolutionaries* (Washington, 1985), 336.
18 In Morgan, *The '60s Experience*, 75; in Mullen, *Blacks and Vietnam*, 18.
19 In Garrow, *Bearing the Cross*, 394–5.
20 In Colaiaco, *Martin Luther King*, 187.
21 Martin Luther King, *Where Do We Go from Here: Chaos or Community?* (Boston, 1967), 58, 2–4.
22 King, *Where Do We Go from Here*, 35.
23 Andrew Young, *An Easy Burden: The Civil Rights Movement and the Transformation of America* (New York, 1996), 414.
24 In Colaiaco, *Martin Luther King*, 170.
25 Stokely Carmichael and Charles Hamilton, *Black Power: The Politics of Liberation in America* (New York, 1967), 44.

26   In David Chalmers, *And the Crooked Places Made Straight* (Baltimore, 1996), 31; Stokely Carmichael, *Stokely Speaks* (New York, 1971), 22–5.

27   James Kirkpatrick Davis, *Assault on the Left: The FBI and the Sixties Antiwar Movement* (Westport, CT, 1997), 8; David Garrow, *The FBI and Martin Luther King, Jr.* (New York, 1983), 207.

28   King, *Where Do We Go from Here*, 36–8.

29   In transcript of interview with Henry Louis Gates on "The Two Nations of Black America," PBS Frontline Series, PBS website.

30   Earl Ofari Hutchinson, *Blacks and Reds: Race and Class in Conflict, 1919–1990* (East Lansing, MI, 1995), 243.

31   King, *Where Do We Go from Here*, 186.

32   William Julius Wilson, Kathleen Cleaver, and Jesse Jackson in "The Two Nations of Black America" transcript, PBS website.

33   Young, *An Easy Burden*, 440–6; McPherson to LBJ, 18 March 1968, Reference File, box 1, McPherson Memos on Vietnam, LBJ Library.

34   Garrow, *Bearing the Cross*, 621.

35   In Miller, *On Our Own*, 229.

36   In William Julius Wilson interview in "The Two Nations of Black America" transcript, PBS website.

37   King in "The Home Front" episode of PBS series "Vietnam: A Television History," transcript on PBS website.

38   "SNCC Position Paper (Women in the Movement)," in Sara Evans, *Personal Politics* (New York, 1979), 233–5, 87; Mary King, *Freedom Song* (New York, 1987), 452–4. King also set the record straight on one of the infamous episodes between men and women in SNCC. The evening after they had presented their memo, King, Hayden, and many other men and women went out to relax. Stokely Carmichael, who was as much a performer as an intellectual, was conducting a monologue on the day's activities and looked at King and said "the position for women in SNCC is prone." While since then most scholars have used this as evidence of Carmichael's insensitivity and misogyny, King says that everyone there, including she and Hayden, laughed at his joke and that in fact he was one of the biggest supporters of women's issues within SNCC.

39   "Sex and Caste: a Kind of Memo," in Evans, *Personal Politics*, 235–8.

40   Linda Gordon and Ann Popkin, "Women's Liberation: 'Let Us Now Emulate Each Other.'" I would like to thank Landon Storrs for bringing this document to my attention.

41   The following section is based on Evans's *Personal Politics*, a path-breaking look at the origins of Women's Lib in the 1960s, especially pp. 158–92.

42   Robin Morgan, "Feminist Guerrilla Theatre, 1968" in Susan Ware, ed., *Modern American Women: A Documentary History* (Belmont, CA, 1989), 341–4; Susan Douglas, *Where the Girls Are* (New York, 1994), 139.

43 For an excellent, and hilarious, treatment of media images of women, see Douglas, *Where the Girls Are.*

Notes to Chapter 8

1 In Timothy Miller, *The Hippies and American Values* (Knoxville, 1991), 10.

2 John Kenneth Galbraith and Nicole Salinger, *Almost Everyone's Guide to Economics* (Boston, 1978), 143–4.

3 See Marty Jezer, *Abbie Hoffman, American Rebel* (New Brunswick, NJ, 1993).

4 In Robert Cantwell, *When We Were Good: The Folk Revival* (Cambridge, MA, 1996), 261.

5 In Jon Wiener, *Come Together: John Lennon in His Time* (New York, 1984), 17.

6 Linda Gordon, *Woman's Body, Woman's Right: Birth Control in America* (New York, 1990), 421.

7 In Miller, *Hippies and American Values*, 65–7; in Douglas Miller, *On Our Own*, 206.

8 In Gitlin, *Years of Hope, Days of Rage*, 360.

9 In Anderson, *The Movement and the Sixties*, 283–4.

10 Tom Frank, *The Conquest of Cool* (Chicago, 1997), 8, 30.

11 Bob Spitz, *Barefoot in Babylon* (New York, 1989), 203, 426.

12 In Frank, *Conquest of Cool*, 2–3.

Bibliography

The historical literature on Vietnam and the 1960s is already quite substantial and growing. The following books listed therefore represent but a selected portion of the sources available. I have organized this bibliographic essay roughly as the book is. First I will discuss Vietnam books, by general category or time period, and then books on the 1960s, including general overviews, books on liberalism, civil rights, Women's Liberation, and the Counterculture.

Vietnam

Overviews

There are already scores of excellent books that cover the war in its entirety. I have made extensive use of my own *Masters of War: Military Dissent and Politics in the Vietnam Era* (New York, 1996) in preparing this text. Among others, the best books include Gabriel Kolko's *Anatomy of a War* (New York, 1985), and Marilyn Young's *The Vietnam Wars: 1945– 1990* (New York, 1991). Stanley Karnow, *Vietnam: A History* (New York, 1983), James Olson and Randy Roberts, *Where the Domino Fell* (New York, 1996), Neil Sheehan, *A Bright Shining Lie: John Paul Vann and America in Vietnam* (New York, 1988), Andrew Krepinevich, *The Army and Vietnam* (Baltimore, 1986), and Phillip Davidson, *Vietnam at War* (New York, 1991) were also useful.

Memoirs

Many of the ranking political and military figures of the Vietnam era have written their own personal narratives of the war, and they are quite useful. Among those used extensively were Lyndon B. Johnson, *The Vantage Point:*

Perspectives of the Presidency, 1963–1969 (New York, 1971), Richard
Nixon, *No More Vietnams* (New York, 1985) and *RN: The Memoirs
of Richard Nixon* (New York, 1978), William Westmoreland, *A Soldier
Reports* (Garden City, NY, 1976), Clark Clifford with Richard Holbrooke,
Counsel to the President (New York, 1991), Henry Kissinger, *White
House Years* (Boston, 1979), U.S.G. Sharp, *Strategy for Defeat* (San Rafael,
CA, 1978), Matthew Ridgway, *Soldier: The Memoirs of Matthew B.
Ridgway* (New York, 1956), and Victor Krulak, *First to Fight* (Annapolis,
MD, 1984).

The Vietnamese

There is a growing literature on both northern and southern Vietnam. Some
of the most important works are David Marr, *Vietnamese Anticolonialism,
1885–1925* (Berkeley, 1971), William Duiker, *The Communist Road to
Power in Vietnam* (Boulder, CO, 1981) and *Sacred War: Nationalism and
Socialism in a Divided Vietnam* (New York, 1995), Neil Jamieson, *Under-
standing Vietnam* (Berkeley, 1995), Jean Lacouture, *Ho Chi Minh: A Po-
litical Biography* (New York, 1968), Bernard Fall, ed., *Ho Chi Minh on
Revolution: Selected Writings, 1920–1966* (New York, 1967), Huynh Kim
Khanh, *Vietnamese Communism, 1925–1945* (Ithaca, NY, 1982), Ngo Vinh
Long, ed., *Before the Revolution: The Vietnamese Peasants Under the French*
(New York, 1991), and Vo Nguyen Giap, *People's War, People's Army* (New
York, 1962).

The Early Years

Among books on US policies toward Vietnam in the aftermath of World
War II until the Kennedy administration, and of events in Vietnam in gen-
eral, I have made valuable use of Gary Hess, *Vietnam and the United States:
Origins and Legacy of War* (Boston, 1990), Lloyd Gardner, *Approaching
Vietnam: From World War II to Dienbienphu* (New York, 1988), Andrew
Rotter, *The Path to Vietnam* (Ithaca, NY, 1987), Bernard Fall, *Street With-
out Joy* (Harrisburg, PA, 1961), Gareth Porter, *The Myth of the Bloodbath:
North Vietnam's Land Reform Reconsidered* (Ithaca, NY, 1972), Arthur
Schlesinger, Jr, *A Thousand Days* (Boston, 1965), George McT. Kahin, *In-
tervention: How the United States Became Involved in Vietnam* (Garden
City, NY, 1987), David Halberstam, *The Best and the Brightest* (New York,
1972), Roger Hilsman, *To Move a Nation* (Garden City, NY, 1967), John
Newman, *JFK and Vietnam* (New York, 1992), Thomas Paterson, ed.,
Kennedy's Quest for Victory (New York, 1989), Tom Wicker, *JFK and LBJ*
(Baltimore, 1973), and especially Noam Chomsky, *Rethinking Camelot*
(Boston, 1993).

The Johnson and Nixon Years

Excellent information can be gained from Doris Kearns, *Lyndon Johnson and the American Dream* (New York, 1976), Larry Berman, *Planning a Tragedy* (New York, 1982), Harold G. Moore and Joseph L. Galloway, *We Were Soldiers Once . . . and Young* (New York, 1992), Seymour Hersh, *The Price of Power* (New York, 1983), Roger Morris, *Uncertain Greatness* (New York, 1977), Arnold Isaacs, *Without Honor* (Baltimore, 1983), and William Shawcross, *Sideshow: Kissinger, Nixon, and the Destruction of Cambodia* (New York, 1987).

Domestic Consequences of the War

There are a good number of books on the anti-war movement, racial and class issues and the war, and other domestic factors relating to Vietnam. Among those used were Noam Chomsky, *American Power and the New Mandarins* (New York, 1969), Charles DeBenedetti with Charles Chatfield, *An American Ordeal* (Syracuse, NY, 1990), I. F. Stone, *The Killings at Kent State* (New York, 1971), Tom Wells, *The War Within* (Berkeley, 1994), Christian Appy, *Working-Class War* (Chapel Hill, NC, 1993), Richard Moser, *The New Winter Soldiers* (New Brunswick, NJ, 1996), Wallace Terry, *Bloods: An Oral History of the War by Black Veterans* (New York, 1984), Stanley Goff and Robert Sanders, *Brothers: Black Soldiers in the Nam* (New York, 1982), and Vietnam Veterans Against the War, *The Winter Soldier Investigation* (Boston, 1972).

The Movements of the 1960s

Overviews

There is already a substantial number of fine books that cover the major movements of the 1960s. Among them are Edward P. Morgan, *The '60s Experience: Hard Lessons for Modern America* (Philadelphia, 1991), Allen Matusow, *The Unraveling of America: A History of Liberalism in the 1960s* (New York, 1984), David Farber, *The Age of Great Dreams* (New York, 1994), Todd Gitlin, *The Sixties: Years of Hope, Days of Rage* (New York, 1987), William Chafe, *The Unfinished Journey* (New York, 1991), Andrew Kopkind, *The Thirty Years' War* (New York, 1995), David Caute, *The Year of the Barricades: A Journey Through 1968* (New York, 1988), David Steigerwald, *The Sixties and the End of Modern America* (New York, 1995), Milton Viorst, *Fire in the Streets* (New York, 1979), Douglas T. Miller, *On Our Own: Americans in the Sixties* (Lexington, MA, 1996), Emily Rosenberg and Norman Rosenberg, *In Our Times* (Englewood, Cliffs, NJ, 1995), and Terry Anderson, *The Movement and the Sixties* (New York, 1995).

Liberalism and its Critics

In addition to those works cited above, books on the politics of the Kennedy and Johnson years and the opposition to it, liberalism, and the New Left include Jim Heath, *Decade of Disillusionment: The Kennedy–Johnson Years* (Bloomington, IN, 1975), James Miller, *Democracy Is In the Streets: From Port Huron to the Siege of Chicago* (New York, 1987), Massimo Teodori, *The New Left: A Documentary History* (Indianapolis, IN, 1969), W. J. Rorabaugh, *Berkeley at War, the 1960s* (New York, 1989), James Simon Kunen, *The Strawberry Statement: Notes of a College Revolutionary* (New York, 1969), Marcy Darnovsky, Barbara Epstein, and Richard Flacks, eds, *Cultural Politics and Social Movements* (Philadelphia, 1995), David Goines, *The Free Speech Movement: Coming of Age in the 1960s* (Berkeley, 1993), Free Speech Movement website, http://www.fsm-a.org, Peter Levy, *The New Left and Labor in the 1960s* (Urbana, IL, 1994), Frances Fox Piven and Richard Cloward, *Poor People's Movements: Why They Succeed, How They Fail* (New York, 1979), and Robert Fisher, *Let the People Decide: Neighborhood Organizing in America* (Boston, 1994).

Civil Rights and Women's Liberation

Perhaps no issue of the 1960s, with the exception of Vietnam, has been covered as extensively as the African-American civil rights struggle. Some of the better books on that subject are Taylor Branch, *Parting the Waters: America in the King Years, 1954–1963* (New York, 1988), David Garrow, *Bearing the Cross: Martin Luther King, Jr. and the SCLC* (New York, 1986), James Colaiaco, *Martin Luther King, Jr.: Apostle of Militant Nonviolence* (New York, 1993), Clayborne Carson, *In Struggle: SNCC and the Black Awakening of the 1960s* (Cambridge, MA., 1981), Eldridge Cleaver, *Soul on Ice* (New York, 1968), Howard Zinn, *SNCC, the New Abolitionists* (Boston, 1964), Kenneth Kusmer, ed., *Black Communities and Urban Race Relations in American History* (New York, 1991), Rhoda Lois Blumberg, *Civil Rights, the 1960s Freedom Struggle* (Boston, 1991), Adolph Reed, Jr, ed., *Race, Politics, and Culture: Critical Essays on the Radicalism of the 1960s* (Westport, CT, 1986), Manning Marable, *How Capitalism Under-developed Black America* (Boston, 1983), The Kerner Commission, *Report of the National Advisory Commission on Civil Disorders* (New York, 1968), James Forman, *The Making of Black Revolutionaries* (Washington, 1985), Andrew Young, *An Easy Burden: The Civil Rights Movement and the Transformation of America* (New York, 1996), Robert Mullen, *Blacks and Viet-*

nam (Washington, 1981), Stokely Carmichael, *Stokely Speaks* (New York, 1971), and with Charles Hamilton, *Black Power: The Politics of Liberation in America* (New York, 1967), Malcolm X, *The Autobiography of Malcolm X* (New York, 1992), and Martin Luther King, Jr, *Why We Can't Wait* (New York, 1963), and *Where Do We Go from Here: Chaos or Community?* (Boston, 1967). On the Women's Liberation Movement, see, among others, Sara Evans, *Personal Politics* (New York, 1979), Mary King, *Freedom Song* (New York, 1987), Blanche Linden-Ward, *American Women in the 1960s: Changing the Future* (Boston, 1993), Sara Davidson, *Loose Change: Three Women of the Sixties* (Garden City, NY, 1977), Alice Echols, *Daring to Be Bad: Racial Feminism in America, 1967–1975* (Minneapolis, 1989), Robin Morgan, ed., *Sisterhood is Powerful* (New York, 1970), Susan Ware, ed., *Modern American Women: A Documentary History* (Belmont, CA, 1989), and Susan Douglas, *Where the Girls Are* (New York, 1994). On other movements see Craig Jenkins, *The Politics of Insurgency: The Farm Workers Movement in the 1960s* (New York, 1985), Troy Johnson, *The Occupation of Alcatraz Island* (Urbana, IL, 1996), Paul Chaat Smith, *Like a Hurricane: The Indian Movement from Alcatraz to Wounded Knee* (New York, 1996), John Hammerback, *A War of Words: Chicano Protest in the 1960s and 1970s* (Westport, CT, 1985), Eric Marcus, *Making History: The Struggle for Gay and Lesbian Equal Rights* (New York, 1992), Barry Adam, *The Rise of a Gay and Lesbian Movement* (Boston, 1995), Martin Duberman, *About Time: Exploring the Gay Past* (New York, 1991), Charles Reich, *The Greening of America* (New York, 1971), and Robert Gottleib, *Forcing the Spring: The Transformation of the American Environmental Movement* (Washington, DC, 1993).

The Counterculture

On cultural politics in the 1960s, see Timothy Miller, *The Hippies and American Values* (Knoxville, 1991), Morris Dickstein, *Gates of Eden: American Culture in the Sixties* (New York, 1977), Abe Peck, *Uncovering the Sixties: The Life and Times of the Underground Press* (New York, 1985), Peter O. Whitman, *Aquarius Revisited: Seven Who Created the Sixties Counterculture that Changed America* (New York, 1987), Marty Jezer, *Abbie Hoffman: American Rebel* (New Brunswick, NJ, 1993), Robert Cantwell, *When We Were Good: The Folk Revival* (Cambridge, MA, 1996), Hedda Garza, *Joan Baez* (New York, 1991), Anthony Scaduto, *Bob Dylan* (New York, 1972), Jon Wiener, *Come Together: John Lennon in His Time* (New York, 1984), Linda Gordon, *Woman's Body, Woman's Right: Birth Control in America* (New York, 1990), Tom Frank, *The Conquest of Cool* (Chicago, 1997), George Martin, *Summer of Love: The Making of Sgt. Pepper* (London, 1994), Bob Spitz, *Barefoot in Babylon* (New York, 1989), Tom Wolfe, *The Electric Kool-Aid Acid Test* (New York, 1976), Martin Lee,

Acid Dreams: The CIA, LSD, and the Sixties Rebellion (New York, 1985), Ethan Mordden, *Medium Cool: The Movies of the 1960s* (New York, 1990), and Lynn Spiegel and Michael Curtin, eds, *The Revolution Wasn't Televised: Sixties Television and Social Conflict* (New York, 1997).

Index

274   *Index*

276